D0935494

MEANING AND SPEECH ACTS

Volume II
FORMAL SEMANTICS
OF SUCCESS AND
SATISFACTION

MEANING AND
SPEECH ACTS

Volume II
FORMAL SEMANTICS
OF SUCCESS AND
SATISFACTION

DANIEL
VANDERVEKEN

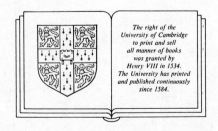

The right of the
University of Cambridge
to print and sell
all manner of books
was granted by
Henry VIII in 1534.
The University has printed
and published continuously
since 1584.

CAMBRIDGE UNIVERSITY PRESS

Cambridge
New York   Port Chester
Melbourne   Sydney

P
95.55
V36
1990
V.2

Published by the Press Syndicate of the University of Cambridge
The Pitt Building, Trumpington Street, Cambridge CB2 1RP
40 West 20th Street, New York, NY 10011, USA
10 Stamford Road, Oakleigh, Melbourne 3166, Australia

© Cambridge University Press 1991

First published 1991

Printed in Great Britain at the University Press, Cambridge

British Library cataloguing in publication data
Vanderveken, Daniel
Meaning and speech acts.
Vol. 2. Formal semantics of success and satisfaction
1. Utterances. Illocutionary force. Related to
structure
1. Title
415

Library of Congress cataloguing in publication data applied for

ISBN 0 521 38216 5 hardback

FLORIDA STATE
UNIVERSITY LIBRARIES   UP

OCT 6 1992

TALLAHASSEE, FLORIDA

For
VINCENT

CONTENTS

vii

Contents

ACKNOWLEDGMENTS

Many colleagues and institutions have been helpful during the writing of this volume. I would like to thank in particular Elias Umberto Alves, Ruth Barcan Marcus, Nuel Belnap, Maître Bayart, Oswaldo Chateaubriand, Charles Daniels, Yvon Gauthier, David Kaplan, Grzegorz Malinowski, Marek Nowak, and Michel de Rougemont for their critical remarks on various aspects of the logical theory. I am especially grateful to David K. Johnston and François Lepage for their collaboration in the completeness proofs. Finally, I would also like to thank the Natural Sciences and Engineering Research Council of Canada, the F.C.A.R. Foundation of Québec, the Communauté Scientifique Réseau de l'Université du Québec, the Ministry of National Defense, and the Social Sciences and Humanities Research Council of Canada for grants that enabled me to work on the logical theory presented in this book and related topics.

INTRODUCTION

In the past few decades, logicians and linguists have used the resources of modern logic extensively in order to contribute to the foundations of the semantics of natural languages. In particular, they have used and further developed the theory of semantic interpretations (or models) originally founded by Tarski for the formal languages in order to interpret directly (or after translation) important fragments of English and of other actual natural languages.

Like Montague and other logicians, I believe that there is no important theoretical difference between natural and formal languages. On the other hand, I reject the idea that the construction of a theory of truth under an arbitrary semantic interpretation is the single most important goal of semantics. In my view, complete illocutionary acts such as assertions, questions, and promises, and not isolated propositions or truth conditions, are the primary units of meaning in the use and comprehension of language. As Searle and I pointed out, most elementary speech acts, which are the meanings of utterances, consist of an illocutionary force and a propositional content. From a logical point of view, they have conditions of success as well as conditions of satisfaction, and these two types of condition are not reducible to truth conditions.

The main purpose of this volume is to formalize by proof- as well as by model-theoretic methods a general success and truth conditional semantics for natural languages that incorporates both a logic of illocutionary acts and a logic of senses and denotations. Until now, most advances that have occurred in contemporary formal semantics have been confined to the interpretation of restricted fragments of natural languages containing only declarative sentences. An integration of illocutionary logic in the theoretical apparatus of formal semantics is necessary in order to analyze adequately the meanings of illocutionary force markers and sentence types as well as the meanings of clauses. It will enable formal semantics to interpret sentences of all types (interrogative, imperative, optative, exclamatory as well as declarative sentences) expressing speech acts with all kinds of illocutionary force.

Given the logical form of illocutionary acts, the two single most important goals of formal semantics are the construction of general theories of success and of satisfaction under an arbitrary interpretation. As I will show, the semantic theory of truth advocated by Montague, Davidson, and others for natural languages is just the particular subtheory for assertive utterances of the more general theory of satisfaction for utterances with an arbitrary illocutionary force.

I do not regard as satisfactory formal treatments of illocutionary force markers or sentential types that have been attempted in previous logics of speech acts, such as Belnap's logic of questions or empirical extensions of Montague grammar. Because these treatments have eliminated illocutionary forces in favor of senses, they have ignored and failed to predict all the non truth conditional types of analyticity, entailment, and consistency that exist in the logical structure of natural languages. Moreover, because they have failed to analyze adequately the logical form of propositions, they have also multiplied false semantic predictions of entailment.

In order to carry out the project of a general formal success and truth conditional semantics for natural languages, I will enrich the theoretical apparatus of formal semantics in various ways. First, I will distinguish two types of meaning: linguistic meaning and meaning in context as in Kaplan's logic of demonstratives. A double semantic indexation is needed in semantics in order to account for the fact that the same sentence can be used to perform different illocutionary acts in different contexts. Second, I will formulate a non-standard definition of the logical type of proposition that takes into account the cognitive aspects of meaning in the apprehension of propositions. Third, I will admit success as well as truth values in the formal ontology of semantics and I will enrich the expressive capacities of the ideal object-language of formal semantics by adding to its theoretical lexicon new logical constants expressing the few primitive notions of illocutionary logic. Finally, I will formulate recursive definitions of success and of satisfaction made by induction on the length of formulas in the canonical notation, and I will ramify fundamental semantic notions such as entailment and consistency. As we will see, such theoretical developments enable formal semantics to derive systematically by standard logical methods all kinds of practical as well as theoretical valid inferences that speakers and hearers are able to make in virtue of their linguistic competence.

I have explained in detail in the first volume of this book the principles underlying the formalization that I will present here. The reader who has not read *Principles of Language Use* is advised to look at chapters 2 and 4 of that volume in order to become acquainted with these principles.

The plan of this second volume is as follows: chapter 1 criticizes previous attempts to formalize the logic of speech acts and the semantics of non-declarative sentences. Chapters 2 and 3 present a complete first order formulation of illocutionary logic which is as simple as possible from a logical point of view. This formulation concentrates on the logical form of speech acts, and formalizes the fundamental laws that govern the successful performance and the satisfaction of elementary illocutionary acts. Chapter 4 defines the ideal perspicuous and disambiguous object-language of general semantics. As I announced earlier, one can translate into that formal conceptual language sentences of natural languages of any possible sentential type. Chapter 5 further develops the model-theory of intensional logic in order to formalize the theory of sentence meaning of general semantics. This chapter defines the structure of a possible interpretation for the ideal object-language. It also enumerates a series of valid laws of synonymy, analyticity, consistency, and entailment which are philosophically or linguistically significant. Chapter 6 is the central chapter of this book. It presents an axiomatic system which is generally complete in the sense that it axiomatizes the set of laws of general semantics which are generally valid. One interesting feature of this proof-theoretic formalization is that general semantics appears to be both a conservative extension and a natural generalization of Montague grammar.

Finally, the last chapter states rules of translation for a series of

3

English performative verbs and analyzes various important modal and tense connectives and propositional attitude verbs. It shows how to apply the theoretical apparatus of general semantics to English. These indirect formal analyses of performative verbs are also intended to facilitate the implementation of illocutionary logic on computers for the purposes of the automatic generation of dialogues between man and machine in artificial intelligence.

1

EARLIER LOGICS
OF SPEECH ACTS

The illocutionary logic that I will develop in this volume is the first attempt to formalize extensively by proof- as well as by model-theoretic methods a general logical theory of speech acts dealing with the conditions of success and of satisfaction of all types of illocutionary act. True, there were a few earlier attempts in past decades to formalize the logic of particular directive speech acts such as commands, orders, and questions. But these logics have been confined to the study of speech acts with one or more isolated illocutionary forces. Moreover, they have tended to *eliminate* rather than to analyze the illocutionary forces of such speech acts. In this chapter, I will first criticize these earlier logics of speech acts and show that they have adopted methodologies and theoretical principles which are incompatible with basic facts about the use of language. Next, I will compare the research program of my general success and truth conditional semantics with that of Montague grammar, which remains to my knowledge the most advanced semantic theory of natural languages. Some logicians or linguists have recently proposed formal treatments of illocutionary force markers or performative verbs in empirical extensions of Montague grammar. I will explain both why these empirical extensions have failed and how I hope to avoid their mistakes by first enriching the theoretical apparatus of Montague's intensional semantics.

I RESCHER'S LOGIC OF COMMANDS

Two important earlier logics of speech acts that were developed before *Foundations*[1] are Rescher's *logic of commands* and Belnap's *logic of questions*. From the point of view of speech act theory, these two logics are not only incomplete in the sense that they only concern a few special types of directive illocutionary acts: they are also inadequate partial formalizations of speech act theory, as I will now argue.

Let us start with Rescher's logic of commands, which was published in 1966. That logic deals with a class of directive speech acts containing not only commands in the proper illocutionary sense of the word, but also orders, requests, injunctions, prohibitions, and so on.[2] Rescher does not analyze the logical differences that exist between the directive speech acts to which his logic applies. In his view, the primary aim of a logical theory of commands is to articulate the various forms of valid inferences that one can make from premise sets consisting of directives, or of both directives and statements.

As Rescher pointed out, some inferences between commands are *valid*, in the sense that:

(1) any speaker who overtly gives the commands and makes the assertions expressed by the premises of those inferences may legitimately *claim* to have *implicitly* given the command expressed by the conclusion;

(2) any hearer who is overtly given the commands and assertions expressed by the premises may legitimately *claim* (or *be claimed*) to have been given the command expressed by the conclusion; and

(3) any future course of action of the hearer which satisfies the commands expressed by the premises must also satisfy the command expressed by the conclusion, when the assertions expressed by the premises are true.[3]

Examples of such valid inferences between commands are:

John, be nice to everyone to whom you speak!
John, speak to Mary!

Therefore, John, be nice to Mary!

---

[1] J. R. Searle and D. Vanderveken, *Foundations of Illocutionary Logic*, Cambridge University Press, 1985.
[2] N. Rescher, *The Logic of Commands*, London: Routledge & Kegan Paul, 1966.
[3] See ibid., p. 77.

6

John, be nice to Tom!
John, be nice to the dog!

Therefore, John, be nice to Tom and to the dog!

John, speak to every guest tonight!
Tom will be a guest tonight.

Therefore, John, speak to Tom tonight!

Rescher also distinguishes in his logic of commands other types of valid inference between commands, including one type that corresponds to what I have called in volume I *truth conditional entailment*.[4] Thus, some inferences involving commands are also valid in the sense that the assertions and directives expressed by their premises cannot be satisfied unless the assertion or directive expressed by their conclusion is also satisfied.

For example, the following truth conditional inference is valid in the logic of commands:

John, be nice to your brother!

John has a brother.

As is clear from Rescher's examples, these different (illocutionary and truth conditional) types of valid inference do not always coincide in extension. One important historical contribution of Rescher's logic of commands has been to emphasize the existence of and the need to study the principles of such valid practical or theoretical inferences involving directive as well as assertive speech acts. On many points, the aims of the logic of commands are similar to those of illocutionary logic.

Unfortunately, Rescher did not try to define formally his semantic notions of valid inferences between commands. On the contrary, he relies heavily on intuition in his investigations. His purpose is to develop a logical theory of commands "in the sense of the every day use of these concepts".[5] Thus, for example, he uses without any explanation the performative verb "to claim" in his definition of a valid inference between commands, instead of using the more basic semantic predicates of success and of satisfaction. Furthermore, there is no general definition of the conditions of success of directive speech

---

[4] See ibid., p. 2.
[5] See ibid., p. 8.

acts in his logic of commands, just as there is no analysis of their particular illocutionary forces. The main reason for this is probably Rescher's methodological prejudice according to which *performances cannot stand in logical relation to one another*. In his view, "specifically, one performance cannot entail or imply another, nor can the description of one performance entail that of another." Thus, his logic of commands is bound to abstract from the proper illocutionary aspect of commands. It cannot study what consists of *the act of giving a command*. Such a prejudice deprives Rescher of the means of defining precisely his notions of valid inference between commands in terms of inclusion of conditions of success or of satisfaction. This is why he is obliged to rely so heavily on intuition in his explanations. Unlike Rescher's logic of commands, the illocutionary logic that—I will formulate in this volume contains a theoretical vocabulary which enables it to analyze the logical form of illocutionary acts and to define recursively their conditions of success. Thus, it will do more than simply enumerate a series of valid inferences between commands. It will try to derive them in a systematic way by axiomatic and model-theoretic means.

II THE LOGIC OF QUESTIONS

In opposition to Rescher's logic of commands, the logic of questions that has been developed in past decades by Belnap,[6] Hamblin,[7] Karttunen[8] and others is much more sophisticated. These logicians have indeed developed model-theoretic semantics for ideal object-languages where questions can be expressed, and, in some cases, they have also presented axiomatizations of laws governing questions. (More recently, linguists, like Groenendijk and Stockhof[9] in Holland and Hausser[10] and Zaefferer[11] in Germany, have also used the intensional logic of Montague grammar in order to interpret in-

---

[6] N. Belnap and T. Steel, *The Logic of Questions and Answers*, Yale University Press, 1976. See also N. Belnap, "Declaratives are not enough", forthcoming in *Philosophical Studies*.

[7] C. L. Hamblin, "Questions", *Australian Journal of Philosophy*, 36 (1958), 159–68, and C. L. Hamblin, "Questions in Montague English", *Foundations of Language*, 10 (1973), 41–53.

[8] L. Karttunen, "Syntax and the semantics of questions", *Linguistics and Philosophy*, 1 (1977), 3–44.

[9] J. Groenendijk and M. Stockhof, "On the semantics of questions and the pragmatics of answers", in F. Landman and F. Veldman (eds.), *Varieties of Formal Semantics*, Dordrecht, Netherlands: Foris, 1984.

[10] R. Hausser: "Surface compositionality and the semantics of mood", in J. R. Searle, F. Kiefer, and M. Bierwisch (eds.), *Speech Act Theory and Pragmatics*, Dordrecht, Netherlands: Reidel, 1980.

[11] D. Zaefferer, *Frageausdrücke und Fragen im Deutschen*, Munich: Wilhelm Fink Verlage, 1984.

8

terrogative sentences. I will discuss these logics of interrogative sentences in the next section.)

Although there are important differences in the logics of questions of Belnap, Hamblin, Karttunen, and others, they all have in common a certain methodology, due to Belnap, which tends to identify a *question* with a set (or a property) of possible *answers* to that question. This is what Harrah[12] calls the *set of answers methodology*. Moreover, they also tend to identify answers to questions with propositions or other senses. Thus, their logic of questions deals in the end only with propositions (or other senses). This *theoretical reduction of questions to senses* is based on principles like the following:

(1) To understand a question is to understand what counts as an answer to that question.

(2) An answer to a question is an assertion or statement.

(3) An assertion is identical with its propositional content.

Thus, for example, in Hamblin's logic a question is identified with the set of propositional contents of its possible answers. On this view, a yes-no question like the question asked by an utterance of the interrogative sentence "Is it raining?" is identical with the set that contains the proposition that it is raining and the proposition that it is not raining. In Karttunen's logic, on the other hand, a question is identified with the smaller set of its true answers.

There are of course differences between the various logics of questions that have been developed on the basis of such a methodology. In certain logics, answers need not be statements: they can be senses of noun phrases. Furthermore, in other logics, not all propositional answers, but only those which are true or direct, are to be taken into consideration. However, all these logics of questions have in common the *reductionist* methodology that I have explained. Thus, in the end, they are only concerned with senses.

Now it is quite obvious that such a reduction of the illocutionary force of a question is incompatible with speech act theory as I have developed it in the first volume of this work. In particular, the three principles underlying the reductionist methodology of these logics of questions are incompatible with basic facts of language use.

First, from a logical point of view, a question is an elementary speech

---

[12] D. Harrah, "The logic of questions", in D. Gabbay and F. Guenthner (eds.), *Handbook of Philosophical Logic*, vol. II, Extensions of Classical Logic, Dordrecht, Netherlands: Reidel, 1984.

act of the form $F(P)$. It has both conditions of success and conditions of satisfaction, and there is no way these conditions can be defined without taking into consideration the nature of the question's illocutionary force. By definition, the *conditions of success* of a question are the conditions under which a speaker can succeed in *asking* that question. On the other hand, the *conditions of satisfaction* of a question are the conditions under which the hearer can succeed in *answering* that question. Obviously, these two types of condition do *not* coincide. Although a question cannot be answered if it has not been asked, it can be asked successfully without being answered. As in the case of other directive speech acts, the conditions of success of a question are a function of its illocutionary force as well as of its propositional content. Thus, there is no way one can hope to characterize adequately all relations of illocutionary commitment and of incompatibility that exist between questions, if their illocutionary force is eliminated.

Second, a linguistic answer to a question is not necessarily an assertion. It can be an utterance with another possible illocutionary force. Thus, for example, an answer to the question "Do you confirm his nomination?" can be a declaration, as in the performative utterance "Yes, I hereby confirm it." Similarly, an answer to the question "Do you promise to come?" can be a promise or a denegation of a promise. On this account, the second principle of the reduction is also clearly false.

Third, even when they are assertions, answers, like other speech acts, cannot be identified with their propositional contents. Any adequate logic of assertion must also analyze what the making of an assertion consists of.

On this account, all the principles underlying the methodology of the logics of questions are incompatible with speech act theory. Furthermore, these logics of questions are also inadequate because of a *lack of generality*.

As Searle and I pointed out, each specific illocutionary force occupies a very precise place in the logical space of all possible illocutionary forces of utterances. It can be obtained from the primitive force with the same illocutionary point by the application of certain operations which consist of adding components or changing the degree of strength. Each illocutionary force stands for that reason in a network of logical relations with respect to other stronger, weaker, or incompatible forces. Thus, it is clearly a mistake to try to develop a logic of questions without integrating it in a general logic of all types of speech acts. Just as one cannot isolate the logic of, for example, truth functional conjunction from the logic of other truth functional operations on propositions, so one cannot isolate the logic of the illocutionary force of questions from the logic of other illocutionary forces.

In particular, one cannot analyze what a *question* is without analyzing the illocutionary forces of *requests* and other simpler directive speech acts. As Frege had already noticed,[13] a question is a special kind of request. A speaker who asks a question requests the hearer to make a future speech act which is a (non-defective or true) answer to that question.[14] In this view, the illocutionary force for a question is a complex directive force obtained from that of a request by adding certain special propositional content conditions. Now, these propositional content conditions are such that the propositional content of a question determines *both* the illocutionary forces and the propositional contents of the possible (direct) answers to that question. Thus, there is no way one can isolate the logic of questions from the logic of other *non-directive* illocutionary forces, since in order to characterize their propositional content conditions one must take into consideration the illocutionary forces of their answers, and these can be of all types.

The necessity of an *integrated logic of speech acts* is shown in language in various ways. First, one can ask questions by uttering non-interrogative sentences whose markers express other illocutionary forces. For example, the question asked by an utterance of the interrogative sentence "Is it raining?" can also be asked by uttering the imperative sentence "Please, tell me if it is raining!" (whose marker expresses the force of a request), or by uttering the performative sentence "I ask you if it is raining" (whose marker expresses the force of a declaration). Second, one can answer questions by uttering various types of sentences. For example, an answer to the question "Are you asking me to help you?" can be a request "Yes, please" or the illocutionary denegation of a request "No, I am not." As I pointed out earlier, an answer to a question need not always be a statement.

---

[13] See "The thought: A logical inquiry", in F. Strawson (ed.), *Philosophical Logic*, Oxford University Press, 1967.

[14] The idea that interrogative sentences are synonymous with the corresponding imperative sentences of the form "Tell me truly" is also defended by D. Lewis and S. Lewis, "Review of Olson and Paul, *Contemporary Philosophy in Scandinavia*", *Theoria*, 41 (1975), 39–60.

In spite of their weaknesses, the logics of questions that I have criticized so far have important merits. They can be used to define the special propositional content conditions of questions. Indeed, they have characterized important logical relations that exist between the propositional contents of questions and answers. Their results on this issue will have to be incorporated into the logic of questions in general semantics. However, more needs to be done. An adequate logic of questions must *also* characterize the logical relations that exist between a question and the illocutionary forces of its possible answers. Moreover, it must deal generally with success conditional types of valid inference involving questions and other types of speech act.

III CRITICISM OF MONTAGUE GRAMMAR

As I said earlier, my research program has many similarities with that of Montague. In carrying out the project of general semantics, I adopt Montague's view that *natural languages can be studied and adequately interpreted by the same rigorous logical methods as those used in meta-mathematics* to study and interpret the artificial object-languages of logic and pure mathematics.[15] According to this view, there is no important *logical* difference between natural and formal languages. Of course, *ordinary language* is not logically perfect: most of its sentences are ambiguous in various ways, and their grammatical structure does not reflect clearly their logical form. On the other hand, *formal languages* are in general both perspicuous and disambiguous. More-over, they impose special theoretical constraints on their linguistic forms of expression. Thus, for example, unlike natural languages, ideal conceptual languages do not in general admit vacuous proper names or several proper names for the same entity. But these grammatical differences between natural and formal languages serve their different purposes and do not affect their logical structure. As Wittgenstein pointed out,[16] ordinary language is perfectly in order as it is. Even if the grammatical form of its sentences can be misleading, their logical form is always apprehended by human speakers and hearers in the process of meaning and understanding. Moreover, these grammatical dif-ferences between natural and formal languages serve their different

---

[15] See "English as a formal language", in R. Montague, *Formal Philosophy*, Yale University Press, 1974.

[16] See his *Tractatus logico-philosophicus*, Routledge & Kegan Paul, 1961.

purposes in human societies. Natural languages must enable human beings to express and communicate their thoughts with precision and efficiency in an endless variety of new situations which can occur in an ever-changing world. In order to be efficient, they must be more flexible than formal languages which are created for the scientific purposes of describing theoretically and as simply as possible fixed aspects of the world.

As I pointed out earlier, the use of ideal languages is convenient for theoretical reasons. The few logical constants and syncategorematic symbols of an ideal conceptual language provide a *theoretical vocabulary* in terms of which linguistic entities and speech acts can be described in a canonical way. Moreover, the translation of sentences in natural languages into an ideal formal language enables semantics to exhibit diagrammatically the logical relations that exist between these sentences in the deep structure of language. This regimentation allows for a major simplification of the theory of meaning.

To my knowledge, Montague himself never tried to apply his logical grammar to the interpretation of fragments of English containing performative or non-declarative sentences. But he was very aware of the necessity of replacing the basic notion of a truth condition by other notions in order to interpret non-declarative sentences. Thus, for example, he proposed to speak of *conditions of fulfillment* rather than of truth conditions in the particular case of imperative sentences.[17] Moreover, one might think that Montague was also aware of the difficulties that his Carnapian definition of the logical type of proposition would raise for the interpretation of performative and non-declarative sentences. Indeed, in his general treatment of *pragmatic languages*,[18] he shows how Carnap's method of intension and extension can be successfully generalized in modal, tense, deontic, and inductive logics, as well as in the logics of non truth functional conditionals and of indexical expressions. But he does not make any reference to the logic of questions and of other directive speech acts.

However, formally minded linguists have tried in recent years to apply Montague grammar *as such* (without making any theoretical extension of its intensional logic) to the interpretation of non-declarative sentences (especially interrogative sentences). Thus,

---

[17] See R. Montague, "The proper treatment of quantification in ordinary English", note 3 in *Formal Philosophy*, Yale University Press, 1974.
[18] See R. Montague, "Pragmatics", in *Formal Philosophy*.

Groenendijk and Stockhof,[19] Hamblin,[20] Hausser,[21] Karttunen,[22] Zaefferer,[23] and others have developed *empirical extensions of Montague grammar*, where Montague's intensional logic is used to interpret indirectly fragments of English (or German) containing non-declarative sentences. In general, these extensions of Montague grammar only deal with one or two isolated types of sentence, usually *interrogatives* and *imperatives*. However, Zaefferer has also used Montague grammar in order to interpret performative and exclamatory sentences.

Among these empirical extensions of Montague grammar theory, Zaefferer's semantic analyses are especially interesting from the point of view of speech act theory. Indeed, Zaefferer adopts a more general approach to language use with the aim of characterizing formally the illocutionary aspects of sentence meaning. In particular, he admits the existence of illocutionary force markers in elementary sentences, and he acknowledges their contribution to the meaning of sentences.[24] As a starting point, he takes the intuitive notion of a *sentence mood* as it can be found in most ordinary grammars. Next, after an overview of sentence moods in various typologically different languages, he proposes an explication of the notion of sentence mood, and states hypotheses about illocutionary universals that are confirmed by his comparative study of illocutionary sentential types in several languages.[25] Thus, Zaefferer's approach is more general: it deals simultaneously with several sentential types in several languages. Moreover, unlike the others, Zaefferer also recognizes explicitly the existence of illocutionary as well as of truth conditional entailments between sentences. According to him, any adequate semantic theory of language should predict accurately both types of entailment.

Unfortunately, from an empirical point of view, these applications of Montague grammar to non-declarative fragments of English have failed. First, they have not succeeded in characterizing adequately the

---

[19] Groenendijk and Stockhof, "On the semantics of questions and the pragmatics of answers".
[20] Hamblin, "Questions in Montague English".
[21] Hausser, "Surface compositionality and the semantics of mood".
[22] Karttunen, "Syntax and the semantics of questions".
[23] D. Zaefferer, "On a formal treatment of illocutionary force indicators", in H. Parret, M. Sbisa, and J. Verschueren (eds.), *Possibilities and Limitations of Pragmatics*, Amsterdam: Benjamins, 1982; "The semantics of non-declaratives: investigating German exclamations", in R. Bäuerle, C. Schwarze, and A. von Stechow (eds.), *Meaning, Use and Interpretation of Language*, Berlin: W. de Gruyter, 1983.
[24] See Zaefferer "On a formal treatment of illocutionary force indicators".
[25] See "The semantics of sentence mood in typologically differing languages", in Shiro Hattori *et al.* (eds.), *Proceedings of the XIIIth International Congress of Linguists*, Tokyo, 1984.

logical structures of the sets of illocutionary forces, of propositions, and of speech acts. For example, they have formulated inadequate definitions of the logical types of speech act and of the meanings of sentential types.

Second, they have also neglected many important success conditional aspects of sentence meaning. In particular, they have ignored or failed to predict many fundamental laws of illocutionary entailment and of incompatibility that hold for the various types of sentence in the use and comprehension of language. Moreover, they have multiplied doubtful or false semantic predictions for sentences of the same type with logically related propositional contents. Finally, they have not recognized to its full extent the variety and the wealth of actual forms of expression for speech acts in English or other actual natural languages. For example, they have not identified the semantic role of modifiers in illocutionary force markers and they have tended to assign to all sentences of the same syntactic type the same illocutionary force.

One can distinguish the following general mistakes in these empirical extensions of Montague grammar:

1 *A methodological mistake*

A general mistake common to all these extensions is that they have been too close to the few illocutionarily significant sentential types of ordinary language. They have studied directly actual illocutionary forces *as they are realized syntactically in sentential types* in English or other languages without first developing an analysis of the logical form of speech acts. This methodology is mistaken for several reasons. First, few actual illocutionary forces are syntactically realized in sentential types. Second, the illocutionary force markers of elementary sentences are often more complex than their sentential type. They contain modifiers like "please" and "alas" whose meaning contributes to determining further the specific illocutionary forces of their utterances. Moreover, it would have been better to start with the analysis of performative verbs, since there are many more performative verbs which name illocutionary forces than sentential types which express such forces. In general, these empirical extensions of Montague grammar have ignored the systematic semantic relations that exist between elementary sentences and the corresponding performative sentences.

Finally, they have also often been misled by the superficial grammatical form of sentences in ordinary language. As I said earlier, the illocutionary force markers of ordinary language can be ambiguous, and their syntactic structure does not always reflect the logical form of the illocutionary forces which they express. Thus, for example, simple sentential types like the interrogative and the optative types express logically complex illocutionary forces with special conditions. On the other hand, logically simple illocutionary forces like the primitive commissive force lack a syntactically simple form of expression in English and most other languages. For all these reasons, it is better to have at the very beginning a general illocutionary logic of the kind developed above, in order to analyze theoretically the illocutionary forces of utterances. Indeed, such a general logical theory of language use provides a *conceptual* analysis of the logical form of illocutionary acts which is relatively independent from their actual contingent linguistic forms of expression. Just as an intensional logic is needed in Montague grammar in order to have a unified theoretical form of description of the truth conditions of utterances, an illocutionary logic is needed in general semantics in order to have a unified theoretical form of description of their conditions of success. (Of course, nothing prevents the improvement of the logical theory in the course of its application.)

A few empirical mistakes follow from the general methodological mistake that I have just criticized.

2 *Inadequate definitions of the logical types of speech acts*

In their semantic analyses of non-declarative sentences, the above-mentioned linguists have assigned to sentential types *senses* whose logical types do not provide the right *criteria of identity*. Thus, for example, Hausser, who accepts utterances of noun phrases as answers to questions, identifies questions with properties of sets of noun phrase denotations in his semantics of interrogatives.[26] Roughly, the semantic value of an interrogative sentence in a context is, according to him, the set of noun phrase denotations which are non-redundant answers to that question. This analysis is just another version of the set of answers reductionist methodology that I have criticized above in my discussion of the logic of questions. In the same vein, Hausser

---

[26] See "Surface compositionality and the semantics of mood".

identifies directive utterances of imperative sentences with properties of individual concepts. Roughly, the semantic value of an imperative sentence in a context is the property that the speaker would want the hearer to acquire if he were using that sentence in that context. An imperative utterance is fulfilled according to Hausser if the hearer acquires the property in question. Similar definitions of the logical types of question and of directive utterance are adopted by Zaefferer and others.

Now, these assignments of logical types to utterances are wrong from the point of view of speech act theory because they do not reflect adequately the nature and linguistic purposes of utterances. Such assignments tend indeed to identify illocutionary acts with their conditions of satisfaction. However, as I have argued repeatedly in volume I, one cannot leave out the general notion of *success* in the semantic interpretation of utterances. Indeed, the linguistic purposes of speech acts are determined by their conditions of success as well as by their propositional content. Thus, speech acts having the same conditions of satisfaction are not necessarily identical. For example, the two utterances "He is dead" and "Alas, he is dead" have the same truth conditions, but different assertive illocutionary forces. Consequently their meanings are also different.

3 *Inadequate analyses of the illocutionary forces of utterances of sentences of the same type*

Because these empirical extensions of Montague grammar have not divided illocutionary forces into their various types of component, they have been unable to analyze adequately the meaning differences that exist between sentences of the same type, such as "Please, come here!" and "Whether you like it or not, come here!", whose markers express different illocutionary forces with the same point. Thus, Hausser recognizes that one can perform different kinds of directive illocutionary acts, such as orders and requests, in the utterance of imperative sentences. However, he is obliged to rely on *pragmatic* criteria, like the status of the speaker (authority), his wishes (sincerity), and so on, in order to differentiate the directive illocutionary forces of imperative utterances.[27] On the other hand, if one incorporates illocutionary logic into formal semantics, then one can differentiate in a much simpler way

[27] See ibid., p. 85.

the illocutionary forces of the literal utterances of sentences of the same type by relying on *semantic* criteria. Indeed, one can then identify the contribution that expressions like "please" and "whether you like it or not" make to the meaning of imperative sentences by saying that they serve to indicate special components of the illocutionary forces of the utterances of these sentences.

Just as there is more to illocutionary force than illocutionary point in the use and comprehension of language, there is more to illocutionary force markers than sentential types in the syntactic structure of sentences.

4 *An unnecessary multiplication of the logical types of speech acts*

Fourth, whenever these empirical extensions of Montague grammar have dealt simultaneously with several illocutionarily significant sentential types, they have also committed the mistake of assigning different logical types to elementary illocutionary acts of the same logical form, like assertions, questions, and directives, which are characteristically expressed by sentences with these types.

Thus, for example, the semantic values of interrogative and imperative sentences are senses of different logical types in these extensions of Montague grammar. Hausser goes as far as to assert that there is no type overlap between syntactic moods.[28] Zaefferer, on the other hand, admits type overlap but only in the case of illocutionary ambiguity.[29] However, it is quite obvious that one can often perform the same speech act by uttering sentences of a different type. One can, for example, literally ask questions by uttering imperative as well as interrogative sentences.

Instead of multiplying the logical types of elementary act of the form $F(P)$ on the contingent basis of their syntactic realizations in sentential types, it is much more natural and simple from a theoretical point of view to assign to all of them a *single logical type* which adequately reflects their criteria of identity. Indeed, one then need only rely formally on the logical structure of the set of all illocutionary acts in order to explain and predict systematically all kinds of entailment and relative inconsistency that exist between sentences (of the same or of different syntactic types). Otherwise, one is obliged to multiply in an

---

[28] See ibid., p. 92.
[29] See "On a formal treatment of illocutionary force indicators".

ad hoc way the number of meaning postulates in order to predict actual illocutionary entailments and relative inconsistencies. The necessity of multiplying enormously the meaning postulates in empirical extensions of Montague grammar appears, for example, in the way they translate performative verbs. Translations of performative verbs with the same point, such as "order", "request", "ask", etc., do not have any syntactic structure in these extensions. They are simply different non-logical constants of the appropriate type of the ideal language.[30]

On the other hand, in general semantics, whenever the illocutionary force named by a performative verb is stronger than the force named by another verb with the same point, the illocutionary entailment is shown diagrammatically in the syntactic structure of their translations. Indeed, the translation of the first performative verb will in general be a syntactically complex formula obtained by combining the translation of the second verb with formulas naming the additional components. Thus, there is no need here of *ad hoc* semantic meaning postulates to predict the corresponding illocutionary entailments between performative sentences. One can simply rely on the recursive definitions of the set of all illocutionary forces and of the conditions of success of utterances of the illocutionary logic of general semantics.

In Montague grammar, the same logical type is assigned to all propositions and the logical structure of the set of all propositions, as described by the intensional logic of that grammar, is heavily relied on in order to predict all kinds of truth conditional entailments between declarative sentences. Similarly, in general semantics, I will assign to all elementary speech acts of the form $F(P)$ the same logical type, and I will rely on the illocutionary logic of that semantics in order systematically to predict all kinds of success conditional entailments. A revised and more detailed model-theoretical approach along the lines of empirical extensions of Montague grammar might well turn out to be equivalent to that of general semantics. However, I suspect that the theory of language use embedded in such an empirical extension would be extremely complicated because of the necessity of the *ad hoc* multiplication of meaning postulates. This is why I advocate first a *theoretical extension* of Montague's intensional logic.

Now, from the point of view of speech act theory, this historical failure of attempts at *empirical* extensions of Montague grammar is not at all surprising. Indeed, there are two major conceptual defects in the

---

[30] See ibid.

theoretical framework of Montague grammar, which make it inapplicable as such to the interpretation of natural languages.

First, Montague's intensional logic identifies, as does Carnap, the *propositional contents* of utterances with their *truth conditions*. For this reason, it cannot adequately characterize the cognitive aspects of meaning in the apprehension of propositions. As I showed earlier, many strictly equivalent propositions are not cognitively apprehended under the same conditions. This is why clauses expressing strictly equivalent propositions are not always substitutable *salva felicitate* within the scope of illocutionary force markers. However, in all these empirical extensions of Montague grammar, sentences with the same markers and strictly equivalent clauses, like "Come here!" and "Come here and either eat or do not eat!", have the same meaning. Moreover, because of their inadequate definition of the logical type of proposition, these empirical extensions of Montague grammar do not have at their disposal a finer relation of implication between propositions than strict implication in order to characterize adequately the laws of illocutionary commitment that are due to the inclusion of truth conditions.

Second, Montague grammar totally ignores in its formalization the logical relations between *success* and *meaning*. Like Tarski, Davidson and other philosophers, Montague emphasizes repeatedly the logical relations that exist between *truth* and *meaning* in the semantic structure of language. In his logical grammar, he attempts to define recursively the notion of a true utterance under an arbitrary semantic interpretation. However, there is no similar attempt to define the general notion of a successful utterance under an interpretation in Montague grammar. Thus, for example, Montague's formal ontology does not admit success values in addition to truth values and individuals in the domain of a model. Similarly, Montague's semantics does not recognize any success conditional type of entailment or of consistency. For such reasons, one cannot represent adequately in Montague grammar basic facts of language-use, like the fact that utterances can either succeed or fail or the fact that the conditions of success of speech acts are not reducible to their conditions of satisfaction or to the truth conditions of their propositional content. On the contrary, most of these empirical extensions of Montague grammar have committed the mistake of tending to identify speech acts with their conditions of satisfaction. As a consequence of this, their analyses of illocutionary force markers and of performative verbs are both materially and formally inadequate.

This historic failure in the achievement of Montague's research program is not at all irremediable. On the contrary, as I will show in this volume, a general success and truth conditional semantics is perfectly compatible with Montague grammar. Indeed, one can theoretically enrich Montague's intensional logic in a natural way and obtain a more general and powerful intensional logic which is adequate for the analysis of speech acts and the interpretation of sentences of all types. In order to do this, one must, however, make the few decisive theoretical moves that I have explained in detail in the preceding volume. In particular, one must (i) ramify the notion of meaning by adopting a double semantic indexation (as in the logic of demonstratives),[31] (ii) enrich the formal ontology of Montague grammar by admitting a set of two success values, (iii) change the definition of the logical type of proposition in order to incorporate cognitive aspects of meaning, (iv) add to the lexicon of formal semantics a few logical constants (like constants for illocutionary points) expressing the primitive notions of speech act theory, and, finally, (v) formulate recursive definitions of the conditions of success and of satisfaction of utterances. As I will show in the rest of this book, one can adequately *derive* in such a *theoretical extension of Montague grammar* (by the usual operations of type theory and without admitting new basic entities other than the two success values) the logical types of illocutionary force and of speech act. Illocutionary acts and forces are *complex set-theoretical entities* of derived types in general semantics. Moreover, one can next obtain, *by rules of abbreviation*, expressions in canonical forms for illocutionary forces, operations on forces, speech acts, and logical relations between such entities. Thus there is a theoretical economy of primitive notions in the logical theory. Finally, one can also *prove by meta-mathematical methods* that this formalized extension of Montague grammar does *not modify* the set of logically valid formulas of the initial sub-language of Montague. As I announced earlier, my general semantics will be a *conservative* extension of Montague grammar.[32] (More on this later.)

---

[31] This double semantic indexation already exists in Montague grammar, e.g. in "Universal grammar", *Theoria*, 36 (1970), 373–98. But it can be developed in a simpler way along the lines of Kaplan's logic of demonstratives.

[32] For the notion of a conservative extension, see J. R. Shoenfield, *Mathematical Logic*, Reading, Mass.: Addison-Wesley, 1967, ch. 4.

2

---·••·---

A SIMPLE FORMULATION OF
ILLOCUTIONARY LOGIC

The aim of this chapter is to develop, on the basis of the general principles that have been stated above, a complete first order illocutionary logic which is as simple as possible from the point of view of logical syntax and semantics, but strong enough to prove most fundamental laws that govern the successful performance and satisfaction of elementary speech acts.

Only the basic notions which are necessary for the calculus of elementary speech acts are expressible in the ideal object-language of the simple illocutionary logic *IL* which is formulated in this chapter. In particular, only first order quantification is allowed, so as to obtain completeness, and there is no logical analysis of the structure of atomic propositions which constitute the contents of propositions. All the results of this first order formalization will later be incorporated and generalized in the higher order intensional logic of general semantics.

The first section of this chapter presents the ideal object-language of the illocutionary logic *IL*, and explains how its terms and sentences can be naively interpreted. The second section enumerates the rules of abbreviation in terms of which other important notions of speech act theory can be derived from the few primitive notions expressed by the logical constants and syncategorematic symbols of the ideal language. The third section defines the model-theoretical structure of a possible interpretation of illocutionary logic. Finally, the last section presents an axiomatic system in which all logically true sentences of first order illocutionary logic are provable.

I THE IDEAL OBJECT-LANGUAGE

Unlike the logics of commands and of questions discussed in the preceding section, the first order illocutionary logic that I will now present is an *integrated logical theory of speech acts*. It deals with elementary illocutionary acts of all types. However, that illocutionary logic is relatively simple from a logical point of view, because it studies the logical forms of elementary illocutionary acts without worrying about the sentential forms of expression that can exist for these acts in natural languages. Thus, there is no need for a double semantic indexation in the interpretation of the object-language of that first order illocutionary logic. Contrary to what is the case for natural languages, all the terms which name illocutionary forces, propositions, or speech acts in that logic are rigid designators which have the same semantic value in all possible contexts of use of an interpretation.

The grammar of the ideal object-language of illocutionary logic *IL* consists of the following rules and definitions:

1 *The primitive type symbols*

The primitive type symbols of *IL* are p, μ, θ, Σ, τ, ψ and ι. p names the type of *propositions*; μ names the type of *illocutionary points* and of *modes of achievement*; θ names the type of *propositional content conditions*; Σ names the type of *preparatory conditions*; τ names the type of *modes of propositional attitudes*; ψ names the type of *sincerity conditions*; and ι names the type of *degrees of strength*.

2 *The vocabulary*

The vocabulary of illocutionary logic *IL* contains:

infinitely many *variables*: x_α, x_α^1, x_α^2, ..., x_α^n, ..., y_α, y_α^1, y_α^2, ..., y_α^n, ..., z_α, z_α^1, z_α^2, ..., of each type $\alpha = p$, τ and ι;
infinitely many *constants*: c_α^1, c_α^2, c_α^3, ... of all primitive types α;
and the *logical constants*: 0_ι, 1_ζ, 0_ζ, for each type $\zeta \in \{\mu, \theta, \Sigma, \psi\}$ and π_μ^1, π_μ^2, π_μ^3, π_μ^4, π_μ^5.
Variables and constants have the type of their subscript. A variable and a constant of type α respectively indicate and denote (or for short hereafter *name*) an entity of that type.

23

In particular, 0_ι names the integer *zero*, 1_ζ and 0_ζ name respectively the *neutral* and the *absorbent component* of illocutionary force of type ζ. (Thus, for example, 1_μ names the neutral mode of achievement.) π_μ^1, π_μ^2, π_μ^3, π_μ^4 and π_μ^5 name respectively the *assertive, commissive, directive, declarative*, and *expressive* illocutionary *points*. Finally, for each k such that $1 \leqslant k \leqslant 5$, c_ψ^k is intended to name the *sincerity conditions determined* by the illocutionary point named by π_μ^k.[1]

The *syncategorematic symbols* of *IL* are: $\maltese$, $\forall$, $\gg$, E, $\sim$, $\vee$, $'$, t, $=$, $\rangle$, $\square$, (, and). These syncategorematic symbols are introduced in the following rules of formation.

3 The rules of formation of IL

Rule of formation of propositional terms

(i) Every constant and variable of type p of the vocabulary is a *propositional term* (or for short hereafter a *P-term*).

(ii) If A and B are propositional terms, then $\sim A$ and $(A \vee B)$ are also propositional terms.

$\sim A$ names the proposition which is the truth functional *negation* of the proposition named by A; $(A \vee B)$ names the truth functional *disjunction* of the two propositions named by A and B. All propositional terms are of type p.

Rules of formation of terms for components of illocutionary forces

(i) Every constant or variable of a type μ, θ, Σ, ψ, or ι is a *term for a component of illocutionary force* (or for short hereafter an *IFC*-term) of *IL*.

(ii) If A is an *IFC*-term of type ι, then $(A)'$ and $'(A)$ are new *IFC*-terms of the same type ι.

$(A)'$ and $'(A)$ name respectively the *immediate successor* and the *immediate predecessor* of the integer named by A.

(iii) if A and B are *IFC*-terms of the same type ζ, then $(A \maltese B)$ is a new *IFC*-term of type ζ of *IL*.

---

[1] Thus, for example, c_ψ^1 names the sincerity condition which contains the psychological mode of belief, c_ψ^2 the sincerity condition that contains the psychological mode of intention, and so on for other illocutionary points.

$(A \divideontimes B)$ names the *conjunction* of the modes of achievement named by A and B, when A and B are of type μ.

$(A \divideontimes B)$ names the *intersection* of the propositional content conditions named by A and B, when A and B are of type θ, the *union* of the preparatory or sincerity conditions named by A and B, when A and B are of type Σ or ψ; and the *sum* of the integers named by A and B, when A and B are of type ι.

Rule of formation of terms for illocutionary forces

If A_μ, A_θ, A_Σ, A_ψ and A_ι are *IFC*-terms respectively of types μ, θ, Σ, ψ and ι and $1 \leqslant k \leqslant 5$, then $[(A_\mu, A_\theta, A_\Sigma, A_\psi), A_\iota, \pi_\mu^k]$ is an *illocutionary force-term* (or for short hereafter an *IF*-term) of *IL* of the derived type ϕ (which is the type of illocutionary forces).

$[(A_\mu, A_\theta, A_\Sigma, A_\psi), A_\iota, \pi_\mu^k]$ names the illocutionary force F which determines the following success conditions: an elementary illocutionary act of the form $F(P)$ is *performed* in a context of utterance under an interpretation if and only if, in that context, according to that interpretation,

first, the proposition P satisfies the propositional content conditions named by A_θ;

second, the speaker achieves the illocutionary point named by π_μ^k on the proposition P with the mode of achievement named by A_μ;

third, he also presupposes all propositions associated by the preparatory condition named by A_Σ with the propositional content P in that context; and finally

fourth, he expresses with the degree of strength measured by the integer named by A_ι all the psychological states of the form $m(P)$, whose mode m belongs to the sincerity conditions which are named by A_ψ or determined by the illocutionary point named by π_μ^k.

Rule of formation of terms for illocutionary acts

If A_ϕ is an illocutionary force term and A_p is a propositional term, then $A_\phi(A_p)$ is an *illocutionary act term* (or for short hereafter an *IA*-term) of *IL* of the derived type Ω (which is the type for illocutionary acts).

$A_\phi(A_p)$ names the elementary speech act with the illocutionary force named by A_ϕ and the propositional content named by A_p.

Rule of formation of sentences

Sentences reporting conditions of success

If A_p, A_μ, A_θ, A_Σ and A_ψ are terms respectively of type p, μ, θ, Σ and ψ of *IL*, and A_τ is a constant or variable of type τ, then the following expressions $(A_\mu A_p)$, $(A_\theta A_p)$, $(A_\Sigma A_p B_p)$, $(A_\psi A_\tau)$ and $(E(A_\tau A_p)A_\iota)$ are *sentences* of *IL*.

A sentence of the form $(A_\mu A_p)$ is true in a context of utterance under an interpretation if and only if in that context the speaker achieves according to that interpretation an illocutionary point with the mode of achievement named by A_μ on the proposition named by A_p.

A sentence of the form $(A_\theta A_p)$ is true in a context under an interpretation if and only if the proposition named by A_p satisfies in that context the propositional content condition named by A_θ according to that interpretation.

$(A_\Sigma A_p B_p)$ is true in a context under an interpretation if and only if the speaker could not perform in that context according to that interpretation an illocutionary act with a force F having the preparatory conditions named by A_Σ and the propositional content named by A_p, without also presupposing the proposition named by B_p.

$(A_\psi A_\tau)$ is true in a context under an interpretation if and only if a speaker could not perform sincerely an illocutionary act $F(P)$ whose force F has the sincerity condition named by A_ψ, without having the psychological state of the mode named by A_τ about the state of affairs that P represents.

Finally, $(E(A_\tau A_p)A_\iota)$ is true in a context under an interpretation if and only if according to that interpretation the speaker in that context expresses with the degree of strength named by A_ι a psychological state with the mode named by A_τ and the propositional content named by A_p.

Sentences about propositions

If A and B are P-terms of *IL*, then $t(A)$, $(\gg A)$ and $(A \succ B)$ are also *sentences* of *IL*.

$t(A)$ is true in a context under an interpretation if and only if the proposition named by A is true in that context according to that interpretation; $\gg A$ is true in a context if and only if the proposition named by A is presupposed in that context; and $(A \geqslant B)$ is true in a context if and only if the content of the proposition named by B is included in the content of the proposition named by A.

Identity sentences

If A and B are terms of IL of the same type, then $(A = B)$ is a *sentence* of IL.

As in the first order predicate calculus with identity, a sentence $(A = B)$ is true in a context of an interpretation if and only if A and B name the same entities according to that interpretation.

Complex sentences

If A and B are sentences of IL, then $\sim A$, $\Box A$ and $(A \lor B)$ are new *sentences* of IL which are interpreted as usual.[2]

A sentence $\sim A$ is true in a context under an interpretation if and only if A is false in that context according to that interpretation; a sentence $(A \lor B)$ is true in a context if and only if at least one of the two sentences A and B is true in that context. Finally, the sentence $\Box A$ is true in a context under an interpretation if and only if A is true in all contexts according to that interpretation.

General sentences

If x is a variable and A is a sentence, then $\forall x\, A$ is a new *sentence* of IL.

As in quantification theory, such a sentence is true in a context under an interpretation if and only if all entities that can be values of x in the domain of that interpretation satisfy A in that context.[3]

Finally, nothing else is a term or a sentence of the illocutionary logic IL.

II RULES OF ABBREVIATION

An interesting feature of the object-language of the illocutionary logic IL is that most fundamental truth functional, modal, propositional, and illocutionary notions which are important for the purposes of the logic of elementary speech acts can be derived from the few primitive notions expressed by the logical constants and syncategorematic symbols of IL by using rules of abbreviation which I will now state. In

---

[2] Thus the logical symbols $\sim$ and $\lor$ are both sentential and propositional connectives.

[3] An occurrence of a variable x is *bound* in a formula (term or sentence) if and only if either it immediately follows $\forall$ in that formula or it is within the scope of a quantifier $\forall$ that is immediately followed by x. Otherwise, an occurrence of x is *free* in that formula. The variable x is free in a formula if and only if it has at least one free occurrence in that formula, and otherwise it is bound in that formula.

these rules, I will often delete exterior parentheses for the sake of brevity. I will also sometimes omit parentheses according to the rule of association to the left as well as type subscripts.

Truth functional conjunction

$(A \wedge B) =_{\text{def}} \sim (\sim A \vee \sim B)$, where A and B are two P-terms or two sentences of *IL*.

Material implication

$(A \rightarrow B) =_{\text{def}} \sim (A \wedge \sim B)$

Material equivalence

$(A \leftrightarrow B) =_{\text{def}} (A \rightarrow B) \wedge (B \rightarrow A)$

Identity of content

$A_p \langle \rangle B_p =_{\text{def}} (A_p \rangle B_p) \wedge (B_p \rangle A_p)$

A logically necessary proposition

$1_p =_{\text{def}} c_p^1 \vee \sim c_p^1$

Propositional necessity

$\square A_p =_{\text{def}} (A_p \leftrightarrow 1_p)$

Logical possibility

$\lozenge A =_{\text{def}} \sim \square \sim A$, where A and B are two P-terms or two sentences

Thus, sentence $\Diamond A_t$ is true in a context under an interpretation if and only if sentence A_t is true in at least one context according to that interpretation. Similarly, propositional term $\Diamond A_p$ names the proposition that A_p is possible.

Strict implication

$$(A \dashv B) =_{\text{def}} \Box(A \rightarrow B)$$

Thus, sentence $(A_t \dashv B_t)$ is true in a context under an interpretation if and only if sentence B_t is true in all contexts where sentence A_t is true according to that interpretation. Similarly, the propositional term $A_p \dashv B_p$ names the proposition that A_p strictly implies B_p.

Strict equivalence

$$(A \Vdash B) =_{\text{def}} (A \dashv B) \wedge (B \dashv A)$$

Tautological propositions

$$\mathbf{T}A_p =_{\text{def}} A_p = (A_p \vee \sim A_p)$$

Sentence $\mathbf{T}A$ means that A names a tautology.

Strong implication

$$(A \vdash B) =_{\text{def}} \mathbf{T}(A \rightarrow B) \wedge (A > B)$$

Sentence $(A \vdash B)$ means that the proposition named by A strongly implies the proposition named by B.

World propositions

$$W(A_p) =_{\text{def}} \Diamond(t(A_p) \wedge \forall x_p (t(x_p) \rightarrow (A_p \vdash x_p)))$$

Sentence $W(A_p)$ means that the proposition named by A_p completely represents the state of the world of one context.[4]

Existential generalization

$$\exists x\, A =_{\mathrm{def}} \sim \forall x \sim A$$

Unique existential generalization

$\exists! x\, A =_{\mathrm{def}} \exists x\, A \wedge (\forall x'\, ([x'/x]A \to x' = x))$ where x' is the first variable of the same type as x which has no occurrence in A, and $[x'/x]A$ is the sentence obtained from A by replacing each free occurrence of x in A by x'.

The primitive illocutionary force of assertion

$$\vdash =_{\mathrm{def}} [(1_\mu, 1_\theta, 1_\Sigma, 1_\psi), 0_\iota, \pi^1]$$

The primitive commissive illocutionary force

$$\perp =_{\mathrm{def}} [(1_\mu, 1_\theta, 1_\Sigma, 1_\psi), 0_\iota, \pi^2]$$

The primitive directive illocutionary force

$$! =_{\mathrm{def}} [(1_\mu, 1_\theta, 1_\Sigma, 1_\psi), 0_\iota, \pi^3]$$

The primitive illocutionary force of declaration

$$\top =_{\mathrm{def}} [(1_\mu, 1_\theta, 1_\Sigma, 1_\psi), 0_\iota, \pi^4]$$

The primitive expressive illocutionary force

$$\dashv =_{\mathrm{def}} [(1_\mu, 1_\theta, 1_\Sigma, 1_\psi), 0_\iota, \pi^5]$$

---

[4] World propositions were first studied by A. N. Prior and Kit Fine in *Worlds, Times and Selves*, Amherst: University of Massachusetts Press, 1977.

The operation of imposing a new mode of achievement on an illocutionary force

$$[B_\mu][(A_\mu,A_\theta,A_\Sigma,A_\psi),A_\iota,\pi^k] =_{\text{def}} [((B_\mu \ast A_\mu),A_\theta,A_\Sigma,A_\psi),A_\iota,\pi^k]$$

$[B_\mu]A_\phi$ names the illocutionary force obtained by adding to the illocutionary force named by A_ϕ the mode of achievement named by B_μ.

The operation of adding a new propositional content condition to an illocutionary force

$$[B_\theta][(A_\mu,A_\theta,A_\Sigma,A_\psi),A_\iota,\pi^k] =_{\text{def}} [(A_\mu,(B_\theta \ast A_\theta),A_\Sigma,A_\psi),A_\iota,\pi^k]$$

$[B_\theta]A_\phi$ names the illocutionary force which is obtained by adding the propositional content condition named by B_θ to the force named by A_ϕ.

The operation of adding a new preparatory condition to an illocutionary force

$$[B_\Sigma][(A_\mu,A_\theta,A_\Sigma,A_\psi),A_\iota,\pi^k] =_{\text{def}} [(A_\mu,A_\theta,(B_\Sigma \ast A_\Sigma),A_\psi)),A_\iota,\pi^k]$$

$[B_\Sigma]A_\phi$ names the illocutionary force obtained by adding the preparatory condition named by B_Σ to the force named by A_ϕ.

The operation of adding a new sincerity condition to an illocutionary force

$$[B_\psi][(A_\mu,A_\theta,A_\Sigma,A_\psi),A_\iota,\pi^k] =_{\text{def}} [(A_\mu,A_\theta,A_\Sigma,(B_\psi \ast A_\psi)),A_\iota,\pi^k]$$

$[B_\psi]A_\phi$ names the illocutionary force obtained by adding the sincerity condition named by B_ψ to the force named by A_ψ.

The operation of increasing or decreasing the degree of strength

$$[B_\iota][(A_\mu,A_\theta,A_\Sigma,A_\psi),A_\iota,\pi^k] =_{\text{def}} [(A_\mu,A_\theta,A_\Sigma,A_\psi),(B_\iota \ast A_\iota),\pi^k]$$

$[B_\iota]A_\phi$ names the illocutionary force obtained by adding the integer named by B_ι to the integer measuring the degree of strength of the force named by A_ϕ.

The success value of an illocutionary act

$$s([(A_\mu,A_\theta,A_\Sigma,A_\psi),A_\iota,\pi^k]A_p) =_{\text{def}} (\pi^k A_p \wedge A_\mu A_p \wedge A_\theta A_p \wedge (\forall x_p \, (A_\Sigma A_p x_p \\ \to \gg x_p) \wedge (\forall x_\tau \, ((A_\psi x_\tau \vee c_\psi^k x_\tau) \to E(x_\tau A_p)A_\iota))$$

Whenever A is an IA-term, the sentence $s(A)$ is true in a context under an interpretation if and only if the illocutionary act named by A is performed in that context according to that interpretation.

The property of having an illocutionary point

$$A_\phi \dashv \pi^k =_{\text{def}} \forall x_p \, (s(A_\phi x_p) \dashv (\pi^k x_p))$$

Sentence $A_\phi \dashv \pi^k$ means that it is not possible for a speaker to perform an illocutionary act with the force named by A_ϕ and a propositional content P without achieving the illocutionary point named by π^k on the proposition P.

The property of having the words-to-world direction of fit

$$\downarrow(A_\phi) =_{\text{def}} (A_\phi \dashv \pi^1)$$

Sentence $\downarrow(A_\phi)$ means that the illocutionary force named A_ϕ has the words-to-world direction of fit.

The property of having the world-to-words direction of fit

$$\uparrow(A_\phi) =_{\text{def}} (A_\phi \dashv \pi^2 \vee A_\phi \dashv \pi^3 \vee A_\phi \dashv \pi^4)$$

The property of having the double direction of fit

$$\updownarrow(A_\phi) =_{\text{def}} (A_\phi \dashv \pi^4)$$

Rules of abbreviation

The property of having the null or empty direction of fit

$$\emptyset(A_\phi) =_{\text{def}} ((A_\phi \dashv \pi^5 \wedge \sim\downarrow(A_\phi)) \wedge \sim\uparrow(A_\phi) \wedge \sim\updownarrow(A_\phi))$$

The satisfaction value of an illocutionary act

$$t(A_\phi A_p) =_{\text{def}} ((\downarrow(A_\phi) \vee \emptyset(A_\phi)) \rightarrow t(A_p)) \wedge ((\uparrow(A_\phi) \vee \downarrow(A_\phi))$$
$$\rightarrow (t(A_p) \wedge s(A_\phi A_p)))$$

A sentence of the form $t(A_\phi A_p)$ is true in a context under an interpretation if and only if the speech act named by $A_\phi(A_p)$ is satisfied in that context according to that interpretation.[5]

The relation of strong illocutionary commitment between illocutionary acts

$$A_\Omega \rhd B_\Omega =_{\text{def}} (s(A_\Omega) \dashv s(B_\Omega)) \text{ for any } IA\text{-term } A_\Omega \text{ and } B_\Omega$$

A sentence of the form $A_\Omega \rhd B_\Omega$ means that the illocutionary act named by A_Ω strongly commits the speaker to the illocutionary act named by B_Ω.

The relation of being a stronger illocutionary force

$$A_\phi \rhd B_\phi =_{\text{def}} \forall x_p (A_\phi(x_p) \rhd B_\phi(x_p)) \text{ for any } IF\text{-term } A_\phi \text{ and } B_\phi$$

Sentence $A_\phi \rhd B_\phi$ means that every illocutionary act with the force named by A_ϕ and a propositional content P strongly commits the speaker to the corresponding illocutionary act with the force named by B_ϕ and the same propositional content.

---

[5] This definition of satisfaction is incomplete from a philosophical point of view, because it does not reflect the necessity of a causal link between the truth of the propositional content and the performance of the illocutionary act in the case of satisfaction of utterances with the double or the world-to-words direction of fit. However, this definition will do for the purposes of the formalization. One could express this causal link by adding the connective of causal necessity to the list of the logical constants of *IL*. See chapter 7 for a semantic analysis of this modal connective.

Inclusion of conditions of satisfaction

$(A_\Omega \dashv B_\Omega) =_{\mathrm{def}} t(A_\Omega) \dashv t(B_\Omega)$ for any IA-term

The relation of being two illocutionary acts which are not simultaneously performable

$(A_\Omega \rangle\langle_s B_\Omega) =_{\mathrm{def}} s(A_\Omega) \dashv \sim s(B_\Omega)$

The relation of being incompatible illocutionary forces

$(A_\phi \rangle\langle B_\phi) =_{\mathrm{def}} \forall x_p \, (s(A_\phi x_p) \dashv \sim s(B_\phi x_p))$

The relation of being two illocutionary acts which are not simultaneously satisfiable

$(A_\Omega \rangle\langle_t B_\Omega) =_{\mathrm{def}} (t(A_\Omega) \dashv \sim t(B_\Omega))$

Addition

$(A_\iota + B_\iota) =_{\mathrm{def}} (A_\iota \not\ast B_\iota)$

The arithmetical relation $\geqslant$ of being equal to or greater than is defined as usual.

III THE STRUCTURE OF A SEMANTIC INTERPRETATION

The formal semantics for illocutionary logic *IL* is *model-theoretical*, in the sense that it specifies how meanings can be assigned to the formulas of its ideal object-language in arbitrary *possible interpretations* or models for that language. In formal semantics, a possible interpretation of a language is also called a *model* of all the sentences of that language which are true in all contexts of that interpretation. While the semantic values of non-logical constants can vary quite arbitrarily from one semantic interpretation to another, all *possible semantic interpretations* must respect certain *meaning postulates* in the assignments of semantic values to the logical constants and to the complex formulas. These meaning postulates guarantee that the logical constants and syncategorematic expressions have their intended theoretical meaning in the set of interpretations over which one quantifies in order to define logical truth, semantic consequence, and entailment. Interpretations which do not respect these meaning postulates are not among the *possible* interpretations that are considered.

The primary aim of this section is to define the logical structure which is common to all *possible (standard) interpretations or models* of illocutionary logic. On the basis of the previous explanations of the meanings of the terms and sentences of *IL*, I will construct a possible interpretation for *IL* as a *set-theoretical structure* which characterizes the meaning of each term A_α of type α of *IL* by determining the entity of type α which is the *denotation* of that term in that interpretation under each possible assignment of values to its free variables. I will first formulate the *rules of assignment of meanings* to terms in a *recursive definition*. Next, I will define inductively the *conditions under which a sentence* of *IL is true* in a context under a possible assignment of values to its free variables in a possible interpretation. Following Frege's principle of composition of denotations, the truth value of a sentence in a context under an assignment in a possible interpretation will be uniquely determined by the denotations of the constituent terms of that sentence under that assignment, and by the meaning postulates governing the logical constants and syncategorematic symbols that occur in that sentence.

For the sake of simplicity, I will hereafter identify in a model the *truth conditions* of a proposition with the set of all possible contexts of use where that proposition is true according to that model, rather than with the function from possible contexts into truth values that is the characteristic function of this set. Similarly, I will also identify in a model the *conditions of success* of an illocutionary act with the set of all possible contexts of use where it is performed according to that model, rather than with the function from possible contexts into success values that is the characteristic function of that set. This set-theoretical formalization is more convenient for the purposes of a *first order illocutionary logic*. Moreover, it is formally equivalent with the formalization in terms of functions that will be used later in the higher order illocutionary logic of general semantics.

Because the content of propositions is left unanalyzed in first order illocutionary logic, there is no direct way to define simply (by elimination) the truth conditions of propositions in terms of their content and of the set of truth value assignments to atomic propositions under which they are (or could be) true. However, one can rely on the fact that propositional terms contain propositional constants and variables to which one can assign truth values in order to represent in models the nature of the *truth function* by the application of which the conditions under which a proposition is true are determined from the truth possibilities of its atomic propositions. Thus, I will identify each *proposition* in a model of first order illocutionary logic with the triple consisting first of its content, second of its truth conditions, and third of the set of all truth value assignments to propositional terms under which it is true in that model. On this account, two propositions are identical in a model if and only if they have the same content, the same truth conditions, and their truth conditions are determined in the same truth functional way from the truth conditions of the atomic propositions. This definition of the logical type of propositions is formally equivalent with the one I have proposed in chapter 3 of volume I. It is the simplest kind of semantic definition of propositions that one can formulate in the first order illocutionary logic *IL*.

Definition of a standard model

From a logical point of view, a *standard possible interpretation or model for IL* has the following structure: it is an eightuple $\mathfrak{M} = \langle I, D, M, U, (\Pi_k), \rangle\rangle, \mathbb{E}, \| \| \rangle$ where I, D and M are three disjoint non-empty sets, (Π_k) is a family of five functions and U, $\rangle\rangle$, $\mathbb{E}$, and $\| \|$ are four other functions. These elements satisfy the following clauses.

(1) I is an arbitrary non-empty set which represents *the set of possible contexts of utterance* considered in the possible interpretation $\mathfrak{M}$.

(2) D is another non-empty set which represents the *set of all possible contents* which are considered in the possible interpretation $\mathfrak{M}$. Thus, each element of the set D represents a set of *atomic propositions*[6] which

---

[6] A finer analysis of the logical form of contents of propositions will be made later in the higher order intensional logic of general semantics. See chapter 7.

is the content of certain propositions. By definition, the set D is partially ordered by a binary relation $\subseteq$ and is closed under a binary operation $\cup$: whenever D contains two elements d_1, and d_2, it also contains a third element $d_1 \cup d_2$ which is their supremum.

(3) M is another arbitrary non-empty set representing *the set of psychological modes* which are considered in the possible interpretation $\mathfrak{M}$.[7]

(4) U is a function whose domain is the set of all primitive type symbols of IL. That function associates with each type α the set U_α of all entities which are *possible denotations* of terms of type α in the possible interpretation $\mathfrak{M}$. The values of that function are determined as follows:

(i) $U_\tau = M$.

(ii) $U_p \subseteq D \times \mathscr{P}(I) \times \mathscr{P}(2^{L_p})$ where L_p is the set of propositional constants and variables of IL and 2 is the set of truth values.

(iii) $U_\mu = \mathscr{P}(I \times U_p)$.

(iv) $U_\theta = (\mathscr{P}(U_p))^I$.

(v) $U_\Sigma = (\mathscr{P}(U_p))^{I \times U_p}$.

(vi) $U_\psi = \mathscr{P}(M)$.

(vii) U_ι is the set Z of integers.

Thus, for example, U_p represents the set of all propositions, and U_θ the set of all propositional content conditions which are considered in the possible interpretation $\mathfrak{M}$. (One can verify easily that these set-theoretical definitions respect the logical types of those denotations.) Moreover, the union of the sets U_α is *the domain* of the possible interpretation $\mathfrak{M}$.

Conventions and definitions

If $P \in U_p$, let $id_k(P)$ be the k-th term of P where $1 \leqslant k \leqslant 3$. Intuitively, $id_1(P)$ represents the set of atomic propositions which belong to the *content* of the proposition P in the interpretation $\mathfrak{M}$. Similarly, $id_2(P)$ represents the set of all possible contexts where the proposition P is true according to that interpretation. Finally, $id_3(P)$ is a set of *truth value assignments* to propositional variables and constants which serves

---

[7] In this simple formulation of illocutionary logic, the set of all possible psychological modes has no particular logical structure.

to represent the nature of the truth function by the application of which the conditions under which P is true are determined. On this account, the proposition P is *true* in a context i under the interpretation $\mathfrak{M}$ if and only if $i \in id_2(P)$; and it is *contingent* if and only if $id_2(P)$ is a proper non-empty subset of I.

Similarly, P is a *tautology* if and only if $id_3(P)$ is the total set of all truth value assignments and P is a *contradiction* if and only if $id_3(P)$ is the empty set. Moreover, a proposition P *strongly implies* another proposition Q if and only if, first, $id_1(Q) \subseteq id_1(P)$ and, second, $id_3(P) \subseteq id_3(Q)$.

As tautologies are necessarily true, the second and third elements of propositions are not independent in a model. Whenever the set of all truth value assignments under which a proposition P is true is included in the set of the truth value assignments under which another proposition Q is true, all truth conditions of Q are also truth conditions of P. Thus, in all possible interpretations of first order illocutionary logic, the set U_p of propositions is a subset of $D \times \mathscr{P}(I) \times \mathscr{P}(2^{L_p})$ which satisfies the following clause: for all propositions P and $Q \in U_p$, $id_3(P) \subseteq id_3(Q)$ only if it is also the case that $id_2(P) \subseteq id_2(Q)$. On this account, all cases of strong implication between propositions are also cases of strict implication.

(5) Π_1, Π_2, Π_3, Π_4 and Π_5 are five subsets of $I \times U_p$ which represent respectively the conditions of achievement of the assertive, commissive, directive, declarative, and expressive *illocutionary points* in the possible interpretation $\mathfrak{M}$. Thus, $\langle i, P \rangle \in \Pi_k$ means that the k-th illocutionary point is achieved on the proposition P in the context i according to the possible interpretation $\mathfrak{M}$.

These five subsets obey the following postulates:
(i) The set $\{P/\langle i, P \rangle \in \Pi_1\}$ of all propositions on which the assertive illocutionary point is achieved in a context i under a possible interpretation is *minimally consistent*, that is to say, it does not contain any contradiction. Moreover, that set is also *closed under strong implication*: whenever it contains a proposition P, it also contains all propositions Q which are strongly implied by P. Finally, whenever it is non-empty, the set $\{P/\langle i, P \rangle \in \Pi_1\}$ contains *a unique supremum*, that is to say, it contains a unique proposition which strongly implies all other propositions that it contains.
(ii) If $k = 2$ or 3, $\{P/\langle i, P \rangle \in \Pi_k\}$ is a set of propositions which is *minimally consistent* and which contains a *unique supremum* whenever it

is non-empty. Moreover, it is closed under strong implication, in the restricted sense that it contains a proposition P if and only if it contains also every non-tautological proposition which is strongly implied by P.[8] Finally, $\Pi_2 \subseteq \Pi_1$.

(iii) $\{P/\langle i, P \rangle \in \Pi_4\}$ is a set of contingent propositions with the following properties: if it is non-empty, it contains a unique supremum which is true in the context i. Moreover, it is closed under strong implication, in the restricted sense that if it contains a proposition then it contains also every contingent proposition which is strongly implied by that proposition. Finally, $\Pi_4 \subseteq \Pi_1$.

(6) $\rangle\rangle$ is a subset of $I \times U_p$ which determines which propositions are *presupposed* under the possible interpretation $\mathfrak{M}$ at each context. Thus, $\langle i, P \rangle \in \rangle\rangle$ means that the proposition P is presupposed in the context i according to possible interpretation $\mathfrak{M}$. By definition, the set of all propositions $\{P/\langle i, P \rangle \in \rangle\rangle\}$ which are presupposed in a context i under the possible interpretation $\mathfrak{M}$ is a *proper* subset of U_p which is closed under strong implication. Moreover, whenever $\langle i, P \rangle \in \rangle\rangle$, it is not the case that $\langle i, \sim P \rangle \in \Pi_1$.

(7) $\mathbb{E}$ is a subset of $I \times U_\tau \times U_p \times U_\iota$ which determines which mental states are *expressed* according to the possible interpretation $\mathfrak{M}$ in each context. Thus, $\langle i, m, P, k \rangle \in \mathbb{E}$ means that the speaker in the context i expresses with the degree of strength measured by the integer k a mental state of the form $m(P)$ in the possible interpretation $\mathfrak{M}$. By definition, the set of all modes m such that $\langle i, m, P, k \rangle \in \mathbb{E}$ is a proper subset of M, and the set of all integers $\{k/\langle i, m, P, k \rangle \in \mathbb{E}\}$ representing the degrees of strength with which a mental state $m(P)$ is expressed in a context i is an initial segment of integers.[9]

Moreover, $\langle i, P \rangle \in \Pi_5$ if and only if, for some $m \in M$ and for some $k \in Z$, $\langle i, m, P, k \rangle \in \mathbb{E}$ in the possible interpretation $\mathfrak{M}$.

(8) Finally, $\| \ \|$ is a function which associates with each term A of type α under each possible assignment σ of values to its free variables the entity $\|A\|^\sigma$ of U_α which is its *denotation* under that assignment in the possible interpretation $\mathfrak{M}$. By a *possible assignment of values to the free variables* of the terms of L, I mean here any function σ whose domain is the set of all variables of IL and which associates with each

---

[8] A finer characterization of the propositional content conditions of illocutionary forces with the world-to-words direction of fit would of course require further development of the logic of action or praxeology.

[9] An initial segment of integers is a set which is either empty or which contains all and only the integers which are smaller than a given integer.

variable of type α of IL an entity of the set U_α of the domain of the interpretation. In case v is a propositional variable, $id_3(\sigma(v))$ must be the set of all truth value assignments $f \in 2^{L_p}$ which are such that $f(v) = 1$.

The evaluation function $\| \ \|$ which defines recursively the *meanings* of all terms in a possible interpretation satisfies the following clauses:

(i) For any variable v of type α of L, $\|v\|^\sigma = \sigma(v)$.

(ii) For any (non-logical) constant of type α of L, $\|c\|^\sigma \in U_\alpha$.

As in the case of propositional variables, $id_3(\|c_p\|^\sigma)$ must be the set of all truth value assignments f such that $f(c_p) = 1$.

Moreover, if $1 \leqslant k \leqslant 5$, $\|c_\psi^k\|^\sigma \neq \varnothing$, and if $\langle i, P \rangle \in \Pi_k$ then for all $m \in \|c_\psi^k\|^\sigma$, there exists an integer n such that $\langle i, m, P, n \rangle \in \mathbb{E}$.

(iii) $\|0_\iota\|^\sigma$ is the integer zero.

(iv) $\|1_\mu\|^\sigma = I \times U_p$ and $\|0_\mu\|^\sigma = \varnothing$.

(v) $\|1_\theta\|^\sigma$ is the function $f \in U_\theta$ such that $f(i) = U_p$, and $\|0_\theta\|^\sigma (i) = \varnothing$.

(vi) $\|1_\Sigma\|^\sigma (i, P) = \varnothing$ and $\|0_\Sigma\|^\sigma$ is the function $f \in U_\Sigma$ such that $f(i, P) = U_p$.

(vii) $\|1_\psi\|^\sigma = \varnothing$ and $\|0_\psi\|^\sigma = M$.

(viii) $\|\pi^k\|^\sigma = \Pi_k$ for each k such that $1 \leqslant k \leqslant 5$.

(ix) $\|A_\mu \star B_\mu\|^\sigma = \|A_\mu\|^\sigma \cap \|B_\mu\|^\sigma$.

(x) $\|A_\theta \star B_\theta\|^\sigma$ is the function f of type θ such that $f(i) = \|A_\theta\|^\sigma(i) \cap \|B_\theta\|^\sigma(i)$.

(xi) $\|A_\Sigma \star B_\Sigma\|^\sigma$ is the function f of the type Σ such that $f(i, P) = \|A_\Sigma\|^\sigma(i, P) \cup \|B_\Sigma\|^\sigma(i, P)$.

(xii) $\|A_\psi \star B_\psi\|^\sigma = \|A_\psi\|^\sigma \cup \|B_\psi\|^\sigma$.

(xiii) $\|A_\iota + B_\iota\|^\sigma$ is the sum of the two integers $\|A_\iota\|^\sigma$ and $\|B_\iota\|^\sigma$, $\|(A_\iota)'\|^\sigma$ and $\|'(A_\iota)\|^\sigma$ are respectively the immediate successor and the immediate predecessor of the integer $\|A_\iota\|^\sigma$.

(xiv) If A_p is a propositional term, $\|\sim A_p\|^\sigma = \langle id_1(\|A_p\|^\sigma), \{i/i \in I$ and $i \notin id_2 (\|A_p\|^\sigma)\}, \{f/f \in 2^{L_p}$ and $f \notin id_3 (\|A_p\|^\sigma)\} \rangle$.

(xv) Similarly, $\|A_p \vee B_p\|^\sigma = \langle id_1(\|A_p\|^\sigma) \cup id_1 (\|B_p\|^\sigma), id_2(\|A_p\|^\sigma) \cup id_2(\|B_p\|^\sigma, id_3(\|A_p\|^\sigma \cup id_3(\|B_p\|^\sigma) \rangle$.

(xvi) $\|[(A_\mu, A_\theta, A_\Sigma, A_\psi), A_\iota, \pi^k]\|^\sigma$ is the function f with domain U_p such that $f(P) = \langle P, \mathcal{J} \rangle$ where $\mathcal{J}$ is the subset of I such that $i \in \mathcal{J}$ if and only if $\langle i, P \rangle \in \|A_\mu\|^\sigma \cap \|\pi^k\|^\sigma$, $P \in \|A_\theta\|^\sigma(i)$, $\|A_\Sigma\|^\sigma(i, P) \subseteq \{Q/\langle i, Q \rangle \in \rangle\}$ and for all m such that $m \in \|A_\psi\|^\sigma \cup \|c_\psi^k\|^\sigma$, $\langle i, m, P, \|A_\iota\|^\sigma \rangle \in \mathbb{E}$.

(xvii) If A_ϕ is an *IF*-term and A_p is a *P*-term, $\|A_\phi(A_p)\|^\sigma = \|A_\phi\|^\sigma(\|A_p\|^\sigma)$.

The truth definition

On the basis of the preceding explanations and definitions, the truth conditions of the sentences of *IL* are defined inductively as follows:

A sentence A of *IL* *is true in a context i under an assignment* σ *of values to its variables in the possible interpretation* $\mathfrak{M}$ (for short hereafter $\|A\|^\sigma(i) = T$) if and only if this follows from the following clauses:

(i) A sentence of the form $(A_\mu A_p)$ is true in a context i under an assignment σ in $\mathfrak{M}$ if and only if $\langle i, \|A_p\|^\sigma \rangle \in \|A_\mu\|^\sigma$.

(ii) A sentence of the form $(A_\theta A_p)$ is true in i under σ in $\mathfrak{M}$ if and only if $\|A_p\|^\sigma \in \|A_\theta\|^\sigma(i)$.

(iii) A sentence of the form $(A_\Sigma A_p B_p)$ is true in i under σ in $\mathfrak{M}$ if and only if $\|B_p\|^\sigma \in \|A_\Sigma\|^\sigma(i, \|A_p\|^\sigma)$.

(iv) A sentence of the form $(A_\psi A_\tau)$ is true in i under σ in $\mathfrak{M}$ if and only if $\|A_\tau\|^\sigma \in \|A_\psi\|^\sigma$.

(v) A sentence of the form $E(A_\tau A_p) A_\tau$ is true in i under σ in $\mathfrak{M}$ if and only if $\langle i, \|A_\tau\|^\sigma, \|A_p\|^\sigma, \|A_\iota\|^\sigma \rangle \in \mathbb{E}$.

(vi) A sentence $t(B_p)$ is true in a context i under σ in $\mathfrak{M}$ if and only if $i \in id_2 (\|B_p\|^\sigma)$.

(vii) A sentence $\gg B_p$ is true in a context i under σ in $\mathfrak{M}$ if and only if $\langle i, \|B_p\|^\sigma \rangle \in \rangle\rangle$.

(viii) A sentence $(A_p \ni B_p)$ is true in a context i under σ in $\mathfrak{M}$ if and only if $id_1(\|B_p\|^\sigma) \subseteq id_1(\|A_p\|^\sigma)$.

(ix) A sentence of the form $(B = C)$ is true in a context i under σ in $\mathfrak{M}$ if and only if $\|B\|^\sigma = \|C\|^\sigma$.

(x) A sentence of the form $\sim B$ is true in a context i under σ in $\mathfrak{M}$ if and only if B is not true in i under σ in $\mathfrak{M}$.

(xi) A sentence of the form $(B_1 \vee B_2)$ is true in a context i under σ in $\mathfrak{M}$ if and only if at least one of the sentences B_1 and B_2 is true in that context under σ in $\mathfrak{M}$.

(xii) A sentence of the form $\square B$ is true in a context i under σ in $\mathfrak{M}$ if and only if B is true in all contexts $j \in I$ under σ in $\mathfrak{M}$.

(xiii) Finally, a sentence of the form $(\forall x) B$ is true in a context i under σ in $\mathfrak{M}$ if and only if B is true in i under all assignments σ' which differ at most from σ by the fact that $\sigma'(x) \neq \sigma(x)$.

41

Logical truth and validity

All other fundamental semantic notions of illocutionary logic are now defined as usual by quantifying over all possible interpretations. A sentence A of IL is *logically true* (or *valid*) (in symbols $\vDash_{IL}A$) if and only if it is true in all possible contexts under all assignments in all possible interpretations of IL. A sentence A of IL is *satisfiable* if and only if it is true in at least one context under at least one assignment of a possible interpretation of IL. Moreover, a sentence A of IL is a *semantic consequence* of a set of sentences Γ of IL (in symbols: $\Gamma \vDash_{IL}A$) if and only if, in all possible interpretations of IL where all sentences $B \in \Gamma$ are true in a context under an assignment, the sentence A is also true in that context under that assignment.

IV A COMPLETE AXIOMATIC SYSTEM

The simple first order illocutionary logic IL that I have formulated in the preceding sections is *complete*. All its logically true sentences are provable in the following axiomatic system V whose language is that of IL. This axiomatic system is also *sound* in the sense that all its theorems are logically true. Thus it axiomatizes *all and only* the logically true sentences of IL.

The axioms of the formal system V

The axioms of V are:

(1) *The axioms of truth functional logic*

These axioms are the instances of the following schemas, where A, B and C are meta-linguistic variables for sentences of IL.

Axiom schema 1 $A \to (B \to A)$

Axiom schema 2 $(A \to (B \to C)) \to ((A \to B) \to (A \to C))$

Axiom schema 3 $(\sim A \to \sim B) \to (B \to A)$

(II) *The axioms of the first-order predicate calculus*[10]

Axiom schema 4 $\forall x\, A \rightarrow [B/x]A$ whenever B is a term of the same type as x which is free for variable x in A[11]

Axiom schema 5 $(\forall x\, (A \rightarrow B)) \rightarrow (A \rightarrow \forall x\, B)$ where x is any variable which is not a free variable of A

(III) *The axioms for identity*

Axiom schema 6 $A = A$ where A is any term

Axiom schema 7 $(x_1 = x_2) \rightarrow (B \leftrightarrow B^x)$ where B^x is like B except that x_2 may replace any occurrence of x_1 in B provided there is no confusion of bound variables[12]

(IV) *The axioms of S5 modal logic*[13]

Axiom schema 8 $\Box A \rightarrow A$

Axiom schema 9 $\Box(A \rightarrow B) \rightarrow (\Box A \rightarrow \Box B)$

Axiom schema 10 $\Diamond A \rightarrow \Box \Diamond A$

(V) *The axioms for propositions*

Axiom schema 11 $A_p \succ A_p$

Axiom schema 12 $(A_p \succ B_p) \rightarrow ((B_p \succ C_p) \rightarrow A_p \succ C_p)$

[10] The first order predicate calculus of illocutionary logic *IL* is that of A. Church in *Introduction to Mathematical Logic*, Princeton University Press, 1956.
[11] In quantification theory, a term B is *free for x in A* first, if B is a variable then B occurs free in $[B/x]A$ wherever x occurs free in A, and second, if B is a term in which a variable occurs, then, wherever B is substituted for free occurrences of x in A, all free occurrences of variables in B remain free. If B is a closed term, B is free for x in A.
[12] See Church, *Introduction to Mathematical Logic*.
[13] The axioms and rules of inference of S5 modal logic are due to C. I. Lewis in *A Survey of Symbolic Logic*, Berkeley and Los Angeles: University of California Press, 1918.

Axiom schema 13 $\quad (A_p \vee B_p) \mathbin{\rangle} A_p$

Axiom schema 14 $\quad (A_p \vee B_p) \mathbin{\rangle} B_p$

Axiom schema 15 $\quad ((C_p \mathbin{\rangle} A_p) \wedge (C_p \mathbin{\rangle} B_p)) \to C_p \mathbin{\rangle} (A_p \vee B_p)$

Axiom schema 16 $\quad (A_p \mathbin{\rangle} \sim A_p) \wedge (\sim A_p \mathbin{\rangle} A_p)$

Axiom schema 17 $\quad A_p \mathbin{\rangle} B_p \to \Box(A_p \mathbin{\rangle} B_p)$

Axiom schema 18 $\quad t(\sim A_p) \leftrightarrow \sim t(A_p)$

Axiom schema 19 $\quad t(A_p \vee B_p) \leftrightarrow (t(A_p) \vee t(B_p))$

Axiom schema 20 $\quad ((A_p \mathbin{\Vdash} B_p) \wedge (B_p \mathbin{\Vdash} A_p)) \to (A_p = B_p)$

Axiom schema 21 $\quad \mathbf{T} A_p$ whenever A_p has the form of an instance of axiom schemas 1, 2 or 3

Axiom schema 22 $\quad \mathbf{T} A_p \to \Box t(A_p)$

Axiom schemas 11 and 12 assert that the relation of inclusion of content is reflexive and transitive. Axiom schemas 13–16 assert that the content of a disjunction of two propositions is the union of the contents of its disjuncts and that the content of the negation of a proposition is the content of that proposition. Axiom schema 17 asserts that a proposition has the same content in all contexts. Axiom schemas 18 and 19 are the familiar axioms for determining the truth values of the negation of a proposition and of the disjunction of two propositions. Axiom schema 20 states the law of propositional identity of illocutionary logic. Axiom schema 21 states that propositional terms which have the forms of the axioms of the propositional calculus name tautologies. Finally, axiom schema 22 states that each tautology is necessarily true.

(VI) *The axioms of the Abelian group for integers*

Axiom 23 $\quad \forall x_1 (x_1 \geqslant 0_1 \to \sim 0_1 = (x_1)')$

Axiom 24 $\quad \forall x_\iota (0_\iota \geqslant x_\iota \rightarrow \sim 0_\iota = {}'(x_\iota))$

Axiom 25 $\quad \forall x_\iota \forall y_\iota (x_\iota + y_\iota) = (y_\iota + x_\iota)$

Axiom 26 $\quad \forall x_\iota \forall y_\iota \forall z_\iota x_\iota + (y_\iota + z_\iota) = (x_\iota + y_\iota) + z_\iota$

Axiom 27 $\quad \forall x_\iota ((x_\iota + 0_\iota) = x_\iota \wedge {}'((x_\iota)') = x_\iota)$

Axiom 28 $\quad \forall x_\iota \forall y_\iota ((x_\iota + (y_\iota)') = (x_\iota + y_\iota)')$

Axiom 29 $\quad \forall x_\iota \forall y_\iota ((x_\iota + {}'(y_\iota)) = {}'(x_\iota + y_\iota))$

Axiom schema 30 $\quad A(0_\iota) \wedge \forall x_\iota (A(x_\iota) \rightarrow (A((x_\iota)') \wedge A({}'(x_\iota)))) \rightarrow \forall x_\iota A(x_\iota)$
where $A(0_\iota)$ is a sentence containing an occurrence of 0_ι and $A(x_\iota)$ is the sentence obtained from $A(0_\iota)$ by replacing one or several occurrences of 0_ι in $A(0_\iota)$ by a variable x_ι which has no occurrence in $A(0_\iota)$

Axiom 31 $\quad \forall x_\iota \exists y_\iota \, x_\iota + y_\iota = 0_\iota$

(VII) *The axioms for components of illocutionary forces*

Axiom schema 32 $\quad (\forall x_p (A_\zeta x_p \rightarrowtail B_\zeta x_p) \rightarrow A_\zeta = B_\zeta)$ if $\zeta = \mu$ or θ

Axiom schema 33 $\quad (\forall x_p \forall y_p (A_\Sigma x_p y_p \rightarrowtail B_\Sigma x_p y_p)) \rightarrow A_\Sigma = B_\Sigma$

Axiom schema 34 $\quad (\forall x_\tau (A_\psi x_\tau \leftrightarrow B_\psi x_\tau)) \rightarrow A_\psi = B_\psi$

Axiom schema 35 $\quad \square (1_\zeta A_p)$ where $\zeta = \mu$ or θ

Axiom schema 36 $\quad \sim \lozenge (0_\zeta A_p)$ where $\zeta = \mu$ or θ

Axiom schema 37 $\quad (A_\zeta \ast B_\zeta) A_p \leftrightarrow (A_\zeta A_p \wedge B_\zeta A_p)$ where $\zeta = \mu$ or θ

Axiom schema 38 $\quad \sim \lozenge 1_\Sigma A_p B_p$

Axiom schema 39 $\quad \square 0_\Sigma A_p B_p$

Axiom schema 40 $\quad (A_\Sigma \ast B_\Sigma) A_p B_p \leftrightarrow (A_\Sigma A_p B_p \vee B_\Sigma A_p B_p)$

Axiom schema 41 $\quad \sim \lozenge 1_\psi A_\tau$

Axiom schema 42 $\quad \square 0_\psi A_\tau$

Axiom schema 43 $\quad ((A_\psi \ast B_\psi) A_\tau) \leftrightarrow (A_\psi A_\tau \vee B_\psi A_\tau)$

Axiom schemas 32–4 state the laws of identity for components of illocutionary force. Axiom schemas 35, 36, 38, 39, 41, and 42 fix the logical properties of the neutral and absorbent components of the different types. Axiom schemas 37, 40, and 43 determine respectively the nature of conjunctions of modes of achievement, of intersections of propositional content conditions and of unions of preparatory and sincerity conditions.

(VIII) *The axioms for illocutionary points*

Axiom schema 44 $(\pi^k A_p \to \sim T \sim A_p)$ where $1 \leqslant k \leqslant 4$

Axiom schema 45 $(\pi^1 A_p \to \exists ! x_p \, \forall y_p \, (\pi^1 y_p \leftrightarrow x_p \vdash y_p))$

Axiom schema 46 $\pi^k A_p \to \exists ! x_p \, (\pi^k x_p \wedge (\forall y_p \, (\pi^k y_p \leftrightarrow$

$(x_p \vdash y_p \wedge \sim T y_p))))$ where $2 \leqslant k \leqslant 3$

Axiom schema 47 And similarly for π^4 except that $\sim \Box t(y_p)$ occurs at the place of $\sim T(y_p)$ in that new axiom schema

Axiom 48 $\forall x_p \, (\pi^4 x_p \to t(x_p))$

Axiom 49 $\forall x_p \, ((\pi^4 x_p \vee \pi^2 x_p) \to \pi^1 x_p)$

Axiom schema 50 $(\exists x_\tau c_\psi^k x_\tau) \wedge ((\pi^k A_p) \dashv \forall x_\tau (c_\psi^k x_\tau \to \exists x_\iota E(x_\tau A_p) x_\iota))$ where $1 \leqslant k \leqslant 4$

Axiom schema 51 $\pi^5 A_p \leftrightarrow \exists x_\tau \, \exists x_\iota \, E(x_\tau A_p) x_\iota$

Axiom schema 44 states the law of the minimal consistency of the speaker. Axiom schema 45 asserts that the set of propositions on which the assertive point is achieved is closed under strong implication. It also states the law of foundation for the assertive point. Axiom schemas 46–7 state similar laws for the commissive, directive, and declarative points, with the additional requirement of the *a posteriority* or of the contingency of the propositions on which these points are achieved. Axiom 48 states the truth of the propositional content of a successful declaration. Axiom 49 states the existence of an assertive commitment in the achievement of the declarative or of the commissive illocutionary point. Axiom schema 50 asserts that each illocutionary point determines non-empty sincerity conditions. Finally, axiom schema 51 states the conditions of achievement of the expressive point.

(IX) *The axioms for presupposition*

Axiom 52 $\sim \forall x_p \gg x_p$

Axiom schema 53 $\gg A_p \rightarrow (A_p \mapsto B_p) \rightarrow \gg B_p)$

Axiom schema 54 $\gg A_p \rightarrow \sim (\pi^1 \sim A_p)$

Axiom 52 states that the set of presuppositions of a speaker is not the total set of propositions. Axiom schema 53 states that it is closed under strong implication. Axiom schema 54 states the law of non-deniability of the preparatory conditions.[14]

(X) *The axioms for psychological expression*

Axiom schema 55 $\sim \forall x_\tau E(x_\tau x_p) A_\tau$

Axiom schema 56

$$E(A_\tau A_p) A_\iota \rightarrow (\exists x_\iota \sim E(A_\tau A_p) x_\iota \wedge (\exists y_\iota (E(A_\tau A_p)) y_\iota \wedge \forall z_\iota (E(A_\tau A_p)) z_\iota \\ \leftrightarrow y_\iota \geqslant z_\iota))))$$

Axiom schema 55 states a law of possible sincerity of the speaker. A speaker cannot express all possible psychological states about the same state of affairs in a context because no speaker can possess all such psychological states. Axiom schema 56 states the law of the existence of a maximal degree of strength of sincerity conditions and the law of transitivity of degree of strength in the expression of sincerity conditions.

(XI) *The axioms for illocutionary forces and acts*

Axiom schema 57 $A_\phi = B_\phi \leftrightarrow \Box (\forall x_p (s(A_\phi x_p) \leftrightarrow s(B_\phi x_p)))$

Axiom schema 58 $A_\phi A_p = B_\phi B_p \leftrightarrow (A_p = B_p \wedge \Box (s(A_\phi A_p) = s(B_\phi B_p)))$

---

[14] The law that one cannot both perform an illocutionary act and deny one of its preparatory conditions is derived in illocutionary logic from the more general law that a speaker cannot both presuppose a proposition *P* and assert that it is false.

These two axiom schemas state the laws of identity for illocutionary forces and elementary speech acts.

The rules of inference of V

The four rules of inference of V are:

(I) *The rule of modus ponens*

From A and $(A \rightarrow B)$ infer B.

(II) *The rule of necessitation*

From A infer $\Box A$.

(III) *The rule of tautologies*

From $\mathbf{T}A$ and $\mathbf{T}(A \rightarrow B)$ infer $\mathbf{T}B$.

(IV) *The rule of generalization*

From A infer $\forall x\, A$.

The syntactic notions of *proof, derivation, theoremhood, and consistency* for the axiomatic system V are defined as usual. Thus, a sentence A of *IL* is a *theorem* of the axiomatic system V (in symbols: $\vdash_V A$) if and only if it can be derived in the usual way from the axioms of V by a finite number of applications of the four rules of inference of V. A set Γ of sentences of *IL* is *consistent* in V if and only if it is not the case that one can derive from that set all sentences B of L. A set Γ of sentences of *IL* is *maximally consistent* in V if and only if it is consistent, and whenever B is a sentence which does not belong to Γ, the set $\Gamma \cup \{B\}$ is inconsistent.

As I said earlier, the axiomatic system V of *IL* has two important meta-logical properties. First, it is *sound*, in the sense that every theorem of V is a logically true sentence of *IL*. This is easily proved by checking that its axioms are valid and that its rules of inference preserve logical truth. Second, the axiomatic system V is *complete*, in the sense that every logically true sentence of IL is a theorem of V. This is proved in appendix 1. Thus, $\vDash_{IL} A$ if and only if $\vdash_V A$.

3

FUNDAMENTAL LAWS OF
ILLOCUTIONARY LOGIC

The aim of this chapter is to enumerate a series of fundamental laws for illocutionary forces, propositions, and speech acts which are valid in illocutionary logic IL and provable in the axiomatic system V.

Most of these laws characterize the logical forms of elementary illocutionary acts. They either state logical properties of utterances which follow from the direction of fit of their illocutionary point, or they exhibit logical relations that exist between speech acts in virtue of their conditions of success and of satisfaction. Many of these laws are also linguistically significant. They can be used to predict and explain in a unified theoretical way universal semantic laws of analyticity, validity, consistency, and entailment, as I will show in chapter 5.

I BASIC LAWS FOR PROPOSITIONS

I will begin this chapter by stating the basic laws of illocutionary logic for propositions. As I explained earlier, propositions have a logical structure in illocutionary logic. They are *complex senses* composed out of attributes and other senses logically related in terms of predication. Moreover, their truth conditions are determined as a function of these predications between their propositional constituents. As a consequence of this, there is a new logical relation of implication between propositions that is sensitive both to their content and to their truth conditions. Most important laws about propositions can be stated in terms of that relation of implication that I have called *strong implication*.

50

1.1 Strong implication is a relation of partial order between propositions.

$\vDash A_p \mathbin{\vdash\!\!\!\dashv} A_p$; $\vDash ((A_p \mathbin{\vdash\!\!\!\dashv} B_p) \wedge (B_p \mathbin{\vdash\!\!\!\dashv} C_p)) \rightarrow (A_p \mathbin{\vdash\!\!\!\dashv} C_p)$ and $\vDash ((A_p \mathbin{\vdash\!\!\!\dashv} B_p) \wedge (B_p \mathbin{\vdash\!\!\!\dashv} A_p)) \rightarrow (A_p = B_p)$

As I said earlier, the anti-symmetry of strong implication provides the criterion of propositional identity of illocutionary logic. Two propositions are identical if and only if each of them strongly implies the other.

Contrary to what is the case in standard intensional logic, strictly equivalent propositions are not identical in illocutionary logic, when they have a different content. Thus, $\vDash ((A_p \mathbin{\vdash\!\!\!\dashv} B_p) \wedge \sim (A_p \mathbin{>} B_p)) \rightarrow \sim (A_p = B_p)$.

1.2 The content of a proposition obtained by the application of a logical truth functional operation from other propositions is identical with the union of the contents of those propositions.

For example, $\vDash ((A_p \mathbin{>} C_p) \leftrightarrow (\sim A_p \mathbin{>} C_p))$

1.3 Nearly all the laws of elimination of truth functional connectives of natural deduction generate strong implication in the sense that the conjunction of their premises strongly implies their conclusion.[1] However only the laws of introduction of truth functional connectives, where the content of the conclusion is necessarily included in the contents of the premises, also generate strong implication.

These laws are as follows:

1.3.1 The law of elimination of conjunction

$\vDash (A_p \wedge B_p) \mathbin{\vdash\!\!\!\dashv} A_p$

$\vDash (A_p \wedge B_p) \mathbin{\vdash\!\!\!\dashv} B_p$

A conjunction of two propositions strongly implies each conjunct.

1.3.2 The law of introduction of conjunction

From two propositional terms A_p and B_p one can infer $(A_p \wedge B_p)$.

1.3.3 The law of elimination of disjunction

$\vDash ((A_p^1 \mathbin{\vdash\!\!\!\dashv} B_p) \wedge (A_p^2 \mathbin{\vdash\!\!\!\dashv} B_p)) \rightarrow ((A_p^1 \vee A_p^2) \mathbin{\vdash\!\!\!\dashv} B_p)$

---

[1] These laws are expounded by G. Gentzen, "Untersuchungen über das Logische Schliessen", *Mathematische Zeitschrift*, 39 (1934).

If two propositions strongly imply another proposition, then the disjunction of these two propositions also strongly implies that proposition.

1.3.4 The law of elimination of material implication

$$\vDash (A_p \land (A_p \to B_p)) \vdash\!\!\!\!\dashv B_p$$

The rule of modus ponens generates strong implication in illocutionary logic.

1.3.5 The law of introduction of negation

Let 0_p be any propositional term of the form $(B_p \land \sim B_p)$

$$\vDash (A_p \vdash\!\!\!\!\dashv 0_p) \to (A_p \vdash\!\!\!\!\dashv \sim A_p)$$

Any proposition which strongly implies a contradiction strongly implies its own negation.

1.3.6 The law of elimination of necessity

$$\vDash \Box A_p \vdash\!\!\!\!\dashv A_p$$

1.4 The following laws of introduction and of elimination of natural deduction generate strict, but not strong, implication.
1.4.1 The failure of the law of introduction of disjunction

$$\nvDash A_p \vdash\!\!\!\!\dashv (A_p \lor B_p) \text{ although } \vDash t(A_p \dashv (A_p \lor B_p))$$

The reason for this failure is of course that the content of the proposition named by B_p might not be included in the content of the proposition named by A_p.

Indeed, $\vDash (\sim(A_p \rangle B_p) \to \sim(A_p \vdash\!\!\!\!\dashv (A_p \lor B_p)))$

However, the law of introduction of disjunction also generates strong implication in the particular cases where the content of the new proposition is included in the content of the premise.

$$\vDash (A_p \vdash\!\!\!\!\dashv (A_p \lor B_p)) \leftrightarrow A_p \rangle B_p$$

For example, $\vDash A_p \vdash\!\!\!\!\dashv (A_p \lor A_p)$. Each proposition strongly implies (and is identical with) its disjunction with itself.

1.4.2 The failure of the law of elimination of negation

$$\nvDash (A_p \land \sim A_p) \vdash\!\!\!\!\dashv B_p$$

The law of elimination of negation only generates strong implication in the particular cases where the content of the conclusion is included in the contents of the premises.

$$\models ((A_p \wedge \sim A_p) \vdash B_p) \leftrightarrow (A_p \rangle B_p)$$

1.4.3 The failure of the law of introduction of possibility

$$\not\models A_p \vdash \Diamond A_p$$

1.5 The failure of the law of contraposition

$$\not\models (A_p \vdash B_p) \rightarrow (\sim B_p \vdash \sim A_p)$$

Unlike the rule of *modus ponens*, the rule of *modus tollens* does not generate strong implication.

1.6 A contradictory proposition strongly implies all and only the propositions whose content is included in its content.

$$\models \mathbf{T} \sim A_p \rightarrow (A_p \vdash B_p \leftrightarrow A_p \rangle B_p)$$

Thus, contrary to what is the case in the propositional calculus, a contradictory proposition (with a finite content) only implies logically (in the strong sense) a *finite* number of other propositions.

Remark. The corresponding semantic law does not hold for impossible propositions. Thus, although $\models \sim \Diamond t(A_p) \rightarrow t(A_p \neg\vdash B_p)$, it is not even the case that $\models \sim \Diamond t(A_p) \rightarrow (A_p \vdash B_p \leftrightarrow A_p \rangle B_p)$. For example, the impossible proposition that arithmetic is complete does not strongly imply the contradictory proposition that arithmetic is both complete and incomplete, although the converse is true.

1.7 A proposition strongly implies all and only the tautological propositions whose content is included in its content.

$$\models T(B_p) \rightarrow (A_p \vdash B_p \leftrightarrow A_p \rangle B_p)$$

Thus, each proposition whose content is finite strongly implies only a *finite* number of tautologies. For example, $\models A_p \vdash (A_p \vee A_p)$ but $\models \sim (A_p \rangle B_p) \rightarrow \sim (A_p \vdash (B_p \vee \sim B_p)))$.

Remark. The corresponding semantic law does not hold for necessary propositions. Thus, although $\models \Box t(B_p) \rightarrow t(A_p \vdash B_p)$, it is not even the case that $\models \Box t(B_p) \rightarrow (A_p \vdash B_p \leftrightarrow A_p \rangle B_p)$. For example, the proposition that arithmetic is complete or incomplete does not strongly imply the necessary proposition that arithmetic is incomplete.

1.8 As I explained in volume I, there are two possible reasons why a proposition could strictly but not strongly imply another proposition. First, the content of the second proposition might not be included in the content of the first. Indeed, $\models t(A_p \dashv B_p) \wedge \sim(A_p \wr B_p) \rightarrow \sim(A_p \vdash\dashv B_p)$. This is why certain laws of introduction of connectives do not generate strong implication. Second, the relation of strict implication between the two propositions might not be due to the truth functional ways in which their truth conditions are determined. Indeed, in illocutionary logic, $\models t(A_p \dashv B_p) \wedge (A_p \wr B_p \wedge \sim T(A_p \rightarrow B_p)) \rightarrow \sim(A_p \vdash\dashv B_p)$. This is why, for example, only contradictions and not all impossible propositions strongly imply their negation.

1.9 Any proposition whose content is finite only strongly implies a finite number of other propositions.
This law describes a philosophically important feature of the logical structure of natural language. Indeed, one can argue that human speakers with their restricted cognitive abilities can only have in mind a finite number of propositional constituents, whenever they express a proposition with an illocutionary force in a context of utterance. Otherwise, their meaning in that context would not be determinable in a finite number of steps. Consequently, the propositions with a finite content are the only propositions which are expressible in natural languages.

1.10 Strong implication is decidable.
There exists an effective method of decision which permits us to determine in a finite number of steps whether $\models A_p \vdash\dashv B_p$. Indeed $A_p \vdash\dashv B_p =_{\mathrm{def}} (A_p \wr B_p) \wedge T(A_p \rightarrow B_p))$, and whether $\models A_p \wr B_p$ and $\models T(A_p \rightarrow B_p)$ is decidable. First, $\models A_p \wr B_p$ if and only if all variables and constants of type p which occur in B_p also occur in A_p. Second, $\models T(A_p \rightarrow B_p)$ if and only if the truth table of the formula $(A_p \rightarrow B_p)$ indicates that it is a tautology.[2]

The fact that strong implication is decidable in illocutionary logic is philosophically important. Indeed, this supports the thesis that strong implication is cognitively realized in the minds of speakers. Any speaker who understands fully two propositions knows *a priori*, solely

---

[2] The method of truth tables was first developed by Wittgenstein in his *Tractatus logico-philosophicus*, Routledge & Kegan Paul, 1961.

on the basis of his apprehension of their logical form, whether or not one of them strongly implies the other.

1.11 A finiteness theorem

For any propositional term A_p, there is only a finite number of other propositional terms B_p which are such that $\models A_p \dashv\vdash B_p$ and it is not the case that $\models B_p = A_p$.

The validity of this theorem is due to the fact that each propositional term is of finite length.

1.12 Illocutionary logic distinguishes sharply between necessary and impossible propositions on the one hand and tautologies and contradictions on the other hand.

Thus, all tautologies are necessarily true but the converse is not true. $\not\models \Box t(A_p) \to \mathbf{T}(A_p)$.

Similarly, all contradictions are necessarily false but the converse is not true. $\not\models \sim \Diamond t(A_p) \to \mathbf{T}(\sim A_p)$.

Such distinctions are important from a cognitive point of view, because tautologies are a special kind of necessary proposition which are also *a priori* true. Any competent speaker who apprehends a tautology knows *a priori* solely in virtue of his apprehension of its logical form that it is true. As Wittgenstein pointed out in the *Tractatus*, the truth of a tautology is certain *a priori*. However, this is not the case for all necessary propositions. For example, the proposition that water is H_2O is necessarily but not *a priori* true.

And similarly for contradictions. Contradictions are both necessarily and *a priori* false, and their falsehood is certain *a priori*. However, this is not the case for all impossible propositions. This is why some impossible propositions imply strictly, but not strongly, their negation.

II BASIC LAWS FOR COMPONENTS OF FORCE

Many fundamental laws of illocutionary logic for illocutionary points have already been stated and explained in the first volume and I will not repeat them here. Here are a few additional logical explanations.

2.1 The set of propositions on which a speaker achieves the assertive point is closed under strong implication.

$$\models (((A_p \wedge B_p) \dashv\vdash C_p) \to ((\pi^1 A_p \wedge \pi^1 B_p) \to \pi^1 C_p))$$

2.2 The set of propositions on which a speaker achieves the commissive, directive, or declarative illocutionary points is partially closed under strong implication.

$$\vDash (((A_p \wedge B_p) \rightarrowtail C_p) \wedge \sim\mathbf{T}C_p) \rightarrow ((\pi^k A_p \wedge \pi^k B_p) \rightarrow \pi^k C_p) \text{ where } 2 \leqslant k$$
$$\leqslant 3$$

And similarly for π^4 except that $\sim\Box t(C_p)$ occurs in place of $\sim\mathbf{T}(C_p)$ in that new theorem schema.

The laws for the components of illocutionary force of type μ, θ, Σ, and ψ are those of a *Boolean algebra*, as I mentioned earlier.

2.3 ⅹ is idempotent, commutative, and associative.

Where $\zeta \in \{\mu, \theta, \Sigma, \psi\}$, $\vDash (A_\zeta \ast A_\zeta) = A_\zeta$; $\vDash (A_\zeta \ast B_\zeta) = (B_\zeta \ast A_\zeta)$; $\vDash (A_\zeta \ast (B_\zeta \ast C_\zeta)) = ((A_\zeta \ast B_\zeta) \ast C_\zeta)$

2.4 There exist neutral and absorbent components of each type.

$$\vDash A_\zeta \ast 0_\zeta = 0_\zeta$$
$$\vDash A_\zeta \ast 1_\zeta = A_\zeta$$

2.5 There exists a complement for these types of component.

For each *IFC*-term A_ζ of type $\zeta \in \{\mu, \theta, \psi, \Sigma\}$, the complement of the component of illocutionary force named by A_ζ is syncategorematically named by the term $\bar{A}_\zeta$ in the following rules of abbreviation:

$$(B_\mu = \bar{A}_\mu) =_{\text{def}} \forall x_p (B_\mu x_p \rightarrowtail \sim A_\mu x_p)$$
$$(B_\theta = \bar{A}_\theta) =_{\text{def}} \forall x_p (B_\theta x_p \rightarrowtail \sim A_\theta x_p)$$
$$(B_\Sigma = \bar{A}_\Sigma) =_{\text{def}} \forall x_p \forall y_p (B_\Sigma x_p y_p \rightarrowtail \sim A_\Sigma x_p y_p)$$
$$(B_\psi = \bar{A}_\psi) =_{\text{def}} \forall x_\tau (B_\psi x_\tau \leftrightarrow \sim A_\psi x_\tau)$$

As in a Boolean algebra, the following laws hold for the complement of a component of illocutionary force:

$$\vDash B_\zeta = \bar{A}_\zeta \rightarrow (B_\zeta \ast A_\zeta = 0_\zeta)$$
$$\vDash B_\zeta = \bar{A}_\zeta \rightarrow ((C_\zeta \ast A_\zeta) = 0_\zeta \rightarrow (C_\zeta \ast B_\zeta = C_\zeta))$$

2.6 The relation that exists between two components of illocutionary force whenever one determines the other can be derived by the following rules of abbreviation.

2.6.1 Determination of a propositional content condition by a mode of achievement.

$$(A_\mu \dashv A_\theta) =_{\text{def}} \forall x_p (A_\mu x_p \dashv A_\theta x_p)$$

And similarly for $(A_\theta \dashv A_\mu)$.

56

2.6.2 Determination of a preparatory condition by a mode of achievement.

$$(A_\mu \dashv A_\Sigma) =_{\text{def}} \forall x_p \, (A_\mu x_p \dashv \forall y_p \, (A_\Sigma x_p y_p \rightarrow \gg y_p))$$

And similarly for $(A_\Sigma \dashv A_\mu)$.

2.6.3 Determination of a sincerity condition by a mode of achievement.

$$(A_\mu \dashv A_\psi) =_{\text{def}} \forall x_p \, (A_\mu x_p \dashv \forall x_\tau \, (A_\psi x_\tau \rightarrow \exists x_\iota E(x_\tau x_p) x_\iota))$$

And similarly for all other cases.

2.7 The absorbent components of illocutionary force determine all components.

$\models 0_\zeta \dashv A_{\zeta'}$, where ζ and $\zeta' \in \{\mu, \theta, \Sigma, \psi\}$.

2.8 The neutral components of illocutionary force are determined by all components

$\models A_\zeta \dashv 1_{\zeta'}$

2.9 Only the neutral component of illocutionary force determines itself.

$\models (1_\zeta \dashv A_\zeta) \leftrightarrow A_\zeta = 1_\zeta$

2.10 Degree of strength

As I said in chapter 4, the set of degrees of strength has the structure of an *Abelian group*.

Thus, + is commutative and associative, there is a neutral element for addition, and there exists an inverse.

III BASIC LAWS FOR ILLOCUTIONARY FORCES

The illocutionary logic *IL* is not only a formalization of the philosophical analysis of illocutionary force and of the principles of the recursive definition of the set of all illocutionary forces formulated in volume I. It also determines how the components of illocutionary forces can be identified in terms of the conditions of success of utterances. Moreover, it enables speech act theory systematically to derive a series of laws of comparative strength and of relative incompatibility for illocutionary forces, as I will now show.

3.1 Whether or not an illocutionary force has a certain component can be expressed in illocutionary logic by the following rules of abbreviation.

3.1.1 The property of having an illocutionary point or mode of achievement.

$$([(A_\mu, A_\theta, A_\Sigma, A_\psi), A_\iota, \pi^k] \dashv B_\mu)$$

$$=_{def} \forall x_p\, (s([(A_\mu, A_\theta, A_\Sigma, A_\psi), A_\iota, \pi^k]\, x_p) \dashv B_\mu\, x_p)$$

And similarly for $[(A_\mu, A_\theta, A_\Sigma, A_\psi), A_\iota, \pi^k] \dashv B_\theta)$.

3.1.2 The property of having a preparatory or sincerity condition.

$$([(A_\mu, A_\theta, A_\Sigma, A_\psi), A_\iota, \pi^k] \dashv B_\Sigma)$$

$$=_{def} \forall x_p\, (s([(A_\mu, A_\theta, A_\Sigma, A_\psi), A_\iota, \pi^k]x_p) \dashv \forall y_p\, (B_\Sigma x_p y_p \to\, \gg y_p))$$

And similarly for $([(A_\mu, A_\theta, A_\Sigma, A_\psi), A_\iota, \pi^k] \dashv B_\psi)$.

3.2 The components of an illocutionary force are uniquely determined from the conditions of success of the speech acts with that force.

One can prove in illocutionary logic *IL* the following laws for the components of illocutionary force.

3.2.1 The illocutionary points of a force are the points which are determined by its components.

$$\models [(A_\mu, A_\theta, A_\Sigma, A_\psi), A_\iota, \pi^k] \dashv \pi^n$$

$$\leftrightarrow (A_\mu \dashv \pi^n \lor A_\theta \dashv \pi^n \lor A_\Sigma \dashv \pi^n \lor A_\psi \dashv \pi^n \lor \pi^k \dashv \pi^n)$$

Thus, for example, $\models (A_\mu \dashv \pi^n \to ([A_\mu, A_\theta, A_\Sigma, A_\psi), A_\iota, \pi^k] \dashv \pi^k \,\chi\, \pi^n)$.

3.2.2 The mode of achievement of an illocutionary force is the conjunction of all modes which are determined by its components.

$$\models [(A_\mu, A_\theta, A_\Sigma, A_\psi), A_\iota, \pi^k] \dashv B_\mu$$

$$\leftrightarrow (A_\mu \dashv B_\mu \lor A_\theta \dashv B_\mu \lor A_\Sigma \dashv B_\mu \lor A_\psi \dashv B_\mu \lor \pi^k \dashv B_\mu)$$

3.2.3 The propositional content conditions of an illocutionary force are the intersection of all propositional content conditions determined by its components.

$$\models ([A_\mu, A_\theta, A_\Sigma, A_\psi), A_\iota, \pi^k] \dashv B_\theta)$$

$$\leftrightarrow (A_\mu \dashv B_\theta \lor A_\theta, \dashv B_\theta \lor A_\Sigma \dashv B_\theta \lor \pi^k \dashv B_\theta)$$

Thus, for example, $\models (A_\mu \dashv B_\theta) \to [(A_\mu, A_\theta, A_\Sigma, A_\psi), A_\iota, \pi^k] \dashv (A_\theta \,\chi\, B_\theta)$.

3.2.4 The preparatory conditions of an illocutionary force are the union of all preparatory conditions determined by its components.
(And similarly for its sincerity conditions.)

3.2.5 The property of having a degree of strength

$$\eta([(A_\mu, A_\theta, A_\Sigma, A_\Psi), A_\iota, \pi^k]) = A_\iota$$

$$=_{\mathrm{def}}(\forall x_p \sim s([(A_\mu, A_\theta, A_\Sigma, A_\Psi), A_\iota, \pi^k]x_p) \wedge A_\iota = 0_\iota)$$

$$\vee ((\exists x_p \; s([(A_\mu, A_\theta, A_\Sigma, A_\Psi), A_\iota, \pi^k]x_p)$$

$$\wedge \exists x_\iota \, (\forall y_\iota \, \forall y_p \, ((s([(A_\mu, A_\theta, A_\Sigma, A_\Psi), A_\iota, \pi^k]y_p) \dashv \forall x_\tau ((c_\Psi^k x_\tau \vee A_\Psi x_\tau)$$

$$\rightarrow (E(x_\tau y_p)y_\iota)) \wedge x_\iota \geqslant y_\iota \wedge x_\iota = A_\iota)))))$$

The degree of strength of an illocutionary force is the neutral degree when that force is impossible. Otherwise, it is the greatest degree of strength with which its sincerity conditions are expressed in the case of a successful performance of an act with that force. Such a greatest degree of strength exists because a speaker expresses with a maximal degree of strength the mental states that he expresses in the context of an utterance.

This definition has the following consequence:

3.2.5.1 The degree of strength of the illocutionary force named by an *IF*-term of the form $[(A_\mu, A_\theta, A_\Sigma, A_\Psi), A_\iota, \pi^k]$ is not smaller than the degree of strength named by A_ι.

$$\models \eta[(A_\mu, A_\theta, A_\Sigma, A_\Psi), A_\iota, \pi^k] \geqslant A_\iota$$

$$\not\models \eta[(A_\mu, A_\theta, A_\Sigma, A_\Psi), A_\iota, \pi^k] > A_\iota$$

3.3 The primitive illocutionary forces are the simplest possible illocutionary forces.

If $A_\phi \in \{\vdash, \perp, !, \top, \dashv\}$ and π^k is the last term of A_ϕ, then $\models (A_\phi \dashv A_\zeta) \leftrightarrow (\pi^k \dashv A_\zeta)$ and $\models \eta(A_\phi) \geqslant 0_\iota$.

A primitive illocutionary force has no other mode of achievement, propositional content, preparatory or sincerity conditions than those which are determined by its illocutionary point, and its degree of strength is the neutral degree of strength.

Definition. Let us say that two illocutionary forces are of *comparative strength* if and only if they are identical or one is stronger than the other.

One very important theorem of illocutionary logic is the following law:

3.4 The law of comparative strength for illocutionary forces

If two forces are respectively the argument and the value for that argument of an application of a logical operation on illocutionary forces, then these two forces are of comparative strength. To put the point more precisely:

$$\vDash [A_\zeta]A_\phi = A_\phi \text{ when } \vDash A_\phi \dashv A_\zeta$$

$$\vDash [B]A_\phi = A_\phi \text{ when } A_\phi \text{ contains } 0_\zeta$$

$$\vDash [A_\zeta]A_\phi \rhd A_\phi$$

$$\vDash (A_\iota \geqslant 0_\iota \rightarrow [A_\iota]A_\phi \rhd A_\phi) \text{ and}$$

$$\vDash 0_\iota \geqslant A_\iota \rightarrow A_\phi \rhd [A_\iota]A_\phi$$

In illocutionary logic, the operations which consist of adding a component to an illocutionary force F generate the same illocutionary force when that component is already part of F. Moreover, any application of an operation to an impossible illocutionary force (that determines impossible conditions of success) generates the same impossible illocutionary force. In the other cases, the operations which consist in restricting the mode of achievement, in increasing the degree of strength or in adding new conditions always generate stronger illocutionary forces, while the operation which consists in decreasing the degree of strength generates weaker illocutionary forces.

The fact that the operations of adding new components or of increasing the degree of strength generate stronger illocutionary forces is *made visible* in the very definition of these operations in the logical syntax of illocutionary logic. For example, an illocutionary force F_2 obtained by adding the preparatory condition named by a term B_Σ to the simpler force F_1 is described in the ideal language by an *IF*-term of the form $[B_\Sigma][(A_\mu, A_\theta, A_\Sigma, A_\psi), A_\iota, \pi^k]$ which is clearly more complex than the *IF*-term $[(A_\mu, A_\theta, A_\Sigma, A_\psi), A_\iota, \pi^k]$ naming the illocutionary force F_1.

Now, given the meaning of that term, it is also clear that the force F_2 must be identical with or stronger than the simpler force F_1. Indeed, by definition, a speaker performs an illocutionary act of the form $F_2(P)$ if and only if he performs the simpler illocutionary act $F_1(P)$, and moreover presupposes the propositions determined by the new preparatory conditions. (Similarly for the other cases.)

3.5 Any illocutionary force which is stronger than another force can be obtained from that force by adding a mode of achievement, propositional content, preparatory or sincerity conditions, or by increasing the degree of strength.

If $\models A_\phi \rhd B_\phi$ then, for some $A_\mu, A_\theta, A_\Sigma, A_\psi$ and $A_\iota, \models A_\iota \geq 0_\iota$ and

$$\models A_\phi = [A_\mu][A_\theta][A_\Sigma][A_\psi][A_\iota]B_\phi.$$

Thus, for example, the reason why the illocutionary force of informing is stronger than the force of assertion is that it is obtained from assertion by adding a special preparatory condition. To inform is indeed to assert a proposition to a hearer while presupposing that he does not already know the truth of that proposition.

This law expresses a certain syntactic *completeness* of the set of the various operations on forces. One can derive from it the following theorem:

Corollary 1. **Any illocutionary force with a positive or zero degree of strength is stronger than the primitive illocutionary force with its illocutionary point.**

$$\models A_\iota \geq 0_\iota \to [(A_\mu, A_\theta, A_\Sigma, A_\psi), A_\iota, \pi_\mu^k] \rhd [(1_\mu, 1_\theta, 1_\Sigma, 1_\psi), 0_\iota, \pi_\mu^k]$$

3.6 The order of application of operations on an illocutionary force has no importance.

$$\models [A_1][A_2]A_\phi = [A_2][A_1]A_\phi$$

3.7 The relation of being a stronger or identical illocutionary force is a relation of partial order between illocutionary forces.

$\models A_\phi \rhd A_\phi; \models ((A_\phi \rhd B_\phi) \wedge (B_\phi \rhd A_\phi)) \to A_\phi = B_\phi$; and $\models ((A_\phi \rhd B_\phi) \wedge (B_\phi \rhd C_\phi)) \to A_\phi \rhd C_\phi$, where A_ϕ, B_ϕ and C_ϕ are any *IF*-term of *IL*.

From the antisymmetry of $\rhd$ follows the law of identity for illocutionary forces:

$$\models A_\phi = B_\phi \leftrightarrow \forall x_p (A_\phi x_p \rhd B_\phi x_p \wedge B_\phi x_p \rhd A_\phi x_p)$$

Two illocutionary forces are identical if and only if they give as value, for any proposition, elementary illocutionary acts with the same conditions of success. Thus, there is a logical relationship between the components of illocutionary forces and the conditions of success that they determine. Illocutionary forces with different components determine different conditions of success for certain propositional contents, and consequently serve different linguistic purposes.

As I pointed out in volume I,[3] the four preceding laws concerning the relation of being a stronger or identical illocutionary force show that the set of all possible illocutionary forces of utterances is much more logically structured than has been commonly supposed in contemporary philosophy of language. Indeed, comparable laws do not hold for the relation of strict implication between propositions. It is not the case, for example, that any proposition which is obtained by applying a unary logical operation on another proposition always strictly implies, or is strictly implied by, that proposition. It is also not the case that whenever a proposition strictly implies another proposition, it can be obtained by applying logical operations on that proposition. Furthermore, the order of application of operations on propositions often affects their truth conditions. The proposition that it is not necessary that $2+2 = 5$ is, for example, different from the proposition that it is necessary that $2+2 \neq 5$. Finally, the relation of strict implication is not an anti-symmetric relation between propositions.

Thus, contrary to what was generally believed until now, the set of illocutionary forces is much more structured by the relation of comparative strength than the set of propositions is structured by strict implication. (More on this later.)

3.8 Any illocutionary force with an absorbent component is impossible.

$$\vDash\; \sim\; \Diamond s([A_\mu, A_\theta, A_\Sigma, A_\psi), A_\iota, \pi_\mu^k]\, A_p) \text{ when } A_\mu \text{ contains } 0_\mu \text{ or} \ldots \text{or } A_\psi \text{ contains } 0_\psi$$

3.9 There exists one and only one empty or impossible illocutionary force.

Let $0_\phi =_{\mathrm{def}} [(0_\mu, 0_\theta, 0_\Sigma, 0_\psi), 0_\iota, \pi^5]$

$$\vDash (\forall x_p \sim \Diamond s(A_\phi x_p)) \to A_\phi = 0_\phi$$

The impossible illocutionary force named by 0_ϕ is a *limit case* of

---

[3] See the conclusions of this volume (p. 220).

illocutionary force which serves no linguistic purpose. In illocutionary logic it plays a role comparable to that of the empty set in set theory. Thus, for example, $\models 0_\phi \triangleright A_\phi$ for any *IF*-term A_ϕ. The empty illocutionary force is stronger than all others.

In *Foundations*, Searle and I did not admit the existence of the empty illocutionary force.[4] We defended the view that each illocutionary force F must serve some linguistic purpose and consequently must be *possible*, in the sense that at least one speech act of the form $F(P)$ must be performable. In general semantics, however, the empty illocutionary force is needed for at least two reasons. First, the admission of that force simplifies greatly the model-theoretic formalization. Second, there are in natural languages illocutionary force markers and performative verbs which respectively express and name that impossible illocutionary force. They could not be interpreted if that force was not admitted. For example, the complex illocutionary force marker of the sentence "Please do it, whether you like it or not" expresses the impossible illocutionary force, since its complex modifier expresses the absorbent mode of achievement.

3.10 The property of being the impossible illocutionary force is decidable.
Indeed, $\models A_\phi = 0_\phi$ if and only if A_ϕ contains a term of the form 0_ζ where $\zeta = \theta, \mu, \Sigma$ or ψ.

3.11 The law of measurability of comparative strength.
The relation of comparative strength between illocutionary forces is also decidable.

As in the case of strong implication, there exists an effective method which permits us to determine in a finite number of steps whether $\models A_\phi \triangleright B_\phi$. To put the point more precisely, $[(A_\mu, A_\theta, A_\Sigma, A_\psi), A_\iota, \pi^n] \triangleright [(B_\mu, B_\theta, B_\Sigma, B_\psi), B_\iota, \pi^k]$ in first order illocutionary logic if and only if at least one of the following conditions obtains:

(1) A_ϕ names the impossible illocutionary force. In that case, A_ϕ must contain a term of the form 0_ζ where $\zeta = \theta, \mu, \Sigma$ or ψ.

(2) A_ϕ names an illocutionary force that has a greater degree of strength or more components than the illocutionary force named by B_ϕ.

[4] See chapters 3 and 6 of J. R. Searle and D. Vanderveken, *Foundations of Illocutionary Logic*, Cambridge University Press, 1985.

In that case, these illocutionary force terms satisfy the following clause: first, $n = k$ or $k = 5$ or (n is even and $k = 1$); and/or second, the integer named by A_ι is identical with or greater than the integer named by B_ι;[5] and/or third, all terms of type μ, θ, Σ or ψ which occur in B_ϕ also occur in A_ϕ.

Thus the question whether the force named by an *IF*-term is stronger than or identical with the force named by another *IF*-term is *decidable* in illocutionary logic solely *on the basis of a simple observation of their syntactic forms*. Whenever $\models A_\phi \rhd B_\phi$, this is *visible* on the surface in the apparent grammatical structure of these *IF*-terms. The fact that the relation of comparative strength between forces is decidable in such a straightforward way in illocutionary logic also confirms the thesis that strong illocutionary commitment is cognitively realized in the minds of speakers. Whenever an illocutionary force is stronger than another force, speakers who are capable of performing speech acts with these forces know this *a priori* solely on the basis of their apprehension of the logical forms of these forces. As is clear in the logical symbolism, they cannot apprehend the nature of the first illocutionary force without understanding *eo ipso* that it has a greater degree of strength, an additional mode of achievement, or more propositional content, preparatory or sincerity conditions than the second force.

3.12 Illocutionary forces with complementary components (in the Boolean sense) are incompatible.

$$\models (A_\phi \dashv A_\zeta \wedge B_\phi \dashv \bar{A}_\zeta) \rightarrow A_\phi \rangle\langle B_\phi$$

Thus, for example, one cannot both entreat and order someone to do some action, because the forces of such directive speech acts have incompatible modes of achievement. Indeed one cannot both give and preclude option of refusal for the same action. Similarly, one cannot both report and predict the same event, because these speech acts have incompatible propositional content conditions. The same event cannot be both future and past or present with respect to the same moment of utterance. Furthermore, one cannot also both promise and threaten someone to do the same action, because such speech acts have incompatible preparatory conditions. One cannot indeed presuppose that the same action is both good and bad for the hearer (under the same aspect). Finally, one cannot both thank and criticize the same

---

[5] This can be determined by counting the numbers of occurrences of primes in these terms.

hearer for having done a certain action, because these speech acts have incompatible sincerity conditions.

3.13 The illocutionary force named by an *IF*-term cannot be identified with a sextuple consisting of the components named by its six constituent terms.

$$\nvDash ([(A_\mu, A_\theta, A_\Sigma, A_\psi), A_\iota, \pi^k] = [(B_\mu, B_\theta, B_\Sigma, B_\psi), B_\iota, \pi^n)$$

$$\leftrightarrow (A_\mu = B_\mu \wedge A_\theta = B_\theta \wedge A_\Sigma = B_\Sigma \wedge A_\phi = B_\phi \wedge A_\iota = B_\iota \wedge \pi^k = \pi^n)$$

The reason for this is that the constituent term of type ζ of an *IF*-term A_ϕ does not necessarily name the whole component of type ζ of the illocutionary force named by A_ϕ. For example, the constituent term A_Σ of an *IF*-term $A_\phi = [(A_\mu, A_\theta, A_\Sigma, A_\psi), A_\iota, \pi^k]$ names only one of the preparatory conditions of the illocutionary force named by A_ϕ, when the components named by other constituent terms of A_ϕ determine other preparatory conditions. If, for example, the term A_ψ names a sincerity condition determining a preparatory condition independent of that named by A_Σ, the preparatory conditions of the illocutionary force named by A_ϕ are stronger than those named by A_Σ.

Thus, $\vDash (A_\psi \dashv B_\Sigma) \wedge \sim(A_\Sigma \dashv B_\Sigma) \rightarrow ([(A_\mu, A_\theta, A_\Sigma, A_\psi), A_\iota, \pi^k]$

$= [(A_\mu, A_\theta, (A_\Sigma \ast B_\Sigma), A_\psi), A_\iota, \pi^k].$

For this reason, the illocutionary forces named by two different *IF*-terms can be identical, although these two *IF*-terms contain constituent *IFC*-terms of the same type which name different components. Because the components of illocutionary force are not necessarily independent, the algebra of illocutionary forces is more complex than that of vector spaces.

IV BASIC LAWS FOR SPEECH ACTS

4.1 The law of identity for speech acts

$$\vDash A_\phi(A_p) = B_\phi(B_p) \leftrightarrow (A_p = B_p \wedge A_\phi(A_p) \rhd B_\phi(B_p) \wedge B_\phi(B_p) \rhd A_\phi(A_p))$$

Two elementary illocutionary acts are identical if and only if they have the same propositional content and the same conditions of success.

This law follows from the definition of the logical type of elementary illocutionary acts. As I said earlier, there is a logical relation between the illocutionary forces and propositional contents of elementary speech acts, their conditions of success and of satisfaction, and the linguistic purposes served by these illocutionary acts. Different forces or propositional contents determine generally different conditions of success or of satisfaction, and consequently they serve different linguistic purposes in the performance of illocutionary acts.

4.2 An illocutionary act is not an ordered pair consisting of an illocutionary force and of a propositional content.

$$\not\models A_\phi(A_p) = B_\phi(B_p) \leftrightarrow (A_\phi = B_\phi \wedge A_p = B_p)$$

Of course, two elementary illocutionary acts with the same force and the same propositional content are identical. However, the converse is not true. Indeed, illocutionary acts with the same propositional content and the same conditions of success can have different illocutionary forces. Thus, for example, suppose the proposition named by A_p satisfies in all contexts the special propositional content condition named by A_θ if and only if it satisfies the propositional content conditions of an illocutionary force named by the term A_ϕ. Then the two illocutionary acts named by $[A_\theta] A_\phi(A_p)$ and $A_\phi(A_p)$ are identical, although their forces can be different. This is why, for example, the yes-no question asked by an utterance of the interrogative sentence " Is it raining?" is identical with the request expressed by the imperative sentence "Please, tell me whether it is raining!" in the context of that utterance.

4.3 The relation of strong illocutionary commitment between illocutionary acts is reflexive and transitive but is not anti-symmetric.

$$\models A_\phi(A_p) \rhd A_\phi(A_p), \text{ and } \models (A_\phi(A_p) \rhd B_\phi(B_p) \wedge B_\phi(B_p) \rhd C_\phi(C_p))$$

$$\rightarrow A_\phi(A_p) \rhd C_\phi(C_p)$$

But, $\not\models (A_\phi(A_p) \rhd B_\phi(B_p) \wedge B_\phi(B_p) \rhd A_\phi(A_p)) \rightarrow A_\phi(A_p) = B_\phi(B_p)$

The reason why the relation of strong illocutionary commitment is not anti-symmetric is that a speech act of the form $F_1(P_1)$ can have stronger conditions of success than another speech act of the form $F_2(P_2)$, while its propositional content P_1 does not strictly imply the proposition P_2.

Thus, every non-performable speech act strongly commits the

speaker to any other illocutionary act. But its propositional content does not *eo ipso* strictly imply any other proposition. For example, an assertion that it is raining and not raining and a promise that $2+2 = 4$ are two different self-defeating illocutionary acts. They have the same conditions of success but different propositional contents. Indeed the content of that assertion is impossible, while the content of the promise is necessary.

It is then a mistake to define the logical type of illocutionary acts as that of functions from possible contexts of utterance into success values, and to identify illocutionary acts with their success conditions.[6] Identical illocutionary acts must have both the same conditions of success and the same conditions of satisfaction. Furthermore, even elementary illocutionary acts with the same conditions of success and of satisfaction can be different, since their propositional contents can be different.

4.4 A law of foundation for strong illocutionary commitment

For any primitive *IF*-term A_ϕ other than $\dashv$, $\models s(A_\phi A_p) \rightarrow$

$$\exists x_p \, (s(A_\phi x_p) \wedge \forall y_p \, (s(A_\phi y_p) \rightarrow x_p \vdash y_p))$$

Thus, for example, every assertion that a speaker makes in a context is made by way of a strong assertion whose propositional content strongly implies the propositional content of all other assertions made in that context. And similarly for all other primitive illocutionary forces of utterances with a non-empty direction of fit. This law of foundation follows from the fact that the set of propositions that a speaker expresses with the intention of achieving a success of fit between language and the world has a unique supremum.

This law has the following corollaries for strong illocutionary commitment:

Corollary 1. **There is a unique strongest illocutionary act in the contexts of successful utterances with a non-empty direction of fit.**

For any primitive *IF*-term A_ϕ other than $\dashv$, $\models s(A_\phi A_p) \rightarrow$

$$\exists x_p \, (s(A_\phi x_p) \wedge \forall y_p \, (s(A_\phi y_p) \leftrightarrow A_\phi x_p \triangleright A_\phi y_p))$$

Corollary 2. **A finiteness theorem**

For any illocutionary force F with a non-empty direction of fit, there

---

[6] I committed this mistake in my paper, "A model-theoretical semantics for illocutionary forces", *Logique et Analyse*, 103–4 (1983), 359–94.

is at most a finite number of speech acts of the form $F(P)$ that a speaker can simultaneously perform in a possible context of utterance of a natural language.

This finiteness theorem is a direct consequence of the finiteness of human speakers who can only express propositions (with a finite content) in the context of an utterance. Thus the propositional content of the strongest illocutionary act that is performed in an utterance can only strongly imply a finite number of propositions. (See theorem 1.9.)

4.5 A law of minimal consistency of the speaker

$$\models (\sim \varnothing(A_\phi) \wedge (A_p \vdash B_p)) \to \sim \Diamond s(A_\phi(A_p \wedge \sim B_p))$$

Speakers are rational. They cannot express two propositions which are strongly incompatible with the aim of achieving a success of fit between language and the world from the same direction of fit. Indeed, they know *a priori* that such linguistic attempts are necessarily condemned to failure.

Apparent counter-examples of this law of minimal consistency are non-literal utterances where the speaker means something other than what he says. A speaker who says, for example, " I order and forbid you to come" might mean to order the hearer to come in the morning and to forbid him to come in the afternoon. However, in this case, the propositional content of his utterance is a *non-literal* proposition which does not have the form of a contradiction.

Corollary. Other laws of minimal rationality

Because there is an assertive commitment in the achievement of the commissive and of the declarative illocutionary points, the law of the minimal consistency of the speaker can also be used to predict the incompatibility of speech acts with different directions of fit.

For example, one important corollary of this law is:

$$\models (A_\phi \dashv \pi^k \wedge B_\phi \dashv \pi^n) \to ((A_p \vdash \sim B_p) \to (A_\phi A_p \rangle\langle_s B_\phi \sim A_p)),$$
where n and $k = 1, 2,$ or 4

Two illocutionary acts with an assertive, commissive, or declarative force, and strongly incompatible propositional contents, are both not simultaneously satisfiable and not simultaneously performable.

Such illocutionary acts with different directions of fit are incompatible because the responsibility for achieving the success of fit depends on the speaker in the three cases.

Remark. Although they cannot be minimally inconsistent, speakers can be *inconsistent* in their use and comprehension of language.

$$\not\models (\uparrow(A_\phi) \vee \downarrow(A_\phi)) \rightarrow (\sim \Diamond t(A_p) \rightarrow \sim \Diamond s(A_\phi A_p))$$

Thus, speakers often make successful promises that it is impossible to keep. Similarly, they can make requests that it is impossible to grant. Illocutionary logic is perfectly compatible with the existence of such inconsistencies that occur in the use of scientific as well as of ordinary languages. Mathematicians, for example, often promise to colleagues or ask their assistants to prove the consistency or completeness of axiomatic systems which are later discovered to be inconsistent or incomplete. However, in such cases, they do not know *a priori* in virtue of their linguistic competence that their promise or directive is unsatisfiable.

4.6 Another law of minimal consistency of the speaker

$$\models (\uparrow(A_\phi) \wedge \mathbf{T}A_p) \rightarrow \sim \Diamond s(A_\phi A_p)$$

Speakers are rational. They cannot express a proposition which is *a priori* true with the aim of getting the speaker or hearer to transform the world in order to match that proposition. Indeed they know *a priori* that such propositions are true absolutely independently of any human action.

4.7 Assertion is entirely compatible with strong implication

$$\models ((A_p \vdash\!\!\dashv B_p) \rightarrow \vdash(A_p) \rhd \vdash(B_p))$$

Any speaker who makes an assertion of a proposition also asserts all propositions strongly implied by that proposition. Indeed, in such a case, he and the hearer mutually know *a priori* that this assertion cannot be true if the other weaker assertions are also not true.

Thus, the following laws of introduction and elimination of truth connectives hold for assertion.

4.7.1 The law of elimination of conjunction

$$\frac{\vdash(A_p \wedge B_p)}{\vdash(A_p)}$$

$$\frac{\vdash(A_p \wedge B_p)}{\vdash(B_p)}$$

4.7.2 The law of introduction of conjunction

$$\frac{\vdash(A_p)}{\vdash(A_p \wedge B_p)}$$

4.7.3 A restricted law of introduction of disjunction

$$\frac{\vdash(A_p)}{A_p \rangle B_p}$$
$$\frac{}{\vdash(A_p \vee B_p)}$$

4.7.4 The law of elimination of disjunction

$$A_p \rightarrowtail C_p$$
$$B_p \rightarrowtail C_p$$
$$\frac{\vdash(A_p \vee B_p)}{\vdash(C_p)}$$

4.7.5 The law of elimination of material implication

$$\frac{\vdash(A_p)}{\vdash(A_p \rightarrow B_p)}$$
$$\frac{}{\vdash(B_p)}$$

And similarly for all other truth functional operations on propositions.

Remark. There are two *cognitive reasons* why an assertion of a proposition P_1 might not contain the assertion of another proposition P_2 which is strictly implied by the first. First, it could be possible for competent speakers to have in mind the first proposition without *eo ipso* having in mind the second proposition. This occurs whenever the content of proposition P_2 is not included in the content of the first proposition. This is why an assertion that $2+2 = 4$ does not contain the assertion that $12-2 = 10$. Second, the relation of strict implication existing between the two propositions might not be known *a priori* by speakers in virtue of their linguistic competence. This can occur even when the content of P_2 is included in the content of P_1. Thus, a mathematician can, for example, assert that Goldbach's conjecture is either true or false without being ready to assert which is the case. Similarly, a mathematician unaware of Gödels' theorem could assert that arithmetic is complete, but he would not be illocutionarily committed *eo ipso* to asserting the *a priori* false contradiction that arithmetic is both complete and incomplete.

4.8 As a consequence of this, an assertion can have more truth conditions than another assertion without *eo ipso* having more success conditions than that other assertion.

$$\nvDash A_p \dashv B_p \rightarrow \vdash(A_p) \rhd \vdash(B_p)$$

4.9 However, the converse is false because of the law of foundation. Indeed, $\vDash (\vdash A_p \rhd \vdash B_p) \wedge \Diamond s(\vdash A_p) \rightarrow (A_p \dashv B_p)$

4.10 Strong illocutionary commitment in the case of commissive, directive, and performative utterances is partially compatible with strong implication.

If $A_\phi = \bot$, ! or $\top$ then $\vDash ((A_p \vdash\!\!\dashv B_p) \wedge \sim \Box t(B_p)) \rightarrow A_\phi(A_p) \rhd$
$$A_\phi(B_p).$$

A speaker who performs an illocutionary act $F(P)$ with the aim of achieving a success of fit between language and the world from the world-to-words direction of fit also performs *eo ipso* all illocutionary acts $F(Q)$ whose propositional content is contingent and strongly implied by P.

Unlike assertive speech acts, commissive, directive, and declarative speech acts do not commit the speaker to other speech acts of the same type with a tautological propositional content. Indeed, a competent speaker knows *a priori* that the tautologies strongly implied by the propositional content of his utterance are true independently of that utterance, and consequently that the world cannot be transformed by a present or future human action in order to match such necessary propositions. Thus, for example, the directive utterance "Do this tomorrow with Mary or Ursula!" strongly commits the speaker to the directive "Do this tomorrow!" However, that directive does not contain the tautological directive: "Either do or do not do this tomorrow!"

4.11 The law of the successful performance of satisfied illocutionary acts with the world-to-words or the double direction of fit

$$\vDash \updownarrow(A_\phi) \vee \uparrow(A_\phi) \rightarrow (t(A_\phi A_p) \rightarrow s(A_\phi A_p))$$

This law is a direct consequence of the definition of conditions of satisfaction of utterances with these directions of fit. By definition, an illocutionary act with the world-to-words or the double direction of fit cannot be satisfied unless the world has been changed by the speaker or hearer in order to satisfy that utterance. Thus, if a commissive, directive, or declarative speech act is satisfied, it must have been performed. Indeed, it is the cause of the corresponding change in the world.

4.12 The existence of an assertive commitment in the performance of a commissive illocutionary act

$$\models [(A_\mu, A_\theta, A_\Sigma, A_\psi), A_\iota, \pi^2] \rhd [(A_\mu, A_\theta, A_\Sigma, A_\psi), A_\iota, \pi^1].$$

Thus, in particular, $\models \bot \rhd \vdash$.

A speaker who commits himself to doing a future action *eo ipso* asserts that he will do it. The main reason for this is that his commitment to the performance of that action contains a commitment to the truth of the proposition that he will perform that action, as is shown by the fact that an utterance of the form "I promise to come, but I will not come" is analytically unsuccessful. Furthermore, a commissive utterance also creates a reason for the speaker to do what he commits himself to doing.

4.13 The law of the truth of the propositional content of a successful declaration

$$\models \mathop{\updownarrow}(A_\phi) \to (s(A_\phi A_p) \to t(A_p))$$

By definition, a successful declaration constitutes the performance by the speaker of the course of action represented by its propositional content. Thus, if a declaration is successful, its propositional content is *eo ipso* true.

This law has the following important corollary:

Corollary 1. **Any type of illocutionary act can be performed by way of a declaration.**

$$\models (t(B_p) \mathbin{\rightarrowtail} s(A_\phi A_p)) \to (\top B_p \rhd A_\phi A_p)$$

In performative utterances, speakers perform illocutionary acts by way of declaring that they perform them.

Corollary 2. **Any successful declaration is also satisfied.**

$$\models \mathop{\updownarrow}(A_\phi) \to (s(A_\phi A_p) \to t(A_\phi A_p))$$

72

Indeed, the propositional content of a declaration is true because of the declaration.

Corollary 3. Declarations are successful if and only if they are satisfied.

$$\models \mathop{\updownarrow}(A_\phi) \rightarrow (s(A_\phi A_p) \leftrightarrow t(A_\phi A_p))$$

4.14 Any declaration strongly commits the speaker to an assertion.

$$\models \top \mathrel{\triangleright} \vdash$$

This law is also a direct consequence of the double direction of fit of declarations. A speaker who declares that a proposition is true makes that proposition true in virtue of his utterance by asserting that he performs in that utterance the course of action that it represents.

4.15 Declarations are the strongest type of speech act.

Because they have the double direction of fit, declarations are the strongest kind of illocutionary act. From a logical point of view, *all successful declarations are eo ipso true, satisfied, sincere, and non defective.* Thus, contrary to what is the case for other speech acts, declarations are *self-guaranteeing utterances.* First, the successful performance of declarations is sufficient to bring about success of fit between language and the world. As I pointed out, illocutionary acts of all types can be performed by declaration in performative utterances. But no other type of illocutionary act strongly commits the speaker to declarations. Second, the *successful* performance of an illocutionary act with the primitive illocutionary force of declaration is necessarily *non defective.* Indeed, if the speaker makes the propositional content true in a successful declarative utterance, then he has the capacity to make it true. Thus, the preparatory conditions obtain in the context of his utterance. Moreover, a speaker who makes such a successful declaration is also necessarily sincere. Indeed, he cannot mean to make the propositional content true in virtue of his utterance without *eo ipso* believing, desiring, and intending this utterance to bring out success of fit between language and the world.

Because declarations are the strongest kind of speech act, it is a mistake to take them as paradigmatic for all illocutionary acts, just as it is a mistake to take performative sentences as paradigmatic forms of expression for illocutionary acts. Every performance of an illocutionary act brings about a new state of affairs in the world, namely the state of affairs that this act has been performed. However, *only* declarations bring about the state of affairs represented by their propositional content. Similarly, *only* successful declarations are also necessarily non defective. Austin's mistake of considering preparatory and sincerity conditions as part of the conditions of felicity of speech acts derives from his tendency to consider declarations as paradigmatic speech acts.[7]

4.16 Any illocutionary act strongly commits the speaker to an expressive illocutionary act.

$$\vDash [(A_\mu, A_\theta, A_\Sigma, A_\Psi), A_\iota, \pi^k] \rhd [(A_\mu, A_\theta, A_\Sigma, A_\Psi), A_\iota, \pi^5]$$

This law follows from the *neutrality* of the expressive illocutionary point. In the sense in which declarations are the strongest type of illocutionary act, *expressives are the weakest illocutionary acts*. In the performance of any type of elementary illocutionary act of the form $F(P)$, the speaker expresses propositional attitudes and consequently also performs an expressive illocutionary act. Thus, any type of illocutionary act strongly commits the speaker to expressives. But the expressive type of illocutionary act does not commit the speaker to any other type. Just as it was a mistake for Austin to think that declarations are paradigmatic speech acts, so it is a corresponding mistake for Bach and Harnish,[8] and for Cohen and Levesque,[9] to think that expressive illocutions are paradigmatic for all speech acts. There is more to a speech act with a non-empty direction of fit than just expressing the mental states which are part of its sincerity conditions. Thus, for example, there is more in a request than the simple expression of a desire.

[7] J. L. Austin, *How to do Things with Words*, Oxford, Clarendon Press, 1962.

[8] See E. Bach and R. Harnish, *Linguistic Communication and Speech Acts*, Cambridge, Mass.: M.I.T. Press, 1979.

[9] See P. R. Cohen and H. J. Levesque, "Rational interaction as the basis for communication", in P. R. Cohen, M. Pollack, and J. Morgan (eds.), *Intentions in Communication*, Cambridge, Mass.: Bradford Books, M.I.T., 1990.

4

THE IDEAL CONCEPTUAL LANGUAGE
OF GENERAL SEMANTICS

The aim of this chapter is to present the logical syntax of the ideal unambiguous and perspicuous object-language of general semantics. As I said earlier, general semantics is a *theoretical extension* of Montague grammar. Its ideal object-language is obtained from that of the intensional logic of Montague by adding new symbols and rules of formation. Moreover, the model-theoretical semantics for that object-language is also a natural generalization of *Montague's semantics*. In this chapter, I will first present the ideal conceptual object-language of general semantics and explain how its formulas can be naively interpreted. As we will see, all logical constants and syncategorematic symbols of that ideal language express primitive theoretical notions which are universals of language. I will also state the rules of abbreviation by the application of which all other fundamental notions of illocutionary and intensional logic can be derived. Finally, I will briefly explain how the different syntactic types of sentence in natural languages are to be translated into the ideal language of general semantics.

I VOCABULARY AND RULES OF FORMATION

I will now proceed to the definition of the object-language L_ω of general semantics. From the point of view of logical syntax, that object-language is an extension of the language of standard intensional logic. It incorporates a *simple modal theory of types*[1] which admits the

---

[1] This simple modal theory is developed in R. Montague, *Formal Philosophy*, Yale University Press, 1974.

primitive types of *success value* and of *atomic proposition*, in addition to the types of *truth value* and of *individual*. The two success values are success and insuccess. They are needed in order to define the conditions of success of illocutionary acts. Atomic propositions are more complex entities than simple truth conditions: they have a structure of constituents which is constructed in accordance with the remarks on propositional identity made in chapter 3 of volume I. As in intensional logic, given any pair of types α and β, general semantics also admits the derived type $(\alpha\beta)$ of *functions* from entities of type α into entities of type β, and the derived type $\#\alpha$ of *intensions* whose extensions are entities of types α.[2] These derived types are needed to analyze the logical form of utterances.

In addition to the constants and syncategorematic symbols of intensional logic, the ideal language of general semantics also contains in its vocabulary a few additional symbols of illocutionary logic which are needed to interpret illocutionary force markers and performative verbs. Because of the context dependent nature of literal illocutionary acts, the formulas of general semantics which name senses or illocutionary forces can have different semantic values in different contexts. Moreover, unlike the simple first order language of illocutionary logic *IL*, the language of general semantics also admits *higher order quantification* over all types of entities.

The expressive powers of general semantics are then much richer than those of the illocutionary logic *IL*. As a consequence of this, many of the primitive notions expressed by logical constants of *IL* can be derived by rules of abbreviation in general semantics.

The *grammar of the ideal language* of general semantics consists of the following rules and definitions:

1 The TYPE SYMBOLS of L_ω

t, s, a, and e are the *primitive type symbols* of L_ω. If α and β are type symbols of L_ω, then $\#\alpha$ and $(\alpha\beta)$ are new *derived type symbols* of L_ω.

t names the type of *truth values*, s the type of *success values*, e the type of *individuals*, and a the type of *atomic propositions*. The derived type symbol $(\alpha\beta)$ names the type of *functions* from entities of type α into

---

[2] Intensions (or Carnapian senses) whose extensions are entities of type α are functions from contexts into entities of type α. This type is named in Montague's object-language by the type symbol (s,α).

entities of type β, and ($\#\alpha$) the type of *intensions* whose extensions are entities of type α. As in Carnap's theory, these intensions are functions from possible contexts of utterances into entities of type α.

Thus, for example, $t(tt)$ names the type of binary truth functions and $\#(et)$ the type of properties of individuals. A type symbol of the form $\#e\ldots(et)$ with n occurrences of e names the type of n-ary *attributes of individuals*. Such simple attributes are *first order attributes*. As in simple type theory, one can ramify attributes into higher orders. Thus, attributes of first order attributes are of the second order, attributes of the second order attributes are of the third order, and so on. By definition, a type symbol for an n-ary *simple attribute of order $m+1$* in general semantics is any type symbol of the form $\#\alpha_1\ldots(\alpha_n t)$, where each α_k ($1 \leqslant k \leqslant n$) is either e, or a type symbol for simple attributes of an order identical with or smaller than m where at least one α_k is a simple attribute of order m. For example, $\#(\#(et)\,(et))$ is an attribute of order 2. For the sake of simplicity, the propositional constituents of propositions over which one quantifies in this simple version of general semantics are individual concepts and simple attributes of finite orders.[3]

Here are a few useful abbreviations for naming certain *derived types* which are important for the purposes of general semantics:

$$\alpha_1\alpha_2 =_{\text{def}} (\alpha_1\alpha_2),\ (\alpha_1\alpha_2\alpha_3) =_{\text{def}} \alpha_1(\alpha_2\alpha_3),\ \gamma =_{\text{def}} (at),\ p =_{\text{def}} \gamma((\gamma t)t),$$

$$\mu =_{\text{def}} \#(ps),\ \theta =_{\text{def}} \#(pt),\ \Sigma =_{\text{def}} \#(p(pt)),\ \xi =_{\text{def}} (p(\#tt)),\ \tau =_{\text{def}} p\xi,$$

$$\psi =_{\text{def}} \tau t,\ \iota =_{\text{def}} ((pt)t)(((pt)t)t),\ \Omega =_{\text{def}} (p(\#st))\ \text{and}\ \phi =_{\text{def}} (p\Omega)$$

Thus, γ is the type of *sets of atomic propositions and of truth value assignments to atomic propositions*; p is the type of (complete) *propositions*, θ is the type of *propositional content conditions*, μ is the type of *illocutionary points* and of *modes of achievement*, Σ is the type of *preparatory conditions*, ξ is the type of *propositional attitudes*, ι is the type of *integers*,[4] τ is the type of *psychological modes*, ψ is the type of

---

[3] A full development of the theory of propositions of general semantics leads to a ramification of the type of proposition. The propositions which are considered here are of the first ramified type. They are the simplest kinds of proposition. Their propositional constituents can only be individuals or simple attributes of finite orders. Propositions of the second ramified type are more complex and have at least one proposition of the first ramified type as a propositional constituent, and so on.

[4] Following Russell's method, I will identify a natural number in the theory of types of general semantics with a set of equipotent sets of propositions, and an integer with an ordered pair of natural numbers. See A. N. Whitehead and B. Russell, *Principia Mathematica*, Cambridge University Press, 1910.

sincerity conditions, Ω is the type of *illocutionary acts*, and ϕ is the type of *illocutionary forces*.

One can easily check that the derived logical types of propositions, illocutionary forces, speech acts, and propositional attitudes satisfy the laws of identity that have been stated earlier. For example, from the way that type p is defined, a proposition consists of a set of atomic propositions and of a set of truth value assignments to atomic propositions. Similarly, from the way that type Ω is defined, two elementary illocutionary acts with the same propositional content and the same success conditions are identical in general semantics. As is the case in type-theoretical semantics, only some entities of a derived type α will be possible semantic values of translations of actual expressions of formulas of that type. For example, not all entities of type Ω are possible elementary illocutionary acts. Indeed, a possible elementary illocutionary act has only one propositional content and only one success value in each context. Thus, only the functions of type Ω which are ordered pairs of a proposition and of a success condition are possible elementary illocutionary acts in general semantics.[5]

Note. I will often hereafter use ζ as a meta-linguistic variable for the type symbols μ, θ, Σ and ψ of components of illocutionary force.

2 The vocabulary

The vocabulary of L_ω consists of the following variables, constants and syncategorematic symbols:

The *variables* of L_ω are: x_α, x_α^1, x_α^2, ..., y_α, y_α^1, y_α^2, ..., z_α, z_α^1, z_α^2, ... for each type symbol α.

The *constants* of L_ω are: c_α, c_α^1, c_α^2, ... for each type symbol α.

The *logical constants* of L_ω are: 1_s, $\{\}_{ts}$, $\simeq_{a(at)}$, $[\,]_{a\#t}$, π_μ^1, π_μ^2, π_μ^3, π_μ^4, $\gg_{pt}$ and $E_{\xi(\iota s)}$.

The variables and constants of type α respectively indicate and denote in each possible context of utterance an entity of type α. 1_s names *success* and $\{\}_{ts}$ the function which associates with truth success and with falsehood insuccess. $\simeq_{a(at)}$ names the relation of having the same propositional constituents and $[\,]_{a\#t}$ names the function that

---

[5] A function h of type $\alpha(\beta t)$ is an ordered pair if and only if there are two and only two u_α and u_β such that $h(u_\alpha, u_\beta) = T$.

associates with each atomic proposition its truth conditions. π_μ^1, π_μ^2, π_μ^3 and π_μ^4 name respectively the *assertive, commissive, directive, and declarative illocutionary points*, $\gg_{pt}$ names the relation of *presupposition* and $E_{\xi(\iota s)}$ the attribute of *expressing* a psychological state with a degree of strength.

The *syncategorematic symbols* of L_ω are those of intensional logic: $=$, λ, $^\vee$, $^\wedge$, (and).

They are introduced in the following rules of formation of general semantics.

3 *The rules of formation of L_ω*

Rule I

A variable, constant, or logical constant alone is a well formed formula (or for short hereafter a *formula*) of L_ω which has the type of its subscript.

Rule II

If $A_{\alpha\beta}$ and B_α are formulas of L_ω of type $\alpha\beta$ and α respectively, then $(A_{\alpha\beta} B_\alpha)$ is a new formula of L_ω of type β.

A complex formula of the form $(A_{\alpha\beta} B_\alpha)$ names the *value of the function* named by $A_{\alpha\beta}$ for the argument named by B_α. Thus, for example, the formula $(\gg_{pt} c_p)$ names truth in a context if and only if the speaker presupposes in that context the proposition named by c_p in that context.

Rule III

If A_β is a formula of type β of L_ω and x_α is a variable of L_ω of the type α, then $(\lambda x_\alpha A_\beta)$ is a new formula of type $\alpha\beta$ of L_ω.

A complex formula of the form $\lambda x_\alpha A_\beta$ names the *function of type* $(\alpha\beta)$ which associates with each entity named by a variable y_α the entity of type β named by the formula $[y_\alpha/x_\alpha]A_\beta$ obtained by replacing each free occurrence of x_α in A_β by an occurrence of y_α (when y_α is free for x_α in A_β).[6]

---

[6] An occurrence of a variable x in a formula A is *bound* if it occurs within a part λxB of A, and it is *free* otherwise. A variable is *free* in a formula if and only if at least one of its occurrences in that formula is free. B is *free for a variable* x in a formula A if and only if no free occurrence of B in A lies within a part $\lambda y\, C$ where y is free in B.

Rule IV

If A and B are formulas of the same type, $(A = B)$ is a new formula of type t of L_ω.

A complex formula of the form $(A = B)$ names the true in a context if and only if the formulas A and B name *the same entity* in that context.

Rule V

If A_α is a formula of type α of L_ω, $({}^\wedge A_\alpha)$ is a new formula of L_ω of type #α.

A complex formula of the form ${}^\wedge A_\alpha$ names the function which associates with each possible context of utterance the entity of type α which is named by A_α in that context. Such a function is the *intension* of A_α.

Rule VI

If A is a formula of type #α, then ${}^\vee A$ is a new formula of L_ω of type α.

A complex formula of the form ${}^\vee A_{\#\alpha}$ names at each context the entity of type α which is the value of the function named by $A_{\#\alpha}$ for that context. That entity is the *extension* which corresponds in that context to the intension named by $A_{\#\alpha}$.

Rule VII

Nothing else is a formula of L_ω.

Note. I will go on using hereafter: $A_\alpha, A_\alpha^1, A_\alpha^2, ..., B_\alpha, B_\alpha^1, B_\alpha^2, ..., C_\alpha, C_\alpha^1, C_\alpha^2, ...$ as *meta-linguistic variables* for formulas of type α of L_ω.

As I said earlier, all logical constants and syncategorematic symbols of the vocabulary of general semantics represent *material or formal universals of language use*.

Thus, the logical constants π_μ^1, π_μ^2, π_μ^3 and π_μ^4 name the four transcendental *illocutionary points* of utterances with a non-empty direction of fit. (The expressive illocutionary point is derived later by a rule of abbreviation.) The logical constants $\simeq_{a(at)}$ and $[\,]_{a\#t}$ serve to represent the facts that atomic propositions have *propositional constituents* as well as *truth conditions*. Similarly, the constants $\gg_{(ps)}$ and $E_{\xi(ts)}$ serve to represent the fact that propositions are *presupposed* and propositional attitudes are *expressed* in the performance of illocutionary acts. Moreover, the logical constants 1_s and $\{\}_{ts}$ are needed to define both *the success* and *the satisfaction conditions* of illocutionary acts.

The *identity symbol* is needed to state the fundamental laws of identity for senses, illocutionary forces, and illocutionary acts, and the λ operator to express *functional abstraction*. (As Tarski pointed out, from λ and $=$, one can derive by rules of abbreviation names for truth values and truth functions.) The cap operator $^\wedge$ expresses *functional abstraction over contexts* and is needed to represent intensional entities such as propositional constituents. The cup operator $^\vee$ is the inverse of the cap operator. It is needed to name in a context the *extensions* which correspond in that context to intensions. Finally, the parentheses ( ) express *functional application* which is a universal mode of composition of meanings.[7] For the sake of simplicity, I have not introduced into the vocabulary of this simple version of general semantics logical constants which express action and the present, future, and past temporal operations on propositions. These notions, which are needed to analyze further the components of illocutionary forces, will be studied later. In the last chapter, I will incorporate an elementary logic of demonstratives and of action in the formal apparatus of general semantics.

II RULES OF ABBREVIATION

The ideal object-language of general semantics does not contain in its vocabulary logical constants or syncategorematic symbols which express directly truth values, truth functions, illocutionary forces, illocutionary acts, or relations between such entities. However, all truth functional, modal, propositional, and illocutionary notions which are important for the purposes of general semantics can be derived from the few primitive notions expressed by the logical constants and syncategorematic symbols of general semantics by using the following rules of abbreviation.[8]

As before, the *type symbols of the logical constants* and *the exterior*

---

[7] As Frege pointed out, predication is represented naturally by functional application in logic. See G. Frege, *Translations from the Philosophical Writings of Gottlob Frege*, Oxford: Basil Blackwell, 1970.

[8] Some of these rules are already in Gallin's intensional logic.

parentheses can be omitted. Parentheses can also be omitted according to the rule of the association to the left. Moreover, we will often write $[A_a]$, $\{A_t\}$ and $(A_a \simeq B_a)$ instead of $[]A_a$, $\{\}A_t$ and $(\simeq A_a B_a)$.

Truth

$1_t =_{\text{def}} \lambda x_t x_t = \lambda x_t x_t$ (1_t names *the true*)

Falsehood

$0_t =_{\text{def}} \lambda x_t x_t = \lambda x_t 1_t$

Truth functional negation

$\sim A_t =_{\text{def}} (A_t = 0_t)$

Truth functional conjunction

$(A_t \wedge B_t) =_{\text{def}} \lambda x_{tt} (x_{tt}(A_t = B_t)) = \lambda x_{tt} (x_{tt} 1_t)$

Material implication

$(A_t \rightarrow B_t) =_{\text{def}} \sim (A_t \wedge \sim B_t)$

Truth functional disjunction

$(A_t \vee B_t) =_{\text{def}} \sim (\sim A_t \wedge \sim B_t)$

Material equivalence

$(A_t \leftrightarrow B_t) =_{\text{def}} (A_t = B_t)$

Universal generalization

$\forall x_\alpha A =_{\text{def}} \lambda x_\alpha A = \lambda x_\alpha 1_t$ ($\forall$ is the *universal quantifier*)

Existential generalization

$\exists x_\alpha A =_{\text{def}} \sim \forall x_\alpha \sim A$ ($\exists$ is the *existential quantifier*)

Unique existential generalization

$$\exists! x_\alpha A =_{\text{def}} \exists x_\alpha (A \wedge \forall y_\alpha ([y_\alpha / x_\alpha] A \to y_\alpha = x_\alpha))$$

Content of propositions

$$A_p(A_a) =_{\text{def}} \exists x_\gamma \exists x_{\gamma t} (A_p x_\gamma x_{\gamma t} \wedge x_\gamma A_a)$$

$$\langle A_p \rangle =_{\text{def}} \lambda x_a A_p(x_a)$$

Thus, $A_p(A_a)$ names the true when A_a names an atomic proposition which is in the content of the proposition named by A_p; and $\langle A_p \rangle$ names the content of the proposition named by A_p.

Inclusion of content

$$A_p \rangle B_p =_{\text{def}} \forall x_a (B_p(x_a) \to A_p(x_a))$$

The truth functional algorithm of a proposition

$$|A_p| =_{\text{def}} \lambda y_\gamma \exists x_{\gamma t} \exists x_\gamma (A_p x_\gamma x_{\gamma t} \wedge x_{\gamma t} y_\gamma)$$

$|A_p|$ names the set of truth value assignments to atomic propositions under which the proposition named by A_p could be true.

The truth value of a proposition

$$^\vee A_p =_{\text{def}} \exists x_\gamma (|A_p| x_\gamma \wedge \forall x_a (\langle A_p \rangle x_a \to (x_\gamma x_a = {}^\vee [x_a])))$$

$^\vee A_p$ names at each context the truth value of the proposition named by A_p in that context.

The truth conditions of a proposition

$$[A_p] =_{\text{def}} \text{⅂} x_{\#t} (\exists x_p (x_p = A_p) \wedge x_{\#t} = {}^{\wedge\vee} x_p)$$ where ⅂ is the operator of definite description to be eliminated with wide scope[9]

Elementary propositions

$$(A_a) =_{\text{def}} \lambda x_\gamma \lambda x_{\gamma t} (\forall x_a (x_\gamma x_a \leftrightarrow x_a = A_a) \wedge \forall y_\gamma (x_{\gamma t} y_\gamma \leftrightarrow y_\gamma A_a = 1_t))$$

[9] See *Principia Mathematica*.

Propositional negation

$$\sim A_p =_{\text{def}} \lambda x_\gamma \lambda x_{\gamma t} (x_\gamma = \langle A_p \rangle \land \forall y_\gamma (x_{\gamma t} y_\gamma \leftrightarrow \sim |A_p| y_\gamma))$$

Propositional conjunction

$$(A_p \land B_p) =_{\text{def}} \lambda x_\gamma \lambda x_{\gamma t} ((\forall x_a (x_\gamma x_a) \leftrightarrow (A_p(x_a) \lor B_p(x_a))) \land (\forall y_\gamma (x_{\gamma t} y_\gamma \leftrightarrow (|A_p| y_\gamma \land |B_p| y_\gamma))))$$

Propositional disjunction

$$(A_p \lor B_p) =_{\text{def}} \sim (\sim A_p \land \sim B_p)$$

And similarly for the other truth functional operations on propositions.

Logical necessity

$$\Box A_t =_{\text{def}} ({}^\wedge A_t = {}^\wedge 1_t)$$

$$\Box A_p =_{\text{def}} A_p \leftrightarrow (\lambda x_\gamma \lambda x_{\gamma t} (\forall x_a (x_\gamma x_a \leftrightarrow [x_a] = {}^\wedge 1_t)) \land \forall y_\gamma (x_{\gamma t} y_\gamma \leftrightarrow \forall x_a (([x_a] = {}^\wedge 1_t) \rightarrow y_\gamma x_a = 1_t)))$$

Logical possibility

$$\Diamond A =_{\text{def}} \sim \Box \sim A$$

Strict implication[10]

$$(A \dashv B) =_{\text{def}} \Box (A \rightarrow B)$$

Strict equivalence

$$(A \dashv\vdash B) =_{\text{def}} (A \dashv B) \land (B \dashv A)$$

Tautological propositions

$$\mathbf{T} A_p =_{\text{def}} A_p = (A_p \rightarrow A_p)$$

---

[10] The more complex definition of propositional necessity is necessitated by the double semantic indexation. It enables general semantics to distinguish analytically true and necessarily true propositions as well as weak and strong truth conditional entailments. For the sake of simplicity, I have defined the content of propositions that attribute logical necessity in such a way that we remain in the first ramified type of propositions. This simplification is made possible by the fact that to each proposition there corresponds at least one atomic proposition with identical truth conditions.

The maximal true proposition

$$\text{Max}_p =_{\text{def}} \lambda x_\gamma \lambda x_{\gamma t} ((\forall x_a\, x_\gamma x_a) \wedge \forall y_\gamma (x_{\gamma t} y_\gamma \leftrightarrow \forall x_a (y_\gamma x_a = {}^\vee [x_a])))$$

Max$_p$ names at each context the true proposition that completely represents the actual state of the world of that context.

Strong implication

$$A_p \vdash\!\!\dashv B_p =_{\text{def}} (A_p \supset B_p) \wedge \mathbf{T}(A_p \rightarrow B_p)$$

Insuccess

$$0_s =_{\text{def}} \{0_t\}$$

A function from success values into truth values

$$[A_s] =_{\text{def}} A_s = 1_s$$

The function named by $\lambda x_s [x_s]$ is the inverse of the function named by $\lambda x_t \{x_t\}$. Thus, $[A_s]$ names the true when A_s names success and the false when A_s names insuccess.

The expressive illocutionary point

$$\pi^5 =_{\text{def}} {}^\wedge (\lambda x_p \{\exists x_\tau \exists x_\iota [E(x_\tau x_p) x_\iota]\})$$

The neutral mode of achievement

$$1_\mu =_{\text{def}} {}^\wedge \lambda x_p 1_s$$

The absorbent mode of achievement

$$0_\mu =_{\text{def}} {}^\wedge \lambda x_p 0_s$$

The neutral propositional content condition

$$1_\theta =_{\text{def}} {}^\wedge \lambda x_p 1_t$$

The absorbent propositional content condition

$$0_\theta =_{\text{def}} {}^\wedge \lambda x_p 0_t$$

The neutral preparatory condition

$$1_\Sigma =_{\text{def}} {}^\wedge \lambda x_p \lambda y_p 0_t$$

The absorbent preparatory condition

$$0_\Sigma =_{\text{def}} {}^\wedge \lambda x_p \lambda y_p 1_t$$

The neutral sincerity condition

$$1_\psi =_{\text{def}} \lambda x_\tau 0_t$$

The absorbent sincerity condition

$$0_\psi =_{\text{def}} \lambda x_\tau 1_t$$

The conjunction of two modes of achievement

$$(A_\mu \divideontimes B_\mu) =_{\text{def}} \text{?} x_\mu \exists y_\mu \exists z_\mu (y_\mu = A_\mu \wedge z_\mu = B_\mu \wedge \Box \forall x_p ([{}^\vee x_\mu x_p] \leftrightarrow ([{}^\vee y_\mu x_p] \wedge [{}^\vee z_\mu x_p])))$$

The property of being an illocutionary point

$$\exists x_\pi (A_\mu = x_\pi) =_{\text{def}} (A_\mu = \pi^1 \vee A_\mu = \pi^2 \vee \dots \vee A_\mu = \pi^5)$$

The intersection of two propositional content conditions

$$(A_\theta \divideontimes B_\theta) =_{\text{def}} \text{?} x_\theta \exists y_\theta \exists z_\theta (y_\theta = A_\theta \wedge z_\theta = B_\theta \wedge \Box \forall x_p ({}^\vee x_\theta x_p \leftrightarrow ({}^\vee y_\theta x_p \wedge {}^\vee z_\theta x_p)))$$

The union of two preparatory conditions

$$(A_\Sigma \divideontimes B_\Sigma) =_{\text{def}} \text{?} x_\Sigma \exists y_\Sigma \exists z_\Sigma (y_\Sigma = A_\Sigma \wedge z_\Sigma = B_\Sigma \wedge \Box \forall x_p \forall y_p ({}^\vee x_\Sigma x_p y_p \leftrightarrow ({}^\vee y_\Sigma x_p y_p \vee {}^\vee z_\Sigma x_p y_p)))$$

The union of two sincerity conditions

$$(A_\psi \divideontimes B_\psi) =_{\text{def}} \lambda x_\tau (A_\psi x_\tau \vee B_\psi x_\tau)$$

The sincerity conditions determined by an illocutionary point

$$\psi(\pi^k) =_{\text{def}} \lambda x_\tau \forall x_p ([{}^\vee \pi^k x_p] \dashv \exists x_\iota [E(x_\tau x_p) x_\iota])$$

86

Elementary illocutionary acts

$$([(A_\mu, A_\theta, A_\Sigma, A_\psi), A_\iota, \pi^k] A_p) =_{\text{def}} \lambda x_p \lambda x_{\#s} (x_p = A_p$$

$$\wedge \ (\exists x_\mu \exists x_\theta \exists x_\Sigma \exists x_\psi \exists x_\iota (x_\mu = A_\mu \wedge x_\theta = A_\theta \wedge x_\Sigma = A_\Sigma \wedge x_\psi = A_\psi$$

$$\wedge \ A_\iota = x_\iota \wedge (x_{\#s} = {}^\wedge\{([{}^\vee\pi^k x_p] \wedge [{}^\vee x_\mu x_p] \wedge ({}^\vee x_\theta x_p)$$

$$\wedge \ (\forall y_p ({}^\vee x_\Sigma x_p y_p \rightarrow \gg y_p)) \wedge (\forall x_\tau ((x_\psi x_\tau \vee \psi(\pi^k) x_\tau) \rightarrow [E(x_\tau x_p) x_\iota]))) \}))$$

Illocutionary forces

$$[(A_\mu, A_\theta, A_\Sigma, A_\psi), A_\iota, \pi^k] =_{\text{def}} \lambda x_p ([(A_\mu, A_\theta, A_\Sigma, A_\psi), A_\iota, \pi^k] x_p)$$

As in the simple illocutionary logic *IL*, the formula $[(A_\mu, A_\theta, A_\Sigma, A_\psi),$ $A_\iota, \pi^k]$ names the weakest illocutionary force *F*, with the illocutionary point named by π^k, the mode of achievement named by A_μ, the propositional content condition named by A_θ, the preparatory condition named by A_Σ, the degree of strength represented by the integer named by A_ι and the sincerity condition named by A_ψ.

The formulas of the form $[(A_\mu, A_\theta, A_\Sigma, A_\psi), A_\iota, \pi^k]$ of L_ω are called *illocutionary force indicating devices* (or for short hereafter *ifids*). They are the translations of illocutionary force markers and of performative verbs of natural languages. I will often use hereafter $A_\phi, A_\phi^1, A_\phi^2, \ldots$ as meta-linguistic variables for ifids of L_ω.

The formulas of the form $(A_\phi A_p)$ name at each context the illocutionary acts with the forces and propositional contents respectively named by A_ϕ and by A_p at that context. They are the translations of elementary sentences of natural languages, and will for that reason also be called *sentences of the ideal language*.

Integers

Let 0_ι, $(A_\iota + B_\iota)$ and $(A_\iota > B_\iota)$ be the Russellian abbreviations of type ι in the object-language L_ω for naming the zero integer, the sum of the integers named by A_ι and B_ι, and the truth value of the proposition that the integer named by A_ι is greater than the integer named by B_ι.[11]

The primitive illocutionary force of assertion

$$\vdash =_{\text{def}} [(1_\mu, 1_\theta, 1_\Sigma, 1_\psi), 0_\iota, \pi^1]$$

[11] See *Principia Mathematica*.

The primitive commissive illocutionary force

$$\perp =_{\text{def}} [(1_\mu, 1_\theta, 1_\Sigma, 1_\psi), 0_\iota, \pi^2]$$

The primitive directive illocutionary force

$$! =_{\text{def}} [(1_\mu, 1_\theta, 1_\Sigma, 1_\psi), 0_\iota, \pi^3]$$

The primitive illocutionary force of declaration

$$\top =_{\text{def}} [(1_\mu, 1_\theta, 1_\Sigma, 1_\psi), 0_\iota, \pi^4]$$

The primitive expressive illocutionary force

$$\dashv =_{\text{def}} [(1_\mu, 1_\theta, 1_\Sigma, 1_\psi), 0_\iota, \pi^5]$$

The addition of a mode of achievement

$$[B_\mu][(A_\mu, A_\theta, A_\Sigma, A_\psi), A_\iota, \pi^k] =_{\text{def}} [((B_\mu \divideontimes A_\mu), A_\theta, A_\Sigma, A_\psi), A_\iota, \pi^k]$$

The addition of a propositional content condition

$$[B_\theta][(A_\mu, A_\theta, A_\Sigma, A_\psi), A_\iota, \pi^k] =_{\text{def}} [(A_\mu, (B_\theta \divideontimes A_\theta), A_\Sigma, A_\psi), A_\iota, \pi^k]$$

The addition of a preparatory condition

$$[B_\Sigma][(A_\mu, A_\theta, A_\Sigma, A_\psi), A_\iota, \pi^k] =_{\text{def}} [(A_\mu, A_\theta, (B_\Sigma \divideontimes A_\Sigma), A_\psi), A_\iota, \pi^k]$$

The addition of a sincerity condition

$$[B_\psi][(A_\mu, A_\theta, A_\Sigma, A_\psi), A_\iota, \pi^k] =_{\text{def}} [(A_\mu, A_\theta, A_\Sigma, (B_\psi \divideontimes A_\psi)), A_\iota, \pi^k]$$

The operations of increasing and decreasing the degrees of strength

$$[B_\iota][(A_\mu, A_\theta, A_\Sigma, A_\psi), A_\iota, \pi^k] =_{\text{def}} [(A_\mu, A_\theta, A_\Sigma, A_\psi), (B_\iota + A_\iota), \pi^k]$$

The success conditions of an illocutionary act

$$\{A_\phi A_p\} =_{\text{def}} \jmath x_{\#s} (\exists x_p \exists x_\mu \exists x_\theta \exists x_\Sigma \exists x_\psi \exists x_\iota ((x_p = A_p \wedge x_\mu = A_\mu \wedge x_\theta = A_\theta$$
$$\wedge \; x_\theta = A_\mu \wedge x_\Sigma = A_\Sigma \wedge x_\psi = A_\psi \wedge x_\tau = A_\iota) \wedge x_{\#s} = {}^\wedge\{([{}^\vee\pi^k x_p]$$
$$\wedge \; [{}^\vee x_\mu x_p] \wedge (\forall y_p ({}^\vee x_\Sigma x_p y_p \rightarrow \gg y_p) \wedge \forall x_\tau ((x_\psi x_\tau \vee \psi(\pi^k) x_\tau)$$
$$\rightarrow [E(x_\tau x_p) x_\iota]))\}) \text{ where } A_\phi = [(A_\mu, A_\theta, A_\Sigma, A_\psi), A_\iota, \pi^k]$$

$\{A_\phi A_p\}$ names at each context *the success conditions* of the act named by $A_\phi A_p$ in that context.

The success value of an illocutionary act

$s(A_\Omega) =_{\text{def}} \{^\vee \{A_\Omega\} = 1_s\}$

Inclusion of success conditions

$A_{\#s} \nleftarrow B_{\#s} =_{\text{def}} \exists x_{\#s} \exists y_{\#s} (x_{\#s} = A_{\#s} \wedge y_{\#s} = B_{\#s} \wedge [^\vee x_{\#s}] \nleftarrow [^\vee y_{\#s}])$

The set of illocutionary points of an illocutionary force

$\pi(A_\phi) =_{\text{def}} \lambda x_\mu (\exists x_\pi (x_\mu = x_\pi) \wedge \forall x_p (\{A_\phi x_p\} \nleftarrow {}^\wedge (^\vee x_\mu x_p)))$

The property of having the words-to-world direction of fit

$\downarrow (A_\phi) =_{\text{def}} (\pi(A_\phi) \, \pi^1)$

The property of having the world-to-words direction of fit

$\uparrow (A_\phi) =_{\text{def}} (\pi(A_\phi) \, \pi^2) \vee (\pi(A_\phi) \, \pi^3) \vee (\pi(A_\phi) \, \pi^4)$

The property of having the double direction of fit

$\updownarrow (A_\phi) =_{\text{def}} \pi(A_\phi) \, \pi^4$

The property of having the null direction of fit

$\varnothing (A_\phi) =_{\text{def}} \pi(A_\phi) \, \pi^5 \wedge \sim \downarrow (A_\phi) \wedge \sim \uparrow (A_\phi)$

The set of modes of achievement of an illocutionary force

$\mu(A_\phi) =_{\text{def}} \lambda x_\mu (\forall x_p (\{A_\phi x_p\} \nleftarrow {}^\wedge (^\vee x_\mu x_p)))$

The set of propositional content conditions of an illocutionary force

$\theta(A_\phi) =_{\text{def}} \lambda x_\theta (\forall x_p (\{A_\phi x_p\} \nleftarrow {}^\wedge \{^\vee x_\theta x_p\}))$

The set of preparatory conditions of an illocutionary force

$$\Sigma(A_\phi) =_{\text{def}} \lambda x_\Sigma \left(\forall x_p (\{A_\phi x_p\} \dashv {}^\wedge \{\forall y_p ({}^\vee x_\Sigma x_p y_p \to \gg y_p)\}) \right)$$

The sincerity conditions of an illocutionary force

$$\psi(A_\psi) =_{\text{def}} \lambda x_\tau \forall x_p \left(\{A_\phi x_p\} \dashv {}^\wedge \{\exists x_\iota [E(x_\tau x_p) x_\iota]\} \right)$$

The degree of strength of an illocutionary force

$$\eta(A_\phi) =_{\text{def}} \imath x_\iota \left((\forall x_p (\{A_\phi x_p\} = {}^\wedge 0_s) \to x_\iota = 0_\iota) \wedge ((\exists x_p (\sim \{A_\phi x_p\} = {}^\wedge 0_s \to \right.$$
$$(x_\iota = \imath y_\iota (\forall x_\tau \psi[A_\phi] x_\tau \to ((\forall x_p (\{A_\phi x_p\} \dashv {}^\wedge \{Ex_\tau x_p y_\iota)) \wedge \forall z_\iota ((\forall x_p (\{A_\phi x_p\}$$
$$\left. \dashv {}^\wedge Ex_\tau x_p z_\iota) \to y_\iota \geqslant z_\iota))) \right.$$

$\eta(A_\phi)$ names the integer which represents *the degree of strength of the sincerity conditions* of the force named by A_ϕ.

The satisfaction value of an illocutionary act

$$t(A_\phi A_p) =_{\text{def}} (\sim \uparrow(A_\phi) \to {}^\vee A_p) \wedge (\uparrow(A_\phi) \to ({}^\vee A_p \wedge s(A_\phi A_p)))$$

The conditions of satisfaction of an illocutionary act

$$[A_\phi A_p] =_{\text{def}} \imath y_{\#t} (\exists x_{\#t} \exists x_{\#s} (x_{\#t} = [A_p] \wedge x_{\#s} = \{A_\phi A_p\} \wedge (\sim \uparrow(A_\phi)$$
$$\to (y_{\#t} = x_{\#t})) \wedge (\downarrow(A_\phi) \to (y_{\#t} = {}^\wedge ({}^\vee x_{\#t} \wedge [{}^\vee x_{\#s}]))))))$$

Strong illocutionary commitment

$$A_\Omega \rhd B_\Omega =_{\text{def}} \{A_\Omega\} \dashv \{B_\Omega\}$$

The relation of being a stronger illocutionary force

$$A_\phi \rhd B_\phi =_{\text{def}} \forall x_p (A_\phi x_p \rhd B_\phi x_p)$$

The relation of being not simultaneously performable

$$A_\phi A_p \rangle\!\langle {}_s B_\phi B_p =_{\text{def}} \exists x_{\#s} \exists y_{\#s} (x_{\#s} = \{A_\phi A_p\} \wedge (y_{\#s} = \{B_\phi B_p\}$$
$$\wedge \square \sim ({}^\vee x_{\#s} = {}^\vee y_{\#s})))$$

The relation of having the same or stronger conditions of satisfaction

$$A_\phi A_p \dashv B_\phi B_p =_{\text{def}} \exists x_{\#t} \exists y_{\#t}(x_{\#t} = [A_\phi A_p] \wedge y_{\#t} = [B_\phi B_p]$$

$$\wedge \ (^\vee x_{\#t} \dashv \ ^\vee y_{\#t}))$$

And similarly for all other relations that exist between illocutionary acts with logically related conditions of success or of satisfaction.

The proposition that an illocutionary act is performed

$$KA_\phi A_p =_{\text{def}} \lambda x_\gamma \lambda x_{\gamma t} (\exists x_{\#s}(x_{\#s} = \{A_\phi A_p\} \wedge \forall x_a(x_\gamma x_a \leftrightarrow (\langle A_p \rangle x_a \vee$$

$$([^\vee x_{\#s}] \dashv \ ^\vee [x_a]))) \wedge \forall y_\gamma (x_{\gamma t} y_\gamma \leftrightarrow \forall x_a (([^\vee x_{\#s}] \dashv \ ^\vee [x_a]) \rightarrow y_\gamma x_a = 1_t))))$$

A complex formula of the form $KA_\phi A_p$ names at each context i the proposition which is true in a context j if and only if the illocutionary act named by $(A_\phi A_p)$ in the context i is performed in that context. Such propositions are the *content of performative utterances*.

The conditions of possession of a psychological state

$$\{A_\xi\} =_{\text{def}} \imath x_{\#t} \exists x_p (A_\xi x_p x_{\#t})$$

Strong psychological commitment

$$A_\xi \triangleright B_\xi =_{\text{def}} \exists x_{\#t} \exists y_{\#t} (x_{\#t} = \{A_\xi\} \wedge y_{\#t} = \{A_\xi\} \wedge (^\vee x_{\#t} \dashv \ ^\vee y_{\#t}))$$

$A_\xi \triangleright B_\xi$ means that the mental state named by A_ξ strongly commits the speaker to the mental state named by B_ξ, in the sense that it is not possible to have the first mental state without also having the second.

III GENERAL INSTRUCTIONS FOR TRANSLATION

In order to facilitate a naive understanding of the ideal language of general semantics and its intended application to English and other natural languages, I will now briefly state informally a few general instructions for translating different syntactic types of natural language sentence into that formal language. I will state more precise rules of translation for particular English illocutionary force markers and performative verbs in chapter 7.

Assertive illocutionary force markers and performative verbs in natural languages (which respectively express and name illocutionary forces with the assertive point) are to be translated into *assertive* ifids containing π^1. Commissive illocutionary force markers and performative verbs are to be translated into *commissive* ifids containing π^2, and so on for the other cases. This can be done recursively by applying rules of the following kind. The *syntactic type of declarative sentence* and the performative verb "assert" are to be translated into the primitive assertive ifid $\vdash$. The *syntactic types of imperative and exclamatory sentences* are to be translated respectively into the primitive directive and expressive ifids ! and $\dashv$. The *syntactic type of conditional sentence* is to be translated into the derived ifid $[^\wedge \lambda x_p \exists y_p x_p = \text{after } y_p]$ $[-1_1] \vdash$ where "after" is the translation of the future connective "It will be the case later" of temporal logic.[12] This indexical temporal connective of type (pp) is analyzed later in chapter 7. Finally, the *syntactic types of optative* and *subjunctive sentences* like "If only it would rain tomorrow!" and "Let there be rain tomorrow!" are to be translated respectively into the complex expressive ifids [tr(wish)] $\dashv$ and [tr(will)] $\dashv$, where tr(wish) and tr(will) are the two formulas of type τ of L_ω which name respectively the psychological modes of wish and of desire. Such formulas are also introduced in the last chapter.

Modifiers of illocutionary force markers are to be translated into formulas of the appropriate type. For example, "alas" is to be translated into a formula of type ψ and "please" into a formula of type μ. In particular, the adverb "hereby" of performative sentences is to be translated into the logical constant π^4. If A' is the translation of an illocutionary force marker A and B' the translation of a modifier B, then $(B'A')$ is the translation of the *complex illocutionary force marker* obtained by combining the modifier B with the marker A. Thus the common feature of all explicit performative sentences is syntactically represented in general semantics by an occurrence of the symbols $[\pi^4]$ $\vdash$ in the translations of their illocutionary force marker. Clauses of elementary sentences are to be translated by a similar induction into formulas of type p.

If A and B are translations of the illocutionary force marker and of the clause of an *elementary sentence*, then (AB) is a translation of that

---

[12] For the sake of simplicity, I neglect here in my rule of translation the usual reserved mode of achievement of the assertive point in utterances of conditional sentences. A speaker who uses a conditional sentence often commits himself with a certain reserve to the truth of the propositional content.

sentence. An elementary sentence is *ambiguous* if and only if it has several translations. For example, the sentence "Let him come in now!" is illocutionarily ambiguous in English. It can be imperative as well as subjunctive. In the imperative sense, it serves to give a directive to the hearer, whereas in the subjunctive sense, it serves to express the speaker's will.

Thus, English *declarative sentences* (which have by definition an assertive illocutionary force marker) have to be translated into formulas of the form $A_\phi A_p$, where A_ϕ is an assertive ifid and A_p is a propositional formula, which are translations of their illocutionary force marker and their clauses. *Imperative sentences* have to be translated into formulas of the form $A_\phi A_p$ where A_ϕ is a directive ifid, *exclamatory sentences* have to be translated into formulas of the form $A_\phi A_p$ with an expressive ifid, and similarly for the other cases.

From a symbolic point of view, the logical forms of corresponding sentences of different syntactic types stand in certain internal relations that are apparent in their translations. Thus if $A_\phi A_p$ is the translation of a sentence then $[\pi^4] \vdash K A_\phi A_p$ is the translation of *the performative sentence* that corresponds to it.[13] For example, if "Come!" is translated into $!A_p$ then "You are hereby directed to come" must be translated into $[\pi^4] \vdash K!A_p$.

Similarly, if $\vdash (A_p \to B_p)$ is the translation of a declarative sentence like "If he helps me, I can do it", then $[-1_\lrcorner] \vdash$ after $(A_p \to B_p)$ is the translation of the corresponding *conditional sentence* "If he helped me, I could do it". Finally, if $\vdash A_p$ is the translation of a declarative sentence like "It will rain tomorrow" then $[\mathrm{tr(wish)}] \dashv A_p$ and $[\mathrm{tr(will)}] \dashv A_p$ are respectively the translations of the corresponding *optative* and *subjunctive sentences* "If only it would rain tomorrow!" and "Let there be rain tomorrow!"

---

[13] Such translations of performative sentences are synonymous with sentences of the form $\top K A_\phi A_p$ since their marker $[\pi^4] \vdash$ also names the illocutionary force of declaration.

5

THE LOGICAL SEMANTICS

OF LANGUAGE

The aim of this chapter is to develop the formal semantics for the ideal object-language of general semantics. The first section defines the set-theoretical structure of a standard model (or possible interpretation) of general semantics. The following sections state universal laws of synonymy, analyticity, entailment, and consistency which are valid in all models of general semantics. Most of these laws are both linguistically and philosophically significant.

I DEFINITION OF A STANDARD MODEL

As in the case of first order illocutionary logic, the formal semantics for the ideal language L_ω is *model-theoretical*. It specifies how meanings can be assigned to the formulas of L_ω in a standard model or possible interpretation for that language. All fundamental semantic notions such as, for example, logical truth, analyticity, and the various types of entailment and consistency, are obtained by quantifying over the set of all possible interpretations of the ideal language. As in intensional logic, the semantic values assigned to the formulas of general semantics in a model are taken out of a non-empty set of entities – called the *domain* of that model – which is *stratified* into the same types as the vocabulary of the ideal language. Thus, variables of a type α range in each model over entities of that type in the domain of that model.[1] In

---

[1] The stratification of formulas into types in the ideal object-languages of logic is necessary to make logical form apparent. Indeed, syntactic categories of actual natural languages are often

order to account for the creative abilities of linguistic competence, the semantic rules of assignment of meanings to formulas in a model are formulated in a *recursive definition*. Since the object language L_ω is ideal, that recursive definition retraces the syntactic construction of the formulas of L_ω. Thus, a model for L_ω first assigns semantic values of the appropriate type to the variables and constants of L_ω, which are the *syntactically simple formulas* of that language. Next, it assigns semantic values to *syntactically complex formulas* in the way determined by the semantic rules that correspond to the various rules of formation of that language. The semantic rule which corresponds to a syntactic rule of formation in the model-theoretical semantics specifies how to assign a semantic value in a model to a complex formula that is constructed by the application of that syntactic rule given the semantic values in that model of the simpler formulas out of which it is composed. Such a semantic rule reflects the intended meaning of the syncategorematic symbols introduced in the rule of formation.

The ideal language of general semantics is both unambiguous and perspicuous. Thus, each formula has one and only one semantic value in each model. The way that semantic value is constructed depends heavily on the syntactic structure of that formula, since that structure reflects diagrammatically the logical form of its denotations.[2]

Because the variables of L_ω can be assigned different values, and the non-logical constants of L_ω can have different denotations in different contexts, a model or possible interpretation for the ideal language L_ω assigns a semantic value to a formula of L_ω only with respect to a possible context of use and under a possible assignment of values to its free variables. Thus, formulas of L_ω can have different denotations in different contexts or under different assignments of values to their variables in a model for that language.

From a logical point of view, a *standard possible interpretation or model* for L_ω is a quadruple $\mathfrak{M} = \langle I, D, U, \| \ \| \rangle$, where I is a set and $D, U,$ and $\| \ \|$ are functions. These elements satisfy the following clauses:

(1) I is a non-empty set which represents the set of all possible *contexts of use* of L_ω which are considered in the possible interpretation $\mathfrak{M}$.

misleading since there is no one-to-one correspondence between them and logical types. Thus, expressions of the same syntactic categories of English can name entities of different logical types and expressions of different syntactic categories can name entities of the same type.
[2] I use here the term "diagram" in Peirce's sense where it means an icon of relations.

(2) D is a function whose domain is the set of type symbols of L_ω for individuals and attributes. It gives as value, for each type symbol α belonging to its domain, the set of D_α of entities which are *propositional constituents* of type α in the possible interpretation $\mathfrak{M}$. D satisfies the following clauses:

(i) D_e is a non-empty set of individuals.

(ii) If $\alpha = \#e,\dots(et)$ is the type symbol of an n-ary attribute (of individuals) of the first order, $D_\alpha = (\mathscr{P}(D_e^n))^I$.

(iii) If $\alpha = \#\alpha_1\dots(\alpha_n t)$ is the type symbol of an n-ary attribute of order $m+1$, $D_\alpha = (\mathscr{P}(D_{\alpha_1} \times \dots \times D_{\alpha_n}))^I$.

The union D^s of all these sets D_α (where α is an attribute) represents the set of entities which are propositional constituents in the domain of the possible interpretation $\mathfrak{M}$.[3]

(3) U is a function whose domain is the set of all type symbols of L_ω which gives as value, for each type symbol α, the set U_α of all *possible denotations* of type α which belong to the domain of the possible interpretation $\mathfrak{M}$. It satisfies the following clauses:

(i) $U_t = \{T, T\}$ is the set of *truth values*, where T is truth and T is falsehood.

(ii) $U_s = \{S, S,\}$ is the set of success values, where S is success and S insuccess.

(iii) $U_e = D_e$ is a non-empty set of *individuals*.

(iv) $U_a = (\mathscr{P}(D^s) \times (U_t)^I)$. U_a is the set of *atomic propositions*. As explained before, the first term $id_1(u)$ of an atomic proposition is the *set of its propositional constituents*, and its second term $id_2(u)$ is the function that represents its *truth conditions*.

(v) $U_{(\alpha\beta)} = (U_\beta)^{U_\alpha}$ is the set of all unary functions whose domain is the set U_α and whose range is the set U_β.

(vi) $U_{\#\alpha} = (U_\alpha)^I$ is the set of all functions from I into U_α.

The union of the sets U_α is the *domain* of the possible interpretation $\mathfrak{M}$. It represents the *universe of discourse* of L_ω under that interpretation.

Note. I will often use hereafter u_α, u_α^1, u_α^2 as *meta-linguistic variables for entities* of type α of the domain of the possible interpretation $\mathfrak{M}$.

---

[3] As I said earlier, in this version of general semantics the propositions which are expressed in models are of the first ramified order. They cannot have other propositions as propositional constituents. One could easily complexify the language and the model-theoretical semantics to express in general semantics propositions of superior ramified orders. As in Russell's theory of types, a certain axiom of reducibility is valid in the logic of propositions of higher ramified orders. Every proposition of any ramified type can be reduced to an elementary proposition of the first ramified type with the same truth conditions.

Definition of a standard model

In order to state the meaning postulates for the logical constants of illocutionary logic, it is necessary to explain first how the sets of propositions and of mental states are formally constructed in each model of general semantics.

Definitions relative to propositions

From a model-theoretic point of view, the set of *propositions* of a possible interpretation $\mathfrak{M}$ is the proper subset of its domain which contains all and only the functions of type p which are ordered pairs of a set of atomic propositions and of a set of truth functional valuations of atomic propositions.

Thus, an entity u of type p of the domain of $\mathfrak{M}$ is a *proposition* if and only if there is a unique u_γ and a unique $u_{\gamma t}$ such that $u(u_\gamma u_{\gamma t}) = T$. Let *content* (P) and *assignments* (P) be respectively the first and the second elements of a proposition P. As in illocutionary logic, *content* (P) represents the set of atomic propositions which belong to the content of P in a model $\mathfrak{M}$. Moreover, *assignments* (P) represent the set of all truth value assignments to atomic propositions under which P is true under that model. On this account, the proposition P is *true in a context* i according to a model $\mathfrak{M}$ if and only if there is a truth value assignment $f \in assignments$ (P) which associates with each atomic proposition of P the truth value that that atomic proposition has in the context i under that model $\mathfrak{M}$. In other words, P is true in the context i under $\mathfrak{M}$ if and only if there exists at least one $f \in assignments$ (P) such that, for all atomic propositions $u_a \in content$ (P), $f(u_a) = id_2(u_a)(i)$.

As in intensional logic, a proposition P is *necessary* according to a possible interpretation $\mathfrak{M}$ if and only if it is true in all contexts under that interpretation. A proposition P is *contingent* according to an interpretation $\mathfrak{M}$ if and only if it is true in some but not all contexts i of $\mathfrak{M}$. Moreover, a proposition P is a *tautology* in a possible interpretation if and only if *assignments* (P) is the total set of all truth functional valuations of atomic propositions, and it is a *contradiction* if and only if *assignments* (P) is the empty set.

As in illocutionary logic, a set Γ of propositions is said to be *minimally consistent* if and only if it does not contain a single contradiction. A proposition P *strongly implies* a proposition Q in a possible interpretation $\mathfrak{M}$ if and only if, in that interpretation, *content* $(Q) \subseteq content$ (P) and *assignments* $(P) \subseteq assignments$ (Q). Thus, a set Γ

97

of propositions is *closed under strong implication* if and only if, whenever it contains a proposition P, it also contains any proposition strongly implied by P.

Definitions relative to mental states

From a model-theoretic point of view, an entity of type ξ of the domain of the possible interpretation $\mathfrak{M}$ is a *propositional attitude* only if it is an ordered pair. The first term of a propositional attitude u_ξ is its propositional content, and its second term $id_2(u_\xi)$ represents its conditions of possession. Thus, a propositional attitude u_ξ *is possessed* by the speaker in a context i in the possible interpretation of $\mathfrak{M}$ if and only if $id_2(u_\xi)\,(i) = \mathrm{T}$.

Moreover, u_ξ is a *possible propositional attitude* in $\mathfrak{M}$ if and only if it is possessed by a speaker in at least one context i. A propositional attitude u_ξ^1 *strongly commits* the speaker to a propositional attitude u_ξ^2 in $\mathfrak{M}$ if and only if, for all contexts $i \in I$, if u_ξ^1 is possessed by the speaker in i then u_ξ^2 is also possessed by the speaker in i. A set of propositional attitudes is *closed under strong psychological commitment* if and only if whenever it contains a propositional attitude, it also contains any propositional attitude to which that attitude strongly commits the speaker.

Given the definitions and explanations relative to propositions and mental states, one can now state as follows the *meaning postulates* that each possible interpretation $\mathfrak{M}$ of general semantics must satisfy.

(4) $\| \ \|$ is a function which associates with each formula A of type α of L_ω under each possible assignment σ of values to its free variables with respect to each context $i \in I$, the entity $\|A\|_i^\sigma$ of U_α which is the *denotation* of that formula under that assignment in that context in the possible interpretation $\mathfrak{M}$. A possible *assignment of values* to free variables of the formulas of L_ω is here any function σ which associates with each variable x_α an entity of the set U_α.

The evaluation function $\| \ \|$ satisfies the following clauses:

(i) If x is a variable of L_ω of type α, $\|x_\alpha\|_i^\sigma = \sigma(x_\alpha)$.

(ii) If c_α is a (non-logical) constant of type α of L_ω, $\|c_\alpha\|_i^\sigma \in U_\alpha$.

(iii) $\|1_s\|_i^\sigma = S$ and $\|\{\ \}_{(ts)}\|_i^\sigma(u_t) = S$ if and only if $u_t = \mathrm{T}$.

(iv) $\|A_{\alpha\beta} B_\alpha\|_i^\sigma = \|A_{\alpha\beta}\|_i^\sigma(\|B_\alpha\|_i^\sigma)$.

(v) $\|\lambda x_\alpha A_\beta\|_i^\sigma(u_\alpha) = \|A_\beta\|_i^{\sigma[u_\alpha/x_\alpha]}$, where $\sigma[u_\alpha/x_\alpha]$ is the assignment σ' which differs at most from σ by the fact that $\sigma'(x_\alpha) = u_\alpha$.

(vi) $\|A = B\|_i^\sigma = T$ if and only if $\|A\|_i^\sigma = \|B\|_i^\sigma$.

(vii) $\|^\wedge A_\alpha\|_i^\sigma = \|A_\alpha\|^\sigma$.

(viii) $\|^\vee A_\alpha\|_i^\sigma = \|A_\alpha\|_i^\sigma(i)$.

(ix) $\|[A_a]\|_i^\sigma = id_2(\|A_a\|_i^\sigma)$.

(x) $\|A_a \simeq B_a\|_i^\sigma = T$ if and only if $id_1(\|A_a\|_i^\sigma) = id_1(\|B_a\|_i^\sigma)$.

(xi) The set $\{P/\|\pi^1\|_i^\sigma\,(j, P) = S\}$ of all propositions on which the *assertive illocutionary point* is achieved in the context of a model is a set of propositions which is minimally consistent, closed under strong implication, and which contains a unique supremum (in case it is not empty).

(xii) If $k = 2$ or 3, the sets $\{P/\|\pi^\kappa\|_i^\sigma(j, P) = \text{S}\}$ of all propositions on which the *commissive* and the *directive illocutionary points* are achieved in the context j of a model are two sets of propositions which do not contain any tautology or contradiction.

Each of these sets contains a unique supremum (in case it is not empty) as well as all the non-tautological propositions which are strongly implied by that supremum.[4]

(xiii) The set $\{P/\|\pi^4\|_i^\sigma(j, P)\}$ of all propositions on which the *declarative illocutionary point* is achieved in the context j of a model is a set of contingent propositions which are true in that context. That set contains a unique supremum (in case it is non-empty) as well as all contingent propositions which are strongly implied by that supremum.

(xiv) *The law of the neutrality of the expressive illocutionary point*

If $\|\pi^5\|_i^\sigma(j, P) = S$ then, for some u_τ and some u_ι, $\|E_{\xi(18)}\|_j^\sigma(u_\tau(P), u_\iota) = S$

(xv) *The law of an assertive commitment in the achievement of the declarative point*

If $\|\pi^4\|_i^\sigma(j, P) = S$ then $\|\pi^1\|_i^\sigma(j, P) = S$

(xvi) *The law of an assertive commitment in the achievement of the commissive point*

If $\|\pi^2\|_i^\sigma(j, P) = S$ then $\|\pi^1\|_i^\sigma(j, P) = S$

(xvii) $\{P/\| \gg \|_i^\sigma(P) = T\}$ is a proper subset of the set of propositions

---

[4] More precise propositional content conditions for the illocutionary points with the world-to-words or double direction of fit will be stated in chapter 7, where tense, action, and modalities are analyzed.

which is closed under strong implication, and is included in the set $\{P/\|\pi^1\|_i^\sigma(i, P) = S\}$.[5]

(xviii) $\{u_\xi/\|E_{\xi(1s)}\|_i^\sigma(u_\xi, u_\iota) = S\}$ is a set of possible propositional attitudes, closed under strong psychological commitment and which contains a unique psychological state which strongly commits the speaker to all psychological states that it contains. Moreover, the set $\{u_\iota/\|E_{\xi(1s)}\|_i^\sigma(u_\xi, u_\iota) = S\}$ is an initial segment of integers.

Definition of the fundamental semantic notions

All fundamental notions of the logical semantics of natural languages can now be defined formally as follows:

The semantic concepts of truth and validity

A formula A_t is *true at a context* i under a possible assignment σ according to the possible interpretation $\mathfrak{M}$ if and only if $\|A\|_i^\sigma = T$ in $\mathfrak{M}$. A_t is *logically true* (for short $\vDash A_t$) if and only if A_t is true at all contexts under all assignments in all possible interpretations. A formula A_t is a *semantic consequence* of a set Γ of formulas of type t (for short $\Gamma \vDash A_t$) if and only if whenever all formulas of Γ are true in a possible context under an assignment σ according to a possible interpretation $\mathfrak{M}$, the formula A_t is also true in that context under that assignment according to that interpretation.

The semantic concepts of success and satisfaction

The *illocutionary act* named by a sentence A_Ω of the form $A_\phi A_p$ at a context i under assignment σ of a possible interpretation $\mathfrak{M}$ is the function $u_\Omega = \|A_\Omega\|_i^\sigma$ of $\mathfrak{M}$. That illocutionary act is *(successfully) performed in a context* $j \in I$ in $\mathfrak{M}$ if and only if there is a unique success condition $u_{\#s}$ such that $u_\Omega(\|A_p\|_i^\sigma, u_{\#s}) = T$ and $u_{\#s}(j) = S$ in $\mathfrak{M}$. On the other hand, the same illocutionary act is *satisfied in a context* $j \in I$ in $\mathfrak{M}$ if and only if, first, the proposition $\|A_p\|_i^\sigma$ is true in the context j in $\mathfrak{M}$ and, second, if $\|\uparrow(A_\phi)\|_i^\sigma = T$ then $\|A_\phi A_p\|_i^\sigma$ is also performed in j according to $\mathfrak{M}$. Whenever A_ϕ is an assertive ifid, the illocutionary act $\|A_\phi A_p\|_i^\sigma$ is *true in the context* i under $\mathfrak{M}$ if it is satisfied in that context

---

[5] According to this view, any asserted proposition is also presupposed.

under $\mathfrak{M}$. Otherwise, that speech act is *false* in i under $\mathfrak{M}$. Whenever A_ϕ is a commissive ifid, the illocutionary act $\|A_\phi A_p\|_i^\sigma$ is *kept* in the context i according to $\mathfrak{M}$ if it is satisfied in that context i under $\mathfrak{M}$, and that speech act is *broken* in context i according to $\mathfrak{M}$ if it is both performed and not kept in i under $\mathfrak{M}$. Whenever A_ϕ is a directive ifid, the illocutionary act $\|A_\phi A_p\|_i^\sigma$ *is fulfilled* in i under $\mathfrak{M}$ if and only if it is satisfied in i under $\mathfrak{M}$. And similarly for the other cases.

The semantic concepts of performability and satisfiability

An illocutionary act $\|A_\phi A_p\|_i^\sigma$ *is satisfiable* in a possible interpretation $\mathfrak{M}$ if and only if it is satisfied in at least one possible context of $\mathfrak{M}$. Similarly, an illocutionary act is *performable* in $\mathfrak{M}$ if and only if it is performed in at least one possible context of $\mathfrak{M}$.

The semantic concepts of analyticity

A sentence A_Ω of the form $(A_\phi A_p)$ is *analytically satisfied* if and only if under all possible interpretations $\mathfrak{M}$, for all contexts i and assignments σ, the illocutionary act $\|A_\Omega\|_i^\sigma$ is satisfied in i according to $\mathfrak{M}$. On the contrary, it is *analytically unsatisfied* if and only if, in all possible interpretations $\mathfrak{M}$, the act $\|A_\Omega\|_i^\sigma$ is not satisfied in i.

Similarly, (the utterance of) a sentence A_Ω is *analytically successful* if and only if, in all possible interpretations $\mathfrak{M}$, for all i and σ, the illocutionary act $\|A_\Omega\|_i^\sigma$ is performed in i. On the contrary, (the utterance of) a sentence A_Ω is *analytically unsuccessful* if and only if, in all possible interpretations $\mathfrak{M}$ for all i and σ, the act $\|A_\Omega\|_i^\sigma$ is not performed in i.[6]

The semantic concepts of consistency

In general semantics, a sentence A_Ω is *truth conditionally inconsistent* if and only if, in all possible interpretations $\mathfrak{M}$, for all i and σ, the illocutionary act $\|A_\Omega\|_i^\sigma$ is not satisfiable in $\mathfrak{M}$. Similarly, a sentence A_Ω is *illocutionarily inconsistent* if and only if, in all interpretations $\mathfrak{M}$, for all i and σ, the illocutionary act $\|A_\Omega\|_i^\sigma$ is not performable in $\mathfrak{M}$. As usual, a sentence is *truth conditionally* (or *illocutionarily*) *consistent* if and only if it is not truth conditionally (or illocutionarily) inconsistent.

---

[6] These definitions of analytically successful or satisfied utterances are extensionally equivalent to those of the first volume.

The semantic concepts of entailment

First, a sentence A_Ω *truth conditionally entails* another sentence B_Ω (for short $A_\Omega \vDash B_\Omega$) if and only if, in all possible interpretations $\mathfrak{M}$, for all contexts i, if $\|A_\Omega\|_i^\sigma$ is satisfied in i under $\mathfrak{M}$ then $\|B_\Omega\|_i^\sigma$ is also satisfied in i under $\mathfrak{M}$. In other words, $A_\Omega \vDash B_\Omega$ if and only if $\vDash t(A_\Omega) \dashv t(B_\Omega)$. Moreover, the sentence A_Ω *strongly truth conditionally entails* the sentence B_Ω (for short $A_\Omega \vDash_s B_\Omega$) if and only if, for all contexts i and j, if $\|A_\Omega\|_i^\sigma$ is performed in j under a possible interpretation, then $\|B_\Omega\|_i^\sigma$ is also performed in j under that interpretation (i.e. if and only if $\vDash A_\Omega \dashv B_\Omega$).

Second, a sentence A_Ω *illocutionarily entails* a sentence B_Ω (for short $A_\Omega \Vdash B_\Omega$) if and only if, in all possible interpretations $\mathfrak{M}$, for all contexts i, if $\|A_\Omega\|_s^\sigma$ is successfully performed in i under $\mathfrak{M}$ then $\|B_\Omega\|_i^\sigma$ is also successfully performed in i under $\mathfrak{M}$. Thus, $A_\Omega \Vdash B_\Omega$ if and only if $\vDash s(A_\Omega) \dashv s(B_\Omega)$. Moreover, the sentence A_Ω *strongly illocutionarily entails the sentence* B_Ω (for short $A_\Omega \Vdash_s B_\Omega$) if and only if, for all contexts i and j, if $\|A_\Omega\|_i^\sigma$ is performed in j under a possible interpretation, then $\|B_\Omega\|_i^\sigma$ is also performed in j under that interpretation (i.e. if and only if $\vDash A_\Omega \rhd B_\Omega$).

Third, a sentence A_Ω *illocutionarily entails the satisfaction* of B_Ω (for short $A_\Omega \Vvdash B_\Omega$) if and only if, in all possible interpretations $\mathfrak{M}$, for all contexts i, if $\|A_\Omega\|_i^\sigma$ is successfully performed in i under $\mathfrak{M}$, then $\|B_\Omega\|_i^\sigma$ is satisfied in i under $\mathfrak{M}$. In other words, $A_\Omega \Vvdash B_\Omega$ if and only if $\vDash s(A_\Omega) \dashv t(A_\Omega)$. Moreover, the sentence A_Ω *strongly illocutionarily entails the satisfaction of* B_Ω (for short $A_\Omega \Vvdash_s B_\Omega$) if and only if $\vDash \exists x_{\#s} \exists x_{\#t}(x_{\#s} = \{A_\Omega\} \wedge x_{\#t} = [B_\Omega] \wedge [^\vee x_{\#s}] \dashv {}^\vee x_{\#t})$.

Finally, a sentence A_Ω *truth conditionally entails the success of* a sentence B_Ω (for short $A_\Omega \dashV B_\Omega$) if and only if in all possible interpretations $\mathfrak{M}$, for all contexts i of $\mathfrak{M}$, if $\|A_\Omega\|_i^\sigma$ is satisfied in i under $\mathfrak{M}$, then $\|B_\Omega\|_i^\sigma$ is successfully performed in i under $\mathfrak{M}$. In other words, $A_\Omega \dashV B_\Omega$ if and only if $\vDash t(A_\Omega) \dashv s(B_\Omega)$. Moreover, A_Ω *strongly truth conditionally entails the success of* B_Ω (for short $A_\Omega \dashV_s B_\Omega$) if and only if B_Ω strongly illocutionarily entails the satisfaction of A_Ω.[7]

---

[7] In this book, I have concentrated on *exact reasoning* and I have assumed for the sake of simplicity that all propositions are either true or false according to the principle of bivalence. But, of course, many propositions like, for example, the proposition that most Swedes are tall contain *fuzzy* quantifiers and attributes. From a logical point of view, they are only true (or false) to a certain extent. As a consequence of this, many speech acts like, for example, the assertion "John often sings", the directive "Bring me a lot of flowers!" and the promise "I promise to check most of the cases" can be more or less satisfied. Clearly, for example, an assertion that John often sings is more true if John sings for seven hours a day than if he sings for one hour a day. In such cases, one can speak of illocutionary acts with *intermediate* satisfaction values.

II LAWS FOR SENTENCE MEANING

In general semantics, I will define the *linguistic meaning* of a formula A by quantifying over its evaluations in all possible interpretations. On the basis of previous considerations on linguistic meaning, I will identify the linguistic meaning of a formula A of L_ω with the function which gives as value, for each standard interpretation $\mathfrak{M} = \langle I, D, U, \| \ \| \rangle$, the function $\|A\|$ which is the particular meaning of that formula in that interpretation. On this account, the linguistic meaning of (a translation of) a *sentence* A in the language L_ω is the function which gives as value, for each possible interpretation $\mathfrak{M}$ for L_ω and each context of utterance i and assignment σ of that interpretation, the *illocutionary act* $\|A\|_i^\sigma$ named by A in that context under that assignment according to that interpretation.

Here are a few laws for linguistic meaning which are valid in general semantics:

2.1 The law of synonymy
Two formulas A and B are *synonymous* in L_ω if and only if $\vDash A = B$.

In particular, two sentences of the form $A_\phi A_p$ and $B_\phi B_p$ are synonymous if and only if $\vDash \Box(A_p = B_p \land \{A_\phi A_p\} = \{B_\phi B_p\})$.

Thus, elementary sentences whose translations express, in all possible interpretations with respect to the same possible contexts of utterance, illocutionary acts with the same propositional content and the same conditions of success have the same meaning in general semantics. Here are some schemas of synonymous sentences:

2.1.1 If $\vDash \Box(A_p \vdash\!\!\prec B_p \land B_p \vdash\!\!\prec A_p)$ then the sentences $A_\phi A_p$ and $A_\phi B_p$ are synonymous.
Thus, all sentences with commutative truth functional connectives like conjunction and disjunction are synonymous with the sentences obtained by permutating the order of the arguments of these connectives. For example, the two sentences "How nice of you to help Mary and John!" and "How nice of you to help John and Mary!" are synonymous.

Human speakers are able to make inferences involving illocutionary acts with an inexact satisfaction value just as they are able to make inferences involving propositions with an inexact truth value. So general semantics could greatly benefit from fuzzy logic which attempts to formulate the principles of *approximate reasoning* involving such propositions. For further information on fuzzy logic which has been founded by Zadeh, see L. A. Zadeh, "Fuzzy logic", *Computer*, 21, 4 (1988), 83–92.

2.1.2 Sentences of the form $[A_\alpha][A_\beta]A_\phi A_p$ and $[A_\beta][A_\alpha]A_\phi A_p$ are synonymous.

The order in which the modifiers of illocutionary force markers occur in elementary sentences is not linguistically significant. For example, the two sentences "Father, please, do it!" and "Please, father, do it!" are synonymous.

Incidentally, the corresponding law is not valid for propositional connectives. Most of them are not commutative. For example, the sentences "It is possible that John will not come" and "It is not possible that John will come" do not have the same meaning.

2.2 Modally closed formulas

Many formulas of L_ω do not have the same denotations in different contexts or under different assignments of a model. A formula which has in each model the same denotation in all contexts and under all assignments is called a *modally closed formula* of L_ω. Such formulas are interesting for the purposes of general semantics because they are *rigid designators* in all possible interpretations.

Extending Gallin's definition for intensional logic,[8] one can define as follows the set of *modally closed formulas of L_ω*. It is the smallest set MC such that:

(i) $x_\alpha \in MC$ for any variable x_α.

(ii) $\simeq_{a(at)}, [\,]_{at}, 1_s, \{\,\}_{ts}, \pi_\mu^1, \pi_\mu^2, \pi_\mu^3, \pi_\mu^4 \in MC$.

(iii) $(A_{\alpha\beta} A_\alpha) \in MC$, whenever $A_{\alpha\beta}$ and $B_\alpha \in MC$.

(iv) $^\wedge A_\alpha \in MC$ for every formula A_α.

(v) $(A_\alpha = B_\alpha) \in MC$, whenever A_α and $B_\alpha \in MC$.

(vi) $\lambda x_\alpha A_\beta \in MC$, whenever $A_\beta \in MC$.

It is easily checked that the evaluation of a modally closed formula A under an assignment σ at a context i in $\mathfrak{M}$ is independent of i. Thus, $\|A\|_i^\sigma = \|A\|_j^\sigma$, for all contexts i and j, whenever A is a modally closed formula. Modally closed formulas are rigid designators[9] in all possible interpretations.

As I pointed out, most actual sentences of natural languages express different illocutionary acts in different contexts. Thus, most formulas of L_ω of the form $A_\phi A_p$ which are translations of actual sentences are *not modally closed*. In general, their ifid A_ϕ or their clause A_p can

[8] See D. Gallin, *Intensional and Higher-Order Modal Logic*, Amsterdam: North-Holland, 1975.
[9] The term "rigid designator" is due to S. Kripke in "Naming and Necessity", in D. Davidson and G. Harman (eds.), *Semantics of Natural Language*, Dordrecht, Netherlands: Reidel, 1972.

express different forces or propositions in different contexts. For example, the clause of the declarative sentence $\vdash \mathrm{Max}_p$ names a different proposition in different contexts. In a context i, Max_p names the maximal proposition that completely represents the actual state of the world of the context i. In context j, Max_p names the maximal proposition that completely represents the actual state of the world of context j. By definition, such maximal propositions must be different if these worlds are different.

For this reason, synonymous sentences can express different illocutionary acts in different contexts, as is shown in the following law of general semantics:

$\vDash \exists x_p \,\square(A_p = x_p) \wedge \exists x_{\#s} \,\square({}^{\wedge}\{A_\phi A_p\} = x_{\#s})$ only if $A_\phi A_p$ is modally closed

Conversely, non-synonymous sentences can express the same illocutionary acts in certain contexts:

$\vDash (A_p = B_p \wedge \sim \square(A_p = B_p)) \rightarrow ((A_\phi A_p = A_\phi B_p) \wedge \sim \square(A_\phi A_p = B_\phi B_p))$

For example, the two sentences "John will do it tomorrow" and "John will do it on November 2, 1986" express the same assertion in a context of utterance where the speaker speaks on November 1, 1986. However, these sentences are not synonymous, since they express different assertions in other contexts.

2.3 Sentences which express in all contexts illocutionary acts with the same conditions of success and of satisfaction are not necessarily synonymous.

Indeed, $\vDash \square(({}^{\vee}A_p = {}^{\vee}B_p) \wedge \{A_\phi A_p\} = \{B_\phi B_p\}) \rightarrow \square(A_\phi A_p = B_\phi B_p)$ only if $\vDash \square(A_p = B_p)$.

For this reason, not all sentences which are both illocutionarily and truth conditionally inconsistent are synonymous in general semantics. Thus, two sentences of the form $!(A_p \wedge \sim A_p)$ and $!(B_p \wedge \sim B_p)$ are not synonymous if it is not the case that $\vDash \square(A_p = B_p)$. For example, the two sentences "If only it would rain and not rain!" and "If only it would snow and not snow!" have different meanings.

2.4 Modally closed sentences have a stable meaning.

As I pointed out there is a ramification of meaning in language so that one must distinguish between linguistic meaning and meaning in context. In general semantics, the *linguistic meaning of a* (translation of

a) *sentence* in an interpretation is a *function* from contexts and assignments into illocutionary acts, while the *meaning of that sentence in a context* of that interpretation is an *illocutionary act*. Using Kaplan's terminology, I will say that the meaning of a sentence is *stable* in an interpretation when that sentence expresses the same illocutionary act in all contexts under all assignments according to that interpretation, and that it is *variable* otherwise.[10] By definition, *only the modally closed sentences* of the form $A_\phi A_p$ have a stable meaning in all possible interpretations in general semantics. Such formulas are the translations of *eternal sentences* in Quine's sense.[11]

2.5 The usual laws of extensionality hold for modally closed formulas in general semantics.

Thus, the laws of *existential generalization* and of the *substitutivity salva veritate* of formulas with the same denotation hold in the following restricted cases:

$$\vDash A(B_\alpha) \to \exists x_\alpha A(x_\alpha), \text{ when } A(B_\alpha) \in MC$$

$$\vDash B_1 = B_2 \to A(B_1) = A(B_2), \text{ when } B_1 \text{ and } B_2 \in MC$$

Two important consequences of the fact that most sentences do not have a stable meaning concern the extensions of the concepts of analyticity, necessity, and consistency.

2.6 Some analytically true declarative sentences do not assert a necessary proposition.

By definition, a declarative sentence $\vdash A_p$ is *analytically true* if and only if $\vDash {}^\vee A_p$ or, what amounts to the same, if and only if $\vDash \Box^\vee A_p$. On the other hand, that sentence is *necessarily true* in general semantics if and only if $\vDash {}^\vee \Box A_p$, i.e. if and only if $\vDash \exists x_{\#t}(x_{\#t} = [A_p] \land \Box^\vee x_{\#t})$. But clearly, $\nvDash \Box^\vee A_p = {}^\vee \Box A_p$ unless A_p is modally closed.

Thus, for example, the sentence $\vdash \text{Max}_p$ is analytically true, but it is not necessarily true, since it serves to assert in each context a proposition that can only be true in that context.

2.7 Sentences which are analytically unsuccessful are not necessarily illocutionarily inconsistent.

By definition, a sentence A_Ω is *analytically unsuccessful* if and only if

[10] See D. Kaplan, "On the logic of demonstratives", *Journal of Philosophical Logic*, 8, 1 (1979). 81–98.

[11] See W. V. Quine, *Word and Object*, Cambridge, Mass.: The M.I.T. Press, 1960.

$\models \sim \Diamond[s(A_\Omega)]$ i.e. if and only if $\models {}^{\wedge\vee}\{A_\Omega\} = {}^{\wedge}0_s$. On the other hand, the sentence A_Ω is *illocutionarily inconsistent* if and only if $\models \{A_\Omega\} = {}^{\wedge}0_s$. However, it is not the case that $\models {}^{\wedge\vee}\{A_\Omega\} = \{A_\Omega\}$ in general semantics, whenever A_Ω is not modally closed. Thus when a sentence does not express the same illocutionary act in all contexts of an interpretation, it can be analytically unsuccessful without being *eo ipso* illocutionarily inconsistent.

For example, a performative sentence like "I declare that I am not making any declaration" is analytically unsuccessful. Because a successful declaration is true, a speaker cannot succeed in declaring in a context of utterance that he does not make any declaration in that context. But someone else could declare in another context that he has not declared anything in the first context. Thus that performative sentence does not express a non-performable declaration.

Other examples of analytically unsuccessful sentences which are not illocutionarily inconsistent are instances of *Moore's paradox*, such as "John, please come; I do not want you to come." Utterances of such sentences are analytically unsuccessful because a speaker who performs an illocutionary act expresses *eo ipso* the mental states corresponding to the sincerity conditions. He cannot deny in the context of his utterance that he has the mental states that he expresses in that very context without contradicting himself. Thus no utterance of the sentence "John, please come; I do not want you to come" can constitute the performance of the literal speech act expressed by that sentence. However, that literal speech act is performable. A speaker, for example, can request that John come and assert simultaneously that someone else does not want him to come. In that case, of course, he will have to use *another* sentence expressing the same speech act.

2.8 Similarly, sentences which are analytically unsatisfied are not necessarily truth conditionally inconsistent.

By definition a sentence A_Ω is *analytically unsatisfied* if and only if $\models \sim \Diamond t(A_\Omega)$ i.e. if $\models {}^{\wedge\vee}[A_\Omega] = {}^{\wedge}0_t$. On the other hand, the sentence A_Ω is *truth conditionally inconsistent* if and only if $\models [A_\Omega] = {}^{\wedge}0_t$. However, it is also not the case in general semantics that $\models A_{\#\alpha} = {}^{\wedge\vee}A_{\#\alpha}$, when $A_{\#\alpha}$ is not modally closed.

Thus, for example, the sentence $\vdash \sim \text{Max}_p$ is analytically false but truth conditionally consistent.

2.9 Some consistent sentences are paradoxical in the sense that they express illocutionary acts which cannot be simultaneously successful and satisfied.

For example, any successful utterance of the declarative sentence "I am not making any assertion" would make its propositional content false. And conversely the truth of any utterance of that sentence implies the failure of that very utterance. The existence of such sentences is shown in the following law of general semantics:

$$\models([A_p] = {}^\wedge \sim \exists x_p\, K(\vdash x_p)) \rightarrow (s(\vdash A_p) \rightarrow \sim {}^\vee A_p)$$

2.10 Imperative, commissive, and performative sentences whose clause is a tautology are both illocutionarily and truth conditionally inconsistent.

$$\models (\mathbf{T}(A_p) \wedge (\uparrow(A_\phi) \vee (\updownarrow A_\phi))) \rightarrow \{(A_\phi A_p)\} = {}^\wedge 0_s$$

This law is a derived consequence of the *a posteriori* truth of the propositional content of a satisfied utterance with the words-to-world direction of fit. A speaker who performs a speech act with the aim of achieving a success of fit from the world-to-words direction must express a propositional content which represents an action of one of the protagonists of the utterance that he presupposes to be contingent. Otherwise, the world could not be transformed by the action of the speaker or hearer in order to match the propositional content of the utterance. Now, any competent speaker knows *a priori* that a tautology is necessarily true absolutely independently of anything he or the hearer could do in the world. This is why performative or imperative sentences like "I promise to come or not to come" and "Please, come or do not come!" are illocutionarily inconsistent. As the conditions of success of utterances with the world-to-words direction of fit are part of their conditions of satisfaction, such imperative or performative sentences with a tautological clause are also truth conditionally inconsistent.

2.11 Elementary sentences of the form $A_\phi(A_p \wedge \sim A_p)$ where A_ϕ expresses an illocutionary force with a non-empty direction of fit are both illocutionarily and truth conditionally inconsistent.

This law is a direct consequence of the rationality of speakers. Speakers must be minimally consistent in their use of language. They cannot use literally with success elementary sentences like "It is raining and not raining", "Come and do not come here!", because they know *a priori* that these utterances are not satisfiable.

Corollary. **Natural languages are not semantically closed (in the sense of Tarski) and the liar's paradox[12] does not imply that their formal semantics is inconsistent.**
The law of the minimal rationality of speakers is important for the research program of general semantics, because it implies that *semantic paradoxes* like the liar's paradox *do not really occur in the use of ordinary language.* Contrary to what Tarski and other logicians tend to believe, it is not the case that self referential utterances like "This assertion is false", "Do not follow this advice!", and "I will not keep this promise" are paradoxical in the sense that they are satisfied if and only if they are not satisfied. Indeed, the satisfaction of such utterances implies their success, and the law of the minimal consistency of the speaker predicts that they are analytically unsuccessful.

From a logical point of view, paradoxical sentences like "Disobey this order!" and "This assertion is false" can be translated in our ideal object-language if we introduce propositional quantification and propositional identity by rules of abbreviation such as these:

$$\exists x_p A_p =_{\text{def}} \lambda x_\gamma \lambda x_{\gamma t}(\exists x_{\#t}(x_{\#t} = [\exists x_p{}^\vee A_p] \wedge \forall x_a(x_\gamma x_a \leftrightarrow (\langle A_p \rangle x_a \vee ({}^\vee x_{\#t} \dashv{}^\vee[x_a]))) \wedge \forall y_\gamma(x_{\gamma t} y_\gamma \leftrightarrow \forall x_a(({}^\vee x_{\#t} \dashv{}^\vee[x_a]) \rightarrow y_\gamma x_a = 1_t))))$$

$$(A_p \equiv B_p) =_{\text{def}} \lambda x_\gamma \lambda x_{\gamma t}(\exists x_{\#t}(x_{\#t} = [A_p = B_p] \wedge \forall x_a(x_\gamma x_a \leftrightarrow (\langle A_p \rangle x_a \vee \langle B_p \rangle x_a \vee ({}^\vee x_{\#t} \dashv{}^\vee[x_a]))) \wedge \forall y_\gamma(x_{\gamma t} y_\gamma \leftrightarrow \forall x_a(({}^\vee x_{\#t} \dashv{}^\vee[x_a]) \rightarrow y_\gamma x_a = 1_t))))$$

Indeed, these paradoxical sentences are of the form $A_\phi \exists x_p(KA_\phi x_p \wedge \sim x_p \wedge (x_p \equiv \exists x_p(KA_\phi x_p \wedge \sim x_p)))$ when they are self referential. They strongly entail a sentence of the form $A_\phi(x_p \wedge \sim x_p)$. Consequently, they are both illocutionarily and truth conditionally inconsistent. Thus general semantics can admit in its formal object-language the translation of such paradoxical sentences without inconsistency. Contrary to what Tarski feared, self-reference does not imply inconsistency in the logical structure of language. On this account, the expressive power of the object-language of formal semantics need not be as limited as Tarski advocated. Like natural languages, formal languages can be (at least up to a certain point) their own meta-languages.

As Prior[13] anticipated, when an utterance of a sentence of the form

---

[12] A. Tarski, "The semantic conception of truth and the foundations of semantics", *Philosophy and Phenomenological Research*, 4 (1944), 341–76.
[13] A. N. Prior, *Objects of Thought*, Oxford: Clarendon Press, 1971.

$A_\phi \exists x_p ((KA_\phi x_p) \wedge \sim x_p)$ is successful, it is not self referential; and when it is self referential, it is not paradoxical but it is both analytically unsuccessful and unsatisfied. According to general semantics, the two following laws are valid for such sentences:

$$\vDash \forall x_p \, (s(A_\phi((KA_\phi x_p) \wedge \sim x_p)) \rightarrow \sim (x_p = ((KA_\phi x_p) \wedge \sim x_p))$$

and

$$\vDash \, \sim \Diamond s(A_\phi \exists x_p (((KA_\phi x_p) \wedge \sim x_p) \wedge x_p \equiv \exists x_p ((KA_\phi x_p) \wedge \sim x_p)))$$

III LAWS OF ENTAILMENT

As I said earlier, one of the primary aims of general semantics is to state the various fundamental laws of truth conditional and illocutionary entailments that exist between sentences in virtue of their logical forms. These laws of entailment are important for the purposes of a semantic theory of natural language. Indeed, they are needed to explain and predict the various forms of valid practical and theoretical inferences that competent speakers make in their use and comprehension of language.

In volume I of this work, I stated that all possible types of entailment are syntactically realized in language. I will now justify that assertion by stating valid laws of inference corresponding to each type of entailment. I will also show that the different types of entailment that I have distinguished conceptually in general semantics do not coincide in extension.

3.1 Any sentence of the form $[B]A_\phi A_p$ with a complex illocutionary force marker strongly illocutionary entails or is strongly illocutionarily entailed by the simpler sentence $A_\phi A_p$.

$$[A_\zeta]A_\phi A_p \Vdash_s A_\phi A_p$$

If $\vDash A_\iota \geqslant 0_\iota$ then $[A_\iota]A_\phi A_p \Vdash_s A_\phi A_p$.

If $\vDash 0_\iota \geqslant A_\iota$ then $A_\phi A_p \Vdash_s [A_\iota]A_\phi A_p$.

For example, the imperative sentences "Please, come!", "Yes, come!", "Frankly, come!", and "Father, come!" all strongly illocutionarily entail the simple sentence "Come!". This law of illocutionary entailment is a linguistically significant corollary of the fact that the operations on illocutionary forces generate stronger or weaker illocutionary forces.

Corollary. **On this account, the following rules of inference are valid in the use and comprehension of language.**

The law of elimination of modifiers that express components of illocutionary force

$$\frac{s([A_\zeta]A_\phi A_p)}{s(A_\phi A_p)} \text{ whenever } \zeta = \theta, \mu, \Sigma, \text{ or } \psi$$

The law of elimination of modifiers that express an increase of degree of strength

$$\frac{s([A_\iota]A_\phi A_p)}{s(A_\phi A_p)} \text{ whenever } A_\iota \text{ names a positive integer}$$

The law of introduction of modifiers that express a decrease of degree of strength

$$\frac{s(A_\phi A_p)}{s([A_\iota]A_\phi A_p)} \text{ whenever } A_\iota \text{ names a negative integer}$$

And similarly for $t([A_\zeta]A_\phi A_p)$, $t(A_\phi A_p)$ and $t([A_\iota]A_\phi A_p)$.

Remark. Incidentally, the corresponding semantic laws do not hold for propositional connectives. It is not in general the case that a sentence of the form $A_\phi(A_{(pp)}A_p)$ strongly entails illocutionarily or truth conditionally the simple sentence $A_\phi A_p$. Indeed, the operations on propositions do not in general generate complex propositions which strictly imply or are strictly implied by their arguments.

3.2 Any simple declarative sentence in the future tense strongly entails both illocutionarily and truth conditionally the conditional sentence corresponding to the same declarative sentence in the present tense.
Thus, for example, the declarative sentence "If you buy a car today, you will find it expensive" strongly entails the conditional sentence "If you bought a car today, you would find it expensive." This semantic law of entailment is a consequence of the preceding law of elimination and of the rule of translation for conditional sentences.

3.3 Any commissive sentence strongly entails both illocutionarily and truth conditionally the corresponding declarative sentence.
$[(A_\mu,A_\theta,A_\Sigma,A_\psi),A_\iota,\pi^2]A_p \Vdash_s [(A_\mu,A_\theta,A_\Sigma,A_\pi),A_\iota,\pi^1]A_p.$

And similarly for $\vDash_s$.

For example, the performative sentence "I promise to come" strongly illocutionarily entails the declarative sentence "I will come." This law is a special case of the preceding law of elimination of modifiers that express components of illocutionary force. Indeed, because of the existence of an assertive commitment in the achievement of the commissive point, $\vDash \bot = [\pi^2]\vdash$.

The validity of this law is shown in English by the fact that speakers often commit themselves to doing a future action A indirectly by using a declarative sentence of the form "I will do action A." In such assertive utterances, they exploit the maxim of quantity in order to commit themselves non literally to an indirect commissive speech act with stronger conditions of success.

3.4 Similarly, any performative sentence strongly entails both illocutionarily and truth conditionally the corresponding declarative sentence.
For example, the performative sentence "You are hereby fired" strongly entails the corresponding declarative sentence "You are fired." This law is also a special case of the law of elimination of modifiers that express modes of achievement. Indeed, because of the existence of an assertive commitment in the achievement of the declarative point, $\vDash \top = [\pi^4]\vdash$.

The validity of this law is shown in English by the fact that the illocutionary force marker of explicit performative sentences which serve to make declarations is a complex marker where the declarative sentential type which expresses assertion is modified by adverbs like "hereby" which express the characteristic mode of achievement of declaration.

3.5 Any elementary sentence strongly entails both illocutionarily and truth conditionally the exclamatory sentence that corresponds to it.

$[(A_\mu,A_\theta,A_\Sigma,A_\psi),A_\iota,\pi^k]A_p \Vdash_s [(A_\mu,A_\theta,A_\Sigma,A_\psi),A_\iota,\pi^5]A_p.$

And similarly for $\vDash_s$.

For example, the sentence "Unfortunately, all good things have an end" strongly entails the exclamatory sentence "How unfortunate that all good things have an end!" This law is a consequence of the neutrality of the expressive illocutionary point.

From a logical point of view, for every ifid $A_\phi = [(A_\mu, A_\theta, A_\Sigma, A_\psi, A_\iota, \pi^k], \vDash A_\phi = [A_\mu][A_\theta][A_\psi][A_\iota][\pi^k] \dashv$.

Just as expressive speech acts are the weakest type of illocutionary act, *exclamatory sentences are the weakest type of sentence.* Sentences of all other syntactic types illocutionarily entail exclamatory sentences. But no illocutionarily consistent exclamatory sentence illocutionarily entails a sentence of another type. Indeed, there is more in the performance of an illocutionary act with a direction of fit than a simple expression of the speaker's mental states about the propositional content.

3.6 Any elementary sentence illocutionarily entails the truth of the corresponding performative sentence.

From $s(A_\phi A_p)$, one can infer $^\vee K A_\phi A_p$.

For example, a successful utterance of the interrogative sentence "Is it raining?" illocutionarily entails the truth of the corresponding performative sentence "I ask you if it is raining". This law is a consequence of my semantic analysis of performative sentences according to which they express literal declarations of performance of illocutionary acts.

3.7 Each performative sentence truth conditionally entails the success of the corresponding non-performative sentence.

From $t(\top K A_\phi A_p)$ one can infer $s(A_\phi A_p)$.

For example, the sentences "I request that you come" and "I assert that it is raining" respectively truth conditionally entail the success of the illocutionary acts expressed by the sentences "Please, come!" and "It is raining".

A linguistically significant corollary of these laws for performative sentences is the following: the semantic relation of equivalence that holds between a sentence $A_\phi A_p$ and the corresponding performative sentence $\top K A_\phi A_p$ is the following: in every interpretation, that sentence expresses at each context an illocutionary act whose conditions of success are identical with the truth conditions of the propositional content expressed by the corresponding performative sentence in the same context. These sentences have related logical forms but do not express identical illocutionary acts.

3.8 Any performative sentence strongly illocutionarily entails its own satisfaction.

From $\updownarrow(A_\phi)$ and $s(A_\phi A_p)$ one can infer $t(A_\phi A_p)$.

This law follows from the double direction of fit of the declarative illocutionary point.

It has the following corollaries for performative sentences.

Corollary 1. **Any sentence is strongly illocutionarily entailed by the corresponding performative sentence.**

$$\top K A_\phi A_p \Vdash_s A_\phi A_p$$

As I have argued in volume I, a literal utterance of a performative sentence expresses a declaration by the speaker that he performs the illocutionary act named by its main performative verb. Since the point of a declaration is to make true the propositional content, each successful utterance of a performative sentence is *eo ipso* performative. It constitutes derivatively the performance by the speaker of the illocutionary act with the force named by the performative verb. Thus, for example, the performative sentence "I request that you come" illocutionarily entails the sentence "Please, come!"

Corollary 2. **Any successful performative utterance is *eo ipso* satisfied.**

$$\vDash \updownarrow(A_\phi) \to (\{A_\phi A_p\} \dashv [^\vee A_\phi A_p])$$

Corollary 3. **Whenever a sentence $A_\phi A_p$ (strongly) illocutionarily entails another sentence $B_\phi B_p$, the performative sentence $\top K A_\phi A_p$ that corresponds to it also (strongly) illocutionarily entails the performative sentence $\top K B_\phi B_p$ corresponding to the other sentence.**

Thus, for example, the performative sentence "I firmly recommend that person to you" strongly illocutionarily entails the performative sentence "I recommend that person to you." Similarly, the performative sentence "I assert that it is raining very much" strongly illocutionarily entails the performative sentence "I assert that it is raining."

3.9 Each imperative, commissive, or performative sentence strongly truth conditionally entails its success.

If $\models \uparrow (A_\phi)$ or $\models \updownarrow (A_\phi)$ then $A_\phi A_p =\parallel_s A_\phi A_p$.

For example, the imperative sentence "Please, be nice!", which expresses at each context a request that is satisfied if and only if the hearer is nice after the moment of utterance in order to grant that request, strongly truth conditionally entails its success.

This law follows from the definition of the conditions of satisfaction of illocutionary acts with the world-to-words or the double direction of fit. It has the following corollary for performative sentences:

An utterance of a performative sentence is successful if and only if it is satisfied.

If, on one hand, an utterance of the performative sentence "I promise to come" is successful, then it is satisfied because the speaker in declaring that he makes a promise thereby makes that promise. If, on the other hand, an utterance of the same performative sentence is satisfied, i.e. if the speaker promises something in an utterance of that sentence, it is because of his declaration of a promise, since the utterance has the double direction of fit. Consequently, that declaration must have been made.

3.10 Performative sentences are the strongest type of sentence.

Just as declarations are the strongest type of illocutionary act, performative sentences are the strongest type of sentence. Indeed, *every successful utterance of a performative sentence is* eo ipso *true, satisfied, non defective, and sincere*.

First, unlike other utterances, performative utterances are *self guaranteeing*, in the sense that the speaker cannot lie or be mistaken about the type of speech act that he performs in these utterances (even if he can lie or be mistaken about the propositional content of that act).[14] A speaker who makes the performative utterance "I congratulate you on your victory" is necessarily sincere about the type of

---

[14] On the self-guaranteeing nature of performative utterances, see Searle's paper, "How do performatives work", forthcoming in *Linguistics and Philosophy*.

illocutionary act that he performs by declaration in that utterance. He necessarily believes, intends, and desires that his performative utterance should constitute a congratulation (even though he might lie secondarily about the propositional content of that congratulation, if, for example, he is not glad about it). On the contrary, a speaker who utters the exclamatory sentence "How glad I am you have won!" can lie and not be at all glad at the hearer's victory, while he succeeds in congratulating the hearer on his victory.

Second, unlike other utterances, performative utterances make their propositional content true in the world and are satisfied. Thus in successful utterances of performative sentences, speakers can perform speech acts with any illocutionary force. This is why performative sentences strongly illocutionarily entail the corresponding sentences of other types whose markers express the illocutionary forces named by their performative verbs. For example, all performative sentences of the form "I ask you if A" illocutionarily entail the corresponding interrogative sentences of the form "Is it the case that A?" All performative sentences of the form "I tell you to do A" illocutionarily entail the corresponding imperative sentences of the form "Whether you like it or not, do A!" All performative sentences with an expressive verb like "I apologize for having done A" illocutionarily entail the corresponding exclamatory sentences "How sorry I am to have done A!" However, no consistent sentence which is not performative can strongly illocutionary entail the corresponding performative sentence.

As a result of this, no sentence is synonymous with the corresponding performative sentence.

It is not the case that $\vDash \Box(A_\phi A_p = \top K(A_\phi A_p))$.

Because speakers can perform illocutionary acts without declaring that they perform these acts, a sentence of the form $A_\phi A_p$ does not illocutionarily entail the corresponding performative sentences $\top K A_\phi A_p$. Thus the success conditions of the illocutionary acts expressed by a sentence and by the corresponding performative sentence are not identical.

Moreover, the conditions of satisfaction of these acts are also different. The propositional content of an utterance of a sentence like "Please, come!" is that the hearer will come sometime after the moment of utterance, while the propositional content of an utterance in the same context of the corresponding performative sentence "I request that you come" is that the speaker requests that the hearer come after the moment of utterance. Consequently, *the performative hypothesis*[15] *is false* in general semantics. Although they have logically related meanings, a sentence and the performative sentences which correspond to it are not synonymous.

All the preceding laws of illocutionary entailment derive from the meaning of illocutionary force markers and sentence types. The following laws of illocutionary entailment derive from the meaning of propositional connectives as well as from the meaning of markers. They establish a link between truth conditional and illocutionary entailments.

3.11 A simple declarative sentence strongly illocutionarily entails all simple declarative sentences whose clauses are strongly implied by its clause.

If $\models A_p \vdash\!\!\!\cdot\, B_p$ then $\vdash A_p \Vdash_s \vdash B_p$.

3.12 A simple imperative or commissive elementary sentence strongly illocutionarily entails all corresponding simple sentences of the same type whose clauses express a non-tautological proposition strongly implied by its clause.

If $A_\phi = \,!$ or $\perp$ and $\models (A_p \vdash\!\!\!\cdot\, B_p) \wedge \sim \mathbf{T} B_p$ then $A_\phi A_p \Vdash_s A_\phi B_p$.

And similarly for performative sentences.

These laws, which are consequences of the rationality of the speaker, have the following corollaries:

Corollary 1. **A law of elimination of conjunction**

A sentence of the form $A_\phi (A_p \wedge B_p)$ whose marker expresses a primitive illocutionary force with a non-empty direction of fit strongly illocutionarily entails the two simpler sentences $A_\phi A_p$ and $A_\phi B_p$.

For example, the imperative sentence "Bring cognac and champagne!" strongly illocutionarily entails the two sentences "Bring cognac!" and "Bring champagne!"[16]

Corollary 2. **A law of introduction of conjunction**

From two sentences of the form $A_\phi A_p$ and $A_\phi B_p$ whose marker

---

[15] See J. R. Ross, "On declarative sentences", in R. A. Jacobs and P. S. Rosenbaum (eds.), *Readings in English Transformational Grammar*, Waltham, Mass., Ginn & Co., 1978.

[16] As Searle and I pointed out, cases where the law of elimination of entailment does not hold are cases like "Sally wants to marry and have children", where the connective "and" expresses more than just truth functional conjunction.

expresses a primitive illocutionary force with a non-empty direction of fit one can infer the sentence $A_\phi(A_p \wedge B_p)$.

$$\vDash ([s(A_\phi A_p)] \wedge [s(A_\phi B_p)]) \rightarrow$$

$$[s(A_\phi(A_p \wedge B_p))], \text{ whenever } A_\phi = \vdash, \bot, ! \text{ or } \top$$

The validity of the laws of elimination and introduction of conjunction is shown in English by the fact that the conjunction of two elementary illocutionary acts of the form $F(P_1)$ and $F(P_2)$ and the elementary illocutionary act of the form $F(P_1 \wedge P_2)$ are in general linguistically realized in the same elementary sentence, when F is a primitive illocutionary force with a non-empty direction of fit. Thus, for example, all occurrences of the mood of the verb express an illocutionary point which is applied to the propositions expressed by the subordinate clauses in sentences like "John likes chocolate and I prefer cakes", and "Learn German and be nice!"

Corollary 3. Failure of the law of introduction of disjunction

A sentence of the form $A_\phi A_p$ does not in general illocutionarily entail a sentence of form $A_\phi(A_p \vee B_p)$ even though $\vDash A_p \rightarrow (A_p \vee B_p)$.

Corollary 4. A law of elimination of disjunction

When the two sentences $A_\phi A_p$ and $A_\phi B_p$ both strongly illocutionarily entail the sentence $A_\phi C_p$ and A_ϕ is $\vdash, \bot, !$ or $\top$, the sentence $A_\phi(A_p \vee B_p)$ also strongly illocutionairly entails the sentence $A_\phi C_p$.

For example, the sentence "Speak to Mary tomorrow in the morning or after dinner!" strongly illocutionarily entails the sentence "Speak to Mary tomorrow!"

Corollary 5. *Failure of the law of distribution of disjunction*

The mood of the verb does not express an illocutionary point which is applied to the propositions expressed by the subordinate clauses in sentences of the form $A_\phi(A_p \vee B_p)$ whose propositional content is a disjunction.

$$\nvDash [s(A_\phi(A_p \vee B_p))] \dashv ([s(A_\phi A_p)] \vee [s(A_\phi B_p)])$$

For example, a speaker who says "Learn German or Russian!" does not at the moment of his utterance make a linguistic attempt to get the hearer to learn one of these two languages in particular. Indeed he leaves the choice to the hearer and his utterance is satisfied if the hearer learns after the moment of his utterance any one of these two languages. Thus in English, and other languages, the imperative and declarative moods only express an illocutionary point which is applied to the complete disjunction (and not to the disjuncts) in sentences of the form $A_\phi(A_p \vee B_p)$.

Corollary 6. The law of elimination of material implication

A sentence of the form $A_\phi(A_p \wedge (A_p \rightarrow B_p))$ whose ifid $A_\phi = \vdash, \perp, !$ or $\top$ strongly illocutionarily entails the sentence $A_\phi B_p$.

For example, the sentence "Speak to Mary and, if you speak to her, don't be rude!" strongly illocutionarily entails the sentence "Don't be rude!"

The preceding laws of strong illocutionary entailment hold for sentences whose marker expresses a primitive illocutionary force with a non-empty direction of fit. From a linguistic point of view, these sentences are *simple* declarative or imperative *sentences*, like "Paul is French" and "Do not smoke here!", whose marker consists of the linguistic features which are characteristic of their sentential type, or simple performative sentences whose performative verb names a primitive illocutionary force.

These laws do not hold for exclamatory sentences because all exclamatory sentences have a complex marker expressing a derived expressive illocutionary force with special sincerity conditions.

As I said earlier, the preceding laws of entailment can however be extended to exclamatory and other more complex elementary sentences whose marker contains modifiers, provided that these modifiers express special components of illocutionary force to which these laws apply. For example, the law of elimination of conjunction can be extended to performative sentences with the verb "predict". For a prediction is an assertion with a special propositional content condition which satisfies that law of elimination. Indeed, if a conjunction of two propositions is future with respect to a moment of utterance, so are its two conjuncts. Thus, a performative sentence like "I predict that it will rain and snow tomorrow" illocutionarily entails the simpler sentence "I predict that it will rain tomorrow." On the contrary, the law of elimination of disjunction cannot be extended to performative sentences with the verb "inform". For to inform is to make an assertion with a special preparatory condition (namely that the speaker does not already know the truth of the propositional content) which does not satisfy that law.

One can, for example, presuppose that the hearer does not already know the truth of the proposition that John will make a declaration tomorrow in Québec or in Trois-Rivières without *eo ipso* presupposing that he does not already know the truth of the proposition that John will make a declaration tomorrow. This is why the performative sentence " I inform you that John will make a declaration tomorrow in Québec or Trois-Rivières" does *not* illocutionarily entail the simpler performative sentence " I inform you that John will make a declaration tomorrow", contrary to what is the case for the corresponding performative sentences with the verb "assert".

The following laws state the conditions under which the preceding laws of illocutionary entailment can be extended to elementary sentences with complex illocutionary force markers or performative verbs expressing derived illocutionary forces.

3.13 The addition of a modifier A_μ expressing a special mode of achievement to a marker A_ϕ preserves the illocutionary entailment $A_\phi A_p \Vdash A_\phi B_p$, when it is not possible to achieve the illocutionary point of the force named by A_ϕ on the proposition named by A_p with the mode named by A_μ without also achieving that point with that mode on the proposition named by B_p.

In other words, if the sentence $A_\phi A_p$ illocutionarily entails the sentence $A_\phi B_p$ and, in all standard models, $\|A_\mu\|_i^\sigma (i, \|A_p\|_i^\sigma) = S$ only if $\|A_\mu\|_i^\sigma (i, \|B_p\|_i^\sigma) = S$, then the more complex sentence $[A_\mu]A_\phi A_p$ also illocutionarily entails the sentence $[A_\mu]A_\phi B_p$.

For example, the imperative sentence "Please, be intelligent and brave!" strongly illocutionarily entails the sentence "Please, be brave!" Indeed, the modifier "please" expresses the special mode of achievement which consists of giving an option of refusal to the hearer, and if an option of refusal is given for a conjunction of two actions then it is given for each of them.

3.14 The addition of a modifier A_Σ expressing a special preparatory condition to a marker A_ϕ preserves the illocutionary entailment $A_\phi A_p \Vdash A_\phi B_p$, when it is not possible to presuppose the propositions associated by that preparatory condition with the propositional content named by A_p, without also presupposing the propositions that it associates with the propositional content named by B_p.

In other words, if the sentence $A_\phi A_p$ illocutionarily entails the sentence $A_\phi B_p$ and, in all standard models, for all propositions $P \in \|A_\Sigma\|_i^\sigma(\|A_p\|_i^\sigma, i)$, $\| \gg \|_i^\sigma(i, P) = T$ only if, for all propositions

$Q \in \|A_\Sigma\|_i^\sigma(\|B_p\|_i^\sigma, i)$, $\| \gg \|_i^\sigma (i, Q) = T$, then the more complex sentence $[A_\Sigma]A_\phi A_p$ also illocutionarily entails the corresponding sentence $[A_\Sigma]A_\phi B_p$.

For example, the sentence "Good, Julie and John are coming" illocutionarily entails the sentence "Good, John is coming." Indeed, if a conjunction of two propositions is presupposed to be good, so are both conjuncts.

3.15 The addition of a modifier A_ψ expressing a special sincerity condition to a marker A_ϕ preserves the illocutionary entailment $A_\phi A_p \Vdash A_\phi B_p$, when it is not possible to express the psychological states associated by that sincerity condition with the proposition named by A_p without also expressing the psychological states that it associates with the proposition named by B_p.
For example, the exclamatory sentence "How nice of you to come and to help her!" illocutionarily entails the sentence "How nice of you to come!" and similarly for other exclamatory sentences.

3.16 The addition of a modifier A_θ expressing a special propositional content condition to a marker A_ϕ preserves the illocutionary entailment $A_\phi A_p \Vdash A_\phi B_p$, when the proposition named by B_p satisfies the propositional content conditions named by A_θ in case the proposition named by A_p does.
Thus, if the sentence $A_\phi A_p$ illocutionarily entails $A_\phi B_p$ and, in all standard models, $\|A_p\|_i^\sigma \in \|A_\theta\|_i^\sigma(i)$ only if $\|B_p\|_i^\sigma \in \|A_\theta\|_i^\sigma(i)$, then the more complex sentence $[A_\theta]A_\phi A_p$ will also illocutionarily entail the sentence $[A_\theta]A_\phi B_p$.

For example, the conditional sentence "If he came, I would leave and you should stay" illocutionarily entails the sentence "If he came, I would leave." Indeed a similar law of entailment holds for the corresponding simple declarative sentences, and the illocutionary force of conditional sentences is obtained from assertion by adding components (like the special condition that the propositional content must be future) which obey a similar law of elimination.

3.17 Similarly for degree of strength.
As Searle and I pointed out in *Foundations*, most modes of achievement and conditions of actual illocutionary forces syntactically realized or named in English preserve the laws of strong illocutionary commitment between illocutionary acts with a primitive illocutionary force of the kind described above.

Thus the laws of illocutionary entailment stated above for sentences with simple illocutionary force markers also hold for many sentences with more complex illocutionary force markers or performative verbs. It is the proper task of the logics of special illocutionary forces to state the particular laws of illocutionary entailment that hold for these forces.

3.18 Strong and weak entailments

As I announced earlier, all different types of strong and weak entailment are realized syntactically in language and do not coincide in extension. Here are a few linguistically and philosophically significant laws on this subject.

The semantic relations of weak and strong truth conditional (or illocutionary) entailment do not coincide in extension.

If $\models A_\phi A_p \rhd B_\phi B_p$ then $A_\phi A_p \Vdash B_\phi B_p$, but the converse is not true. Similarly if $\models A_\phi A_p \dashv B_\phi B_p$ then $A_\phi A_p \models B_\phi B_p$, but the converse is not true. Indeed, the weak and strong types of entailment are represented by non-equivalent formulas in the ideal object-language of general semantics.

By definition, a sentence $A_\phi A_p$ *illocutionarily entails* a sentence $B_\phi B_p$ if and only if $\models [^\vee\{A_\phi A_p\}] \dashv [^\vee\{B_\phi B_p\}]$. Similarly, it *truth conditionally entails* the sentence $B_\phi B_p$ if and only if $\models {}^\vee[A_\phi A_p] \dashv {}^\vee[B_\phi B_p]$. On the other hand, the sentence $A_\phi A_p$ *strongly illocutionarily entails* the sentence $B_\phi B_p$ if and only if $\models \exists x_{\#s} \exists y_{\#s} (\{A_\phi A_p\} = x_{\#s} \wedge \{B_\phi B_p\} = y_{\#s} \wedge ([^\vee x_{\#s}] \dashv [^\vee y_{\#s}]))$. Similarly, $A_\phi A_p$ *strongly truth conditionally entails* $B_\phi B_p$ if and only if $\models \exists x_{\#t} \exists y_{\#t} ((x_{\#t} = [A_\phi A_p]) \wedge (y_{\#t} = [B_\phi B_p]) \wedge (^\vee x_{\#t} \dashv {}^\vee y_{\#t}))$.

Now, in general semantics, these formulas are *not* logically equivalent unless the sentences $A_\phi A_p$ and $B_\phi B_p$ are both modally closed. (In such cases these sentences are eternal: they express the same illocutionary act in all contexts of each possible interpretation.) However, very few sentences of natural language are eternal. Consequently, one must distinguish weak from strong entailments in the logical semantics of language. Each instance of strong entailment between two sentences is of course also an instance of weak entailment between those sentences. However, the converse is not true. Indeed, in some cases, a successful or satisfied utterance of a sentence in a context can logically imply the success or the satisfaction of the illocutionary act expressed by another sentence in the same context, although the success or satisfaction conditions of that utterance are *not* stronger than the success or satisfaction conditions of the other illocutionary act.

For example, the performative sentence "I assert that John won yesterday" illocutionarily entails the sentence "I report that John won yesterday." Indeed, its clause expresses in each possible context of utterance a proposition which represents a state of affairs which is past with respect to the moment of utterance of that context. Thus, if it is uttered on October 14, 1987, it expresses the proposition that John won on October 13, 1987. For this reason, it is not possible to make a successful literal utterance of the first performative sentence without *eo ipso* performing the illocutionary act expressed by the second sentence in the same context. However, it is not the case that the literal declaration of *assertion* made by a successful utterance of the first sentence on October 14, 1987 *strongly commits* the speaker to the declaration of *report* expressed by the second sentence in the context of that utterance. Indeed, there are other anterior contexts of utterance (that take place, for example, on October 10, 1984) in which one can *assert* and *predict* but not *report* John's victory of October 13 since that victory is future with respect to their moment of utterance. This is why the first performative sentence does *not also strongly* illocutionarily entail the second.

This law has the following important consequence as regards literal speaker's meaning:

The literal illocutionary act is not necessarily the strongest speech act performed in the context of an utterance.

Because strong and weak illocutionary entailment do not coincide in extension, the primary literal illocutionary act performed by a successful literal utterance of a sentence does not necessarily strongly commit the speaker to all illocutionary acts that he is performing in the context of that utterance. Suppose, for example, a speaker says "It rained yesterday in Paris" on October 14, 1985, and then literally asserts the proposition that it rains in Paris on October 13, 1985. He thereby also makes a report, since the proposition that he asserts represents a past state of affairs with respect to the moment of his utterance. But that *non-literal report* is stronger than his *literal assertion* from the point of view of illocutionary logic. Indeed, that report contains the literal assertion, but the converse is not true, since there are anterior contexts where one can assert without reporting the literal propositional content.

In certain contexts of general semantics, the primary and the literal illocutionary acts are different from the point of view of their type, since the primary illocutionary act has stronger conditions of success than the literal illocutionary act. However their tokens are identical in these contexts from the point of view of philosophy of action, since the speaker performs the stronger primary illocutionary act by way of making the literal speech act.

On the basis of the preceding considerations, I will make the following conjecture:

Conjecture. **The sentence (or the conjunction of the sentences) uttered in a context of use where the speaker means to perform the literal illocutionary act *illocutionarily entails* (but not necessarily strongly) all sentences which express illocutionary acts which are successfully performed in that context. Thus speaker meaning remains well founded in general semantics.**

All other cases of differences in the extension of weak and strong types of entailment can also be illustrated in English. They are consequences of the fact that language has a genuine system of double semantic indexation. In general semantics, they can be derived straightforwardly by exploiting the fact that the law $^{\wedge\vee}A_{\#\alpha} = A_{\#\alpha}$ is not valid in intensional logic, unless $A_{\#\alpha}$ is modally closed.

6

THE AXIOMATIC SYSTEM

Because it is possible to construct arithmetic within general semantics, it follows from Gödel's theorem[1] that there is no complete axiomatization of the set of all formulas of type t of L_ω which are logically true in that semantics. But there is another more restricted notion of logical truth, called *general validity* and discovered by Henkin,[2] which allows for completeness. In this chapter, I will first define that semantic notion of general validity. Next, I will specify the axioms and rules of inference of the axiomatic system of general semantics.

As I will show in appendix 2 by extending Gallin's general completeness proof for intensional logic,[3] that axiomatic system is *generally complete*, in the sense that all generally valid formulas of L_ω are theorems of that system. Finally, I will enumerate a series of theorems which exhibit basic features of the intensional and illocutionary logics of general semantics.

I DEFINITION OF A GENERAL MODEL

The notion of general validity which allows for the completeness of higher order logical theories, like simple type theory and intensional logic, is based on a more liberal definition of a model for the ideal

---

[1] The discovery that arithmetic is incomplete is due to K. Gödel. See his paper "On formally undecidable propositions of *Principia Mathematica* and related systems I", in J. van Heijenoort (ed.), *From Frege to Gödel*, Harvard University Press, 1967.

[2] See L. Henkin, "Completeness in the theory of types", *Journal of Symbolic Logic*, 15 (1950).

[3] See D. Gallin, *Intensional and Higher-Order Modal Logic*, Amsterdam: North-Holland, 1975.

object-languages of these theories. In order to evaluate the axiomatic power of such theories, one considers a wider class of models called *general models* which are not necessarily standard. *A generally valid formula* is a formula which is true in all contexts under all possible assignments in all these general models.

General models can differ from standard models in various aspects. First, the *domain* of a general model can be a proper subset of the domain of corresponding standard models with the same individuals. Indeed, a general model of general semantics contains in its domain a non-empty set of individuals and the sets of truth and success values. However, it need not contain the set of all atomic propositions and the sets of all functions that one can construct from such entities by the usual type-theoretical operations. It can contain only arbitrary proper subsets of these sets of functions. Thus, the ranges of variables of types p, $\#\alpha$ and $(\beta\alpha)$ in a general model need not be the *total* set of all entities of the appropriate type as in standard models. The general models must however assign a denotation $\|A\|_i^\sigma$ to all formulas A of L_ω under all possible assignments σ of values to their free variables and with respect to all possible contexts considered in these models. Consequently, the sets of functions of their domains, which are the ranges of variables of derived types, must be big enough to secure an assignment of meaning to all formulas.[4] Moreover, the assignments of denotations in a general model must also satisfy the meaning postulates of standard interpretations.

Second, unlike standard models, *all entities of the domain of a general model must have a name* in the object-language which is a rigid designator of that entity under that model. Thus, general models must secure a certain expressive completeness in their assignment of denotations to the formulas of their ideal object-language.

Third, in the particular case of general semantics, general models also differ from standard models by the fact that the structure of the contents of propositions is left undefined as in the semantics of illocutionary logic *IL*. The reason for this is that one cannot attribute in the object-language L_ω propositional constituents to atomic propositions. Thus general completeness would not be possible without enriching the expressive powers of the object-language if that

---

[4] Thus the domains of variation of functional variables cannot be selected in a totally arbitrary way, and must be closed under certain operations corresponding to rules of formation, if semantic values are to be assigned to all formulas.

feature of the structure of standard models was present in general models.[5]

These considerations lead to the following definition of the structure of a general model:

The *domain* of a general model is a *frame* based on a non-empty set I which represents in that model the set of possible contexts of use of the ideal language L_ω.

By a *frame* based on a non-empty set, I mean here a family of sets (U_α), for each type symbol α of L_ω, such that:

(i) U_e is an arbitrary set of individuals,
(ii) U_t is the set of truth values T and $\mathcal{T}$,
(iii) U_s is the set of success values S and $\mathcal{S}$,
(iv) $U_{\alpha\beta}$ is a non-empty subset of $(U_\beta)^{U_\alpha}$,
(v) $U_{\#\alpha}$ is a non-empty subset of $(U_\alpha)^I$, and
(vi) U_a is a non-empty subset of $(\mathcal{P}(D) \times (U_t)^I)$ where D is an arbitrary non-empty set.

As before, for each atomic proposition u, $id_1(u)$ and $id_2(u)$ represent respectively the set of propositional constituents and the truth conditions of proposition P.

Now, a *general model* of general semantics is a set-theoretical structure $(U_\alpha, f)_\alpha$ for each type symbol α of L_ω where

(1) $(U_\alpha)_{\alpha \in L_\omega}$ is a frame of the type just described;
(2) f (the meaning function) is a function which assigns to each (logical or non-logical) constant an element of $(U_\alpha)^I$;
(3) there exists an evaluation function $\| \ \|$ such that, for any assignment σ of values of the variables of L_ω, for each $i \in I$, and for each formula A, the denotation $\|A\|_i^\sigma$ is well defined, belongs to U_α and satisfies the meaning postulates of the definition of $\| \ \|$ of a standard model $\mathfrak{M}$.

A formula A_t is *true* at a context i under an assignment σ in a general model $\mathfrak{M}$ if and only if $\|A_t\|_i^\sigma = T$ in $\mathfrak{M}$. A_t is *satisfiable* in $\mathfrak{M}$ if and only if for at least one σ and one i, $\|A_t\|_i^\sigma = T$.

Now a formula A_t *is valid in the general sense* (for short $\vDash_g A_t$) if and

---

[5] Thus, in a general model of general semantics the content of propositions is left unanalyzed as in illocutionary logic *IL*. This is needed to obtain general completeness.

only if A_t is true in all contexts under all assignments in all general models. Similarly, a formula A_t *is satisfiable in the general sense* if and only if for at least one σ and one i, A_t is true at i under σ in a general model $\mathfrak{M}$. The primary aim of this chapter is to specify an axiomatic system in which all generally valid formulas of the ideal language L_ω of general semantics are provable.

II AXIOMS AND RULES OF INFERENCE

As I announced earlier, the *axiomatic system GS* of general semantics is a *conservative extension* of Gallin's axiomatic system for Montague's intensional logic.[6] All formulas of L_ω which are provable in Gallin's intensional logic are theorems of this axiomatic system.[7]

Moreover, if we consider the sub-language of general semantics which corresponds to that of Montague's intensional logic, then all the formulas of that sub-language which are theorems of the axiomatic system *GS* are also provable in Montague's logic. This is important from the point of view of logical semantics, because it shows that *the research project of general semantics is a continuation and a further theoretical development of that of Montague.* Given the richer expressive powers of the language L_ω, many axioms and rules of inference of simple illocutionary logic *IL* are derivable in the axiomatic system *GS* of general semantics. Thus, only a few proper axioms for success values, illocutionary points, propositions, and mental states need to be added to the axioms of intensional logic in the axiomatic system *GS*. However, some theorems of the illocutionary logic *IL* like, for example, the law of universal instantiation, are not derivable in that system, because the intensional logic of general semantics admits a double system of semantic indexation. As in standard intensional logic, the failure of such laws is due to referential opacity.

Axioms of GS

The axioms of the axiomatic system *GS* are:

---

[6] See his book, *Intensional and Higher-Order Modal Logic*, p. 19.
[7] More precisely, all formulas of L_ω which would be provided in Gallin's intensional logic if that logic were formulated in the language L_ω are provable in the axiomatic system *GS* which is a conservative extension of Gallin's formal system.

(1) *The instances in L_ω of the axioms of Gallin's intensional logic*

Axiom 1 $\quad x_{tt} 1_t \rightarrow (x_{tt} 0_t \rightarrow \forall x_t \, x_{tt} x_t)$

Axiom 2 $\quad x_\alpha = y_\alpha \rightarrow (x_{\alpha t} x_\alpha \rightarrow x_{\alpha t} y_\alpha)$

Axiom 3 $\quad (\forall x_\alpha (x_{\alpha t} x_\alpha = y_{\alpha t} x_\alpha)) \rightarrow x_{\alpha t} = y_{\alpha t}$

Axiom schema 4 $\quad (\lambda x_\alpha A_\beta) A_\alpha = [A_\alpha / x_\alpha] A_\beta$ where $[A_\alpha / x_\alpha] A_\beta$ is the
formula obtained from A_β by replacing all free occurrences of x_α
by the formula A_α, and no free occurrence of x_α in A_α lies within
a part $\lambda y \, C$ where y is free in A_α and either (2) no free occurrence
of x_α in A_α lies within the scope of $^\wedge$ or else (3) A_α is modally
closed.

Axiom 5 $\quad \square(^\vee x_{\#\alpha} = {}^\vee y_{\#\alpha}) = (x_{\#\alpha} = y_{\#\alpha})$

Axiom schema 6 $\quad {}^{\vee\wedge} A_\alpha = A_\alpha$

Axiom 1 is Meredith's single axiom for truth functional prototetics.
It asserts that there are only two distinct truth values. Axiom 2 states
the law of substitutivity of identicals, and axiom 3 is an extensional
formulation of Leibnitz's law of identity. Axiom schema 4 specifies in
which cases the law of λ reduction holds. Indirectly, it also specifies
when the laws of universal instantiation and of existential generalization hold. Axiom 5 expresses the law of identity for intensions of
entities of type α. Finally, axiom schema 6 expresses the standard law
of reduction of intensional logic for $^\wedge$ and $^\vee$.

(2) *The axioms for success values*

Axiom 7 $\quad \{1_t\} = 1_s$

Axiom 8 $\quad (\sim[x_s]) = (x_s = 0_s)$

Axiom 7 specifies the success value that the function named by the
logical constant $\{\}$ associates with truth. Axiom 8 states the law that
there are two distinct success values.

(3) *The axioms for atomic propositions*

Axiom schema 9 $\quad A_a \simeq A_a$

Axiom schema 10 $\quad A_a \simeq B_a \rightarrow B_a \simeq A_a$

Axiom schema 11 $\quad A_a \simeq B_a \rightarrow (B_a \simeq C_a \rightarrow A_a \simeq C_a)$

Axiom schema 12 $\quad (A_a \simeq B_a \wedge [A_a] = [B_a]) \rightarrow A_a = B_a$

Axiom schemas 9–11 state that the relation of having the same propositional constituents is an equivalence relation between atomic propositions. Axiom schema 12 states the law of identity for atomic propositions.

(4) *The axioms for illocutionary points*

Axiom schema 13 $[^{\vee}\pi^k A_p] \to \exists!x_\gamma \exists!x_{\gamma t}(A_p x_\gamma x_{\gamma t})$, where $1 \leqslant k \leqslant 4$

Axiom schema 14 $[^{\vee}\pi^k A_p] \to \sim T \sim A_p$, where $1 \leqslant k \leqslant 4$

Axiom schema 15 $[^{\vee}\pi^1 A_p] \to (\exists!x_p \forall y_p ([^{\vee}\pi^1 y_p] \leftrightarrow (x_p \vdash y_p)))$

Axiom schema 16 $[^{\vee}\pi^k A_p] \to \exists!x_p ([^{\vee}\pi^k x_p] \wedge \forall y_p (^{\vee}\pi^k y_p \leftrightarrow ((x_p \vdash y_p)$
$\wedge \sim T y_p)))$, where $k = 2$ or 3

Axiom schema 17 $[^{\vee}\pi^4 A_p] \to \exists!x_p([^{\vee}\pi^4 x_p] \wedge \forall y_p(^{\vee}\pi^4 y_p \leftrightarrow ((x_p \vdash y_p)$
$\wedge (\Diamond^{\vee}y_p \wedge \sim \Box^{\vee}y_p))))$

Axiom 18 $\pi^k \divideontimes \pi^1 = \pi^k$, when $k = 2$ or 4

Axiom schema 19 $[^{\vee}\pi^4 A_p] \to (^{\vee}A_p = 1_t)$

Axiom 20 $\pi^5 \divideontimes \pi^k = \pi^5$, where $1 \leqslant k \leqslant 4$

Axiom schema 13 states that illocutionary points can only be achieved on propositions. Axioms 14–17 are instances in L_ω of axioms of illocutionary logic for illocutionary points. Axiom schema 14 states the minimal consistency of speakers. Axiom schemas 15–17 describe the logical structure of the sets of propositions on which speakers achieve illocutionary points with a non-empty direction of fit. Axiom 18 states the existence of an assertive commitment in the achievement of the commissive or declarative illocutionary point. Axiom schema 19 states the truth of the propositional content of a successful declaration. Axiom 20 states the law of the neutrality of the expressive point.

(5) *The axioms for presupposition*

Axiom 21 $\sim \forall x_p \gg x_p$

Axiom schema 22 $\gg A_p \to ((A_p \vdash B_p) \to \gg B_p)$

Axiom 23 $[^{\vee}\pi^1 x_p] \to \gg x_p$

(6) *The axioms for sincerity conditions*

Axiom 24 $[Ex_\xi x_\iota] \to \Diamond^\vee \{x_\xi\}$

Axiom schema 25 $[EA_\xi A_\iota] \to \exists! x_\xi \forall y_\xi ([Ey_\xi A_\iota] \leftrightarrow x_\xi \triangleright y_\xi)$

Axiom schema 26 $EA_\xi A_\iota \to (\exists x_\iota (\forall y_\iota ([EA_\xi y_\iota] \leftrightarrow x_\iota \geqslant y_\iota)) \wedge x_\iota \geqslant A_\iota)$

Axiom 24 states the law of possible sincerity of the speaker. Axiom schema 25 states a law of foundation and a law of closure under psychological commitment for the expression of propositional attitudes. Axiom schema 26 states the law of existence of a maximal degree of strength and the law of transitivity of degree of strength in the expression of sincerity conditions.

The axiomatic system *GS* has no other axioms than those which have just been stated. In addition to these axioms, it has the following unique rule of inference:

The rule of substitution

From $A_\alpha = B_\alpha$ and the formula C, infer the formula C^1 where C^1 comes from C by replacing one occurrence of A_α (not immediately preceded by λ) by the formula B_α.

This rule of inference is also the rule of inference of Gallin's intensional logic.

Fundamental notions of the logical syntax

The fundamental notions of proof, theoremhood and consistency in *GS* are defined in the usual way.

A *proof* in *GS* is a finite non-empty sequence of formulas of L_ω each of which is either an axiom of *GS* or else is obtainable by the rule of inference of *GS* from two earlier formulas in the sequence. A formula A_t of L_ω is *provable* in *GS* or is a *theorem* of *GS* (for short: $\vdash_{GS} A$) if and only if it is the last term of a proof of *GS*.

A formula A_t is *derivable* from a set Γ of formulas of type t of L_ω in *GS* (for short hereafter: $\Gamma \vdash_{GS} A_t$) if and only if there exist n formulas $B_1, ..., B_n \in \Gamma$ such that $\vdash_{GS} (B_1 \wedge ... \wedge B_n) \to A$. Furthermore, a set Γ of formulas is *consistent* in *GS* if and only if it is not the case that $\Gamma \vdash_{GS} 0_t$. Finally, Γ is *maximally consistent* in *GS* if and only if, for any formula A_t, if $A_t \notin \Gamma$ then the set obtained by adding A_t to Γ is inconsistent in *GS*.

As we will see, the axiomatic system *GS* has the two following important meta-logical properties from the point of view of logical syntax and semantics. First, it is *generally sound* in the sense that all its theorems are generally valid. This is easily proved by proving that all its axioms are generally valid and that its rule of inference preserves general validity. Second, it is *generally complete* in the sense that all generally valid formulas of L_ω are provable in *GS*. This is proved in appendix 2.

III THEOREMS

I will now enumerate without comment a series of theorem schemas of the axiomatic system *GS* which exhibit basic features of the intensional and illocutionary logics of general semantics.[8] Some of these theorems are used in the proof of general completeness of axiomatic system *GS*. All of them are philosophically and linguistically significant, because they characterize syntactically the logical semantic structure of natural languages. (The reader can skip this section without interrupting the larger course of the book.)

Theorem schema 1 $\vdash_{GS} A = A$

Theorem 2 $\vdash_{GS} 1_t$

Theorem 3 $\vdash_{GS} \Box 1_t$

Theorem 4 $\vdash_{GS} \forall x_\alpha 1_t$

Theorem schema 5 $\vdash_{GS} A$ if and only if $\vdash_{GS} \forall x_\alpha A$

Theorem schema 6 If $\vdash_{GS} \forall x_\alpha A$ then $\vdash_{GS} [B_\alpha/x_\alpha]A$, where $[B_\alpha/x_\alpha]A$ comes from A by replacing all free occurrences of x_α by the formula B_α, and (i) B_α is free for x_α in A, and either (ii) no free occurrence of x_α in A lies within the scope of $^\wedge$ or else (iii) B_α is modally closed

Theorem schema 7 If $\vdash_{GS} A$ then $\vdash_{GS} [B_\alpha/x_\alpha]A$ when A and B_α satisfy the conditions of theorem schema 6

Theorem schema 8 $\vdash_{GS} \forall x_\alpha A \to [B_\alpha/x_\alpha]A$ when A and B_α satisfy the conditions of theorem schema 6

Theorem schema 9 $\vdash_{GS} [B_\alpha/x_\alpha]A \to \exists x_\alpha A$ when A and B_α satisfy the conditions of theorem schema 6

Theorem schema 10 $\vdash_{GS} \lambda x_\alpha A(x_\alpha) = \lambda y_\alpha A(y_\alpha)$ where $A(x_\alpha)$ and $A(y_\alpha)$ are identical except that $A(x_\alpha)$ has free occurrences of x_α where $A(y_\alpha)$ has free occurrences of y_α, and vice versa.

---

[8] See Gallin, *Intensional and Higher-Order Modal Logic*, for more theorems of intensional logic.

Theorem schema 11 $\vdash_{GS} \forall x_\alpha A_t(x_\alpha) \leftrightarrow \forall y_\alpha A_t(y_\alpha)$ under the same conditions

Theorem schema 12 $\vdash_{GS} \exists x_\alpha (A_\alpha = x_\alpha)$, where x_α is any variable not free in A_α

Theorem schema 13 $\vdash_{GS} (B_\alpha = C_\alpha) \rightarrow [B_\alpha/x_\alpha] A = [C_\alpha/x_\alpha] A$, where B_α, C_α, and A satisfy the conditions of theorem schema 6

Theorem schema 14 $\vdash_{GS} (B_\alpha = C_\alpha) \rightarrow A_{\alpha\beta} B_\alpha = A_{\alpha\beta} C_\alpha$

Theorem schema 15 $\vdash_{GS} (A_{\alpha\beta} = B_{\alpha\beta}) \rightarrow A_{\alpha\beta} C_\alpha = B_{\alpha\beta} C_\alpha$

Theorem schema 16 $\vdash_{GS} (A_\alpha = B_\alpha) \rightarrow {}^\vee A_\alpha = {}^\vee B_\alpha$, where $\alpha = p$ or is of the form #β

Theorem schema 17 $\vdash_{GS} ({}^\wedge B_\alpha = {}^\wedge C_\alpha) \rightarrow ([B_\alpha/x_\alpha]A = [C_\alpha/x_\alpha]A)$, where $[B_\alpha/x_\alpha]A$ and $[C_\alpha/x_\alpha]A$ come from A by replacing all free occurrences of x_α in A by the formulas B_α, C_α respectively, and B_α and C_α are free for x_α in A

Theorem schema 18 $\vdash_{GS} ({}^\wedge A_\alpha = {}^\wedge B_\alpha) \rightarrow \Box (A_\alpha = B_\alpha)$

Theorem schema 19 $\vdash_{GS} A_t \rightarrow \Box A_t$, where A is modally closed

Theorem 20 $\vdash_{GS} \forall x_t (x_t = 1_t \vee x_t = 0_t)$

Theorem 21 $\vdash_{GS} \forall x_s (x_s = 1_s \vee x_s = 0_s)$

Theorem 22 $\vdash_{GS} x_{st} 1_s \rightarrow (x_{st} 0_s \rightarrow \forall x_s\, x_{st} x_s)$

Theorem schema 23 $\vdash_{GS} \sim (0_\alpha = 1_\alpha)$, where $\alpha = s$ or t

Theorem schema 24 $\vdash_{GS} \{0_t\} = 0_s$

Theorem schema 25 $\vdash_{GS} \Box A_t \rightarrow A_t$

Theorem schema 26 $\vdash_{GS} \Box (A_t \rightarrow B_t) \rightarrow (\Box A_t \rightarrow \Box B_t)$

Theorem schema 27 $\vdash_{GS} \sim \Box A_t \rightarrow \Box \sim \Box A_t$

Theorem schema 28 If $\vdash_{GS} A_t$ then $\vdash_{GS} \Box A_t$

Theorem schema 29 $\vdash_{GS} \Diamond \Box A_t \leftrightarrow \Box A_t$

Theorem schema 30 $\vdash_{GS} \forall x_\alpha \Box A_t \leftrightarrow \Box \forall x_\alpha A_t$

Theorem schema 31 $\vdash_{GS} \mathbf{T} A_p$, where A_p has the form of a tautology according to the method of truth tables

Theorem schema 32 $\vdash_{GS} A_p = B_p \leftrightarrow (A_p \vdash\!\!\!\dashv B_p \wedge B_p \vdash\!\!\!\dashv A_p)$

Theorem schema 33 $\vdash_{GS} A_p = B_p \leftrightarrow (A_p \!>\! B_p \wedge B_p \!>\! A_p \wedge |A_p| = |B_p|)$

Theorem schema 34 $\vdash_{GS} A_p \vdash\!\!\!\dashv B_p \rightarrow (\mathbf{T} A_p \rightarrow \mathbf{T} B_p)$

Theorem schema 35 $\vdash_{GS} A_p \vdash\!\!\!\dashv B_p \rightarrow (\Box A_p \rightarrow \Box B_p)$

Theorem schema 36 $\vdash_{GS} A_p \vdash\!\!\!\dashv B_p$ where all free propositional variables and all propositional constants that occur in B_p also occur in A_p and the formula $A_p \rightarrow B_p$ has the form of a tautology

Theorem schema 37 $\vdash_{GS} A_p \vdash\!\!\!\dashv B_p \leftrightarrow ((A_p \wedge B_p) = A_p)$

Theorem schema 38 $\vdash_{GS} (A_p \wedge B_p) \vdash\!\!\!\dashv A_p$

Theorem schema 39 $\vdash_{GS} (A_p \wedge B_p) \vdash\!\!\!\dashv B_p$

Theorem schema 40 $\vdash_{GS} (A_p \vdash\!\!\!\cdot B_p \land A_p \vdash\!\!\!\cdot C_p) \to (A_p \vdash\!\!\!\cdot (B_p \land C_p))$

Theorem schema 41 $\vdash_{GS} A_p \vdash\!\!\!\cdot (A_p \lor B_p) \leftrightarrow A_p \rangle B_p$

Theorem schema 42 $\vdash_{GS} (A_p \vdash\!\!\!\cdot C_p \land B_p \vdash\!\!\!\cdot C_p) \to ((A_p \lor B_p) \vdash\!\!\!\cdot C_p)$

Theorem schema 43 $\vdash_{GS} A_p \vdash\!\!\!\cdot 0_p \to A_p \vdash\!\!\!\cdot \sim A_p$ where 0_p is any formula B_p such that $\vdash_{GS} \mathbf{T} \sim B_p$

Theorem schema 44 $\vdash_{GS} (A_p \land \sim A_p) \vdash\!\!\!\cdot B_p \leftrightarrow (A_p \rangle B_p)$

Theorem schema 45 $\vdash_{GS} (B_p \vdash\!\!\!\cdot (A_p \lor B_p)) \leftrightarrow B_p \rangle A_p$

Theorem schema 46 $\vdash_{GS} (A_p \vdash\!\!\!\cdot B_p) \to \exists x_p((A_p \rangle x_p) \land ((B_p \land x_p) = A_p))$

Theorem schema 47 $\vdash_{GS} {}^\lor\Box A_p \leftrightarrow \Box {}^\lor A_p$ where A_p is modally closed

Theorem schema 48 $\vdash_{GS} \forall x_p((\mathrm{Max}_p \vdash\!\!\!\cdot x_p) \leftrightarrow {}^\lor x_p)$

Theorem schema 49 $\vdash_{GS} \Box {}^\lor \mathrm{Max}_p$, whereas it is not the case that $\vdash_{GS} {}^\lor\Box \, \mathrm{Max}_p$

Theorem schema 50 $\vdash_{GS} \exists x_a [A_p] = [x_a]$

Theorem schema 51 $\vdash_{GS} \Box A_p \vdash\!\!\!\cdot A_p$

Theorem schema 52 $\vdash_{GS} ((A_p \dashv B_p) \land \Box A_p) \vdash\!\!\!\cdot \Box B_p$

Theorem schema 53 $\vdash_{GS} \Box A_p \vdash\!\!\!\cdot \Box \, \Box A_p$

Theorem schema 54 $\vdash_{GS} \Diamond A_p \vdash\!\!\!\cdot \Box \Diamond A_p$

Theorem schema 55 $\vdash_{GS} 1_\zeta \ast A_\zeta = A_\zeta$, where $\zeta = \mu, \theta, \Sigma$ or ψ

Theorem schema 56 $\vdash_{GS} 0_\zeta \ast A_\zeta = 0_\zeta$

Theorem schema 57 $\vdash_{GS} (A_\zeta \ast B_\zeta) = (B_\zeta \ast A_\zeta)$

Theorem schema 58 $\vdash_{GS} A_\zeta \ast (B_\zeta \ast C_\zeta) = (A_\zeta \ast B_\zeta) \ast C_\zeta$

Theorem schema 59 $\vdash_{GS} A_\zeta \ast \bar{A}_\zeta = 0_\zeta$, where $\bar{A}_\mu =_{\mathrm{def}} \imath x_\mu \exists y_\mu (y_\mu = A_\mu \land \forall x_p ([{}^\lor x_p x_p] \vdash\!\!\!\cdot \sim [{}^\lor y_\mu x_p]))$ and similarly for the other cases

Theorem schema 60 $\vdash_{GS} \forall x_\mu (\pi(A_\phi) x_\mu \to \pi^k \dashv x_\mu)$, where A_ϕ is $\vdash, \bot, !, \mathbf{T}$ or $\dashv$ and π^k occurs in A_ϕ

Theorem schema 61 $\vdash_{GS} \theta(A_\phi) = \lambda x_\theta \forall x_p ([{}^\lor\pi^k x_p] \dashv x_\theta x_p)$, where A_ϕ satisfies the conditions of theorem schema 60

Theorem schema 62 $\vdash_{GS} \Sigma(A_\phi) = \lambda x_\Sigma \forall x_p ([{}^\lor\pi^k x_p] \dashv \forall y_p (x_\Sigma x_p y_p \to \geqslant y_p))$, where A_ϕ satisfies the conditions of theorem schema 60

Theorem schema 63 $\vdash_{GS} \mu(A_\phi) = \lambda x_\mu \forall x_p ([{}^\lor\pi^k x_p] \dashv [x_\mu x_p])$, where A_ϕ satisfies the conditions of theorem schema 60

Theorem schema 64 $\vdash_{GS} \Psi(A_\phi) = \lambda x_\tau \forall x_p ([{}^\lor\pi^k x_p] \dashv \exists x_\iota [E(x_\tau x_p) x_\iota])$, where A_ϕ satisfies the conditions of theorem schema 60

Theorem schema 65 $\vdash_{GS} \zeta([A_\zeta] A_\phi) = A_\zeta \ast \zeta(A_\phi)$, where $\zeta = \mu, \theta, \Sigma$ or ψ

Theorem schema 66 $\vdash_{GS} [A_\zeta] A_\phi \triangleright A_\zeta$, where ζ is as before

Theorem schema 67 $\vdash_{GS} (\zeta(A_\phi) A_\zeta) \to [A_\zeta] A_\phi = A_\phi$ where ζ is as before

Theorem schema 68 If $\vdash_{GS} A_\iota > 0_\iota$ then $\vdash_{GS} [A_\iota] A_\phi \triangleright A_\phi$.

Theorem schema 69 If $\vdash_{GS} 0_\iota < A_\iota$ then $\vdash_{GS} A_\phi \triangleright [A_\iota] A_\phi$.

Theorem schema 70 $\vdash_{GS} [0_\iota] A_\phi = A_\phi$

Theorem schema 71 $\vdash_{GS} \sim \Diamond A_\phi \to \eta(A_\phi) = 0_\iota$, where $\Diamond A_\phi =_{\text{def}}$
$\sim \forall x_p \{A_\phi x_p\} = {}^\wedge 0_s$

Theorem schema 72 $\vdash_{GS} \eta([A_\iota] A_\phi) \geqslant A_\iota + \eta(A_\phi)$

Theorem schema 73 $\vdash_{GS} \sim \Diamond A_\phi \to [B] A_\phi = A_\phi$

Theorem schema 74 $\vdash_{GS} [B][C] A_\phi = [C][B] A_\phi$

Theorem schema 75 $\vdash_{GS} A_\phi \triangleright B_\phi \leftrightarrow (\exists x_\mu \exists x_\theta \exists x_\Sigma \exists x_\psi \exists x_\iota (x_\iota \geqslant 0_\iota \wedge A_\phi$
$= [x_\mu][x_\theta][x_\Sigma][x_\psi][x_\iota] B_\phi))$

Theorem schema 76 $\vdash_{GS} A_\phi = B_\phi \leftrightarrow (A_\phi \triangleright B_\phi \wedge B_\phi \triangleright A_\phi)$

Theorem schema 77 $\vdash_{GS} A_\phi = B_\phi \leftrightarrow \forall x_p \{A_\phi x_p\} = \{B_\phi x_p\}$

Theorem schema 78 If $A_\phi = \vdash, \perp, !, \top$ or $\dashv$ and π^k is the last term
of A_ϕ and B_ϕ then $\vdash_{GS} \eta(B_\phi) \geqslant 0_\iota \to B_\phi \triangleright A_\phi$

Theorem schema 79 $\vdash_{GS} (\eta(A_\phi) \geqslant 0_\iota) \to A_\phi \triangleright \dashv$

Theorem schema 80 $\vdash_{GS} (\vdash = [\pi^1] \dashv)$

Theorem schema 81 $\vdash_{GS} (\perp = [\pi^2] \vdash)$

Theorem schema 82 $\vdash_{GS} (\top = [\pi^4] \vdash)$

Theorem schema 83 $\vdash_{GS} \perp \triangleright \vdash$

Theorem schema 84 $\vdash_{GS} \top \triangleright \vdash$

Definition of a redex

Any formula of the form $(\lambda x_\alpha A) B$ such that $\vdash_{GS} (\lambda x_\alpha A) B = [B/x_\alpha] A$,
is called a *redex*, and $[B/x_\alpha] A$ is called its *contractum*.

Definition of a normal form

For each ifid A_ϕ, let the normal form of A_ϕ be the ifid $(A_\phi)^c$ such that
$(A_\phi)^c = [(A_\mu, A_\theta, A_\Sigma, A_\psi), A_\iota, \pi^k]$, where $A_\mu, A_\theta, A_\Sigma, A_\psi, A_\iota$ and π^k are the
first formulas without any redex in a Gödelian enumeration of L_ω
which are such that $\vdash_{GS} \pi(A_\phi) = \pi^k$, $\vdash_{GS} (\zeta(A_\phi) B_\zeta) \leftrightarrow (A_\zeta \ast B_\zeta = A_\zeta)$,
and $\vdash_{GS} \eta(A_\phi) = A_\iota$.

Theorem schema 85 $\vdash_{GS} A_\phi = (A_\phi)^c$

Theorem schema 86 $\vdash_{GS} A_\phi = B_\phi \leftrightarrow (A_\phi)^c = (B_\phi)^c$

Theorem schema 87 If $A_\phi = [(A_\mu, A_\theta, A_\Sigma, A_\psi), A_\iota, \pi^k]$, $B_\phi = [(B_\mu, B_\theta,$
$B_\Sigma, B_\psi), B_\iota, \pi^n]$ and A_ϕ and B_ϕ are in normal form, then $\vdash_{GS} A_\phi =$
$B_\phi \leftrightarrow (A_\mu = B_\mu \wedge A_\theta = B_\theta \wedge A_\Sigma = B_\Sigma \wedge A_\psi = B_\psi \wedge A_\iota = B_\iota \wedge \pi^k$
$= \pi^n)$

Theorem schema 88 If $\vdash_{GS} A_\phi \triangleright B_\phi$ then $\vdash_{GS} A_\phi A_p \triangleright B_\phi B_p$

Theorem schema 89 $\vdash_{GS} A_p \vdash\hspace{-0.3em}\dashv B_p \to \vdash A_p \triangleright \vdash B_p$

Theorem schema 90 $\vdash_{GS} x_p \mathbin{\vdash\!\!\!\dashv} y_p \to (^\vee x_\theta x_p \mathbin{-\!\!\!\!\in} {}^\vee x_\theta y_p \to [x_\theta] \vdash x_p \rhd [x_\theta] \vdash y_p)$ and similarly for x_μ, x_Σ, and x_ψ

Theorem schema 91 $\vdash_{GS} A_p \mathbin{\vdash\!\!\!\dashv} B_p \to (\sim \mathbf{T} B_p \to A_\phi A_p \rhd A_\phi B_p)$ where $A_\phi = \bot$ or !

Theorem schema 92 $\vdash_{GS} A_p \mathbin{\vdash\!\!\!\dashv} B_p \to (\sim \Box B_p \to \mathbf{T} A_p \rhd \mathbf{T} B_p)$

Theorem schema 93 $\vdash_{GS} [s(\vdash A_p)] \to \exists ! x_p ([s(\vdash x_p)] \wedge \forall y_p ([s(\vdash y_p)] \leftrightarrow x_p \mathbin{\vdash\!\!\!\dashv} y_p))$

Theorem schema 94 $\vdash_{GS} [s(\vdash A_p)] \to \exists ! x_p ([s(\vdash x_p)] \wedge \forall y_p ([s(\vdash y_p)] \leftrightarrow (\vdash x_p \rhd \vdash y_p)))$

Theorem schema 95 $\vdash_{GS} s(A_\phi A_p) \to \exists ! x_p ([s(A_\phi x_p)] \wedge \forall y_p ([s(A_\phi y_p)] \leftrightarrow (x_p \mathbin{\vdash\!\!\!\dashv} y_p \wedge \sim \mathbf{T} y_p)))$ where $A_\phi = \bot$ or !

Theorem schema 96 And similarly for $A_\phi = \top$ except that $\sim \Box^\vee y_p$ occurs at the place of $\sim \mathbf{T} y_p$ in the new theorem schema

Theorem schema 97 $\vdash_{GS} A_\phi A_p \rhd B_\phi B_p \to \mathbf{T} K A_\phi A_p \rhd \mathbf{T} K B_\phi B_p$

Theorem schema 98 $\vdash_{GS} ([s(A_\phi A_p)] \wedge (A_p = B_p)) \to [s(A_\phi B_p)]$

Theorem schema 99 $\vdash_{GS} [s(A_\phi A_p)] \to \exists x_p [s(A_\phi x_p)]$

Theorem schema 100 $\vdash_{GS} A_\phi A_p = B_\phi B_p \leftrightarrow (A_p = B_p \wedge \{A_\phi A_p\} = \{B_\phi B_p\})$

Theorem schema 101 $\vdash_{GS} \zeta(A_\phi) \ast \zeta(B_\phi) = 0_\zeta \to A_\phi \rangle\langle B_\phi$, where $\zeta = \mu, \theta, \Sigma$ or ψ

Theorem schema 102 If $\vdash_{GS} A_\phi \rangle\langle B_\phi$ then $\vdash_{GS} A_\phi A_p \rangle\langle B_\phi A_p$

Theorem schema 103 $\vdash_{GS} (\pi(A_\phi) \pi^k \wedge \pi(B_\phi) \pi^n) \to (A_p \mathbin{\vdash\!\!\!\dashv} \sim B_p \to A_\phi A_p \rangle\langle B_\phi B_p)$, where $1 \leqslant k \leqslant 4$, $1 \leqslant n \leqslant 4$ and either $k = n$ or ($k = 1$ and n is even).

7

RULES OF
TRANSLATION

In this last chapter, I will apply the logical apparatus of general semantics to English and state rules of translation for a series of English performative verbs which name illocutionary forces or kinds of elementary speech acts. These rules of translation will be based on the direct lexical analyses of performative verbs which were formulated in chapter 6 of volume I. As I said earlier, performative verbs are analyzed *indirectly* in general semantics via their translations into formulas of the type $(p\Omega)$ of the ideal language. The purpose of the translation of a performative verb is to exhibit clearly in the syntactic structure of its translation the logical form of the illocutionary acts which it names.

In translating English speech act verbs, my first aim is to make visible in the conceptual perspicuous formal language of general semantics the logical relations of comparative strength that exist between actual English illocutionary forces. A second aim of this formal analysis is to facilitate the implementation of illocutionary logic on computers. One important task of artificial intelligence is to simulate the generation of dialogues between users and computers in the use of query languages. In order to fulfill this task, it is necessary to enable the computer to make practical as well as theoretical valid inferences concerning the conditions of success and of satisfaction of utterances. For example, a computer which "understands" the imperative utterance "Connect me with this network in the morning or in the evening tomorrow!" should also understand that it contains the weaker directive "Connect me with this network tomorrow!" Indeed, if for some reason that computer is unable to establish the connection tomorrow at the time requested, it would be most helpful if it could then propose another moment of time on the same day in an answer to that query. Moreover, general semantics should also facilitate the automatic translation of actual natural languages via their translation in its ideal object-language. Since illocutionary acts are the basic units of meaning in the use and comprehension of language, they are also the *units* of indirect or direct *translation*. Any adequate translation of an utterance of a sentence of a language into another language should use the resources of the language of translation with the greatest possible efficiency to express as completely and precisely as possible the nature of the intended primary illocutionary force of that utterance. Thus adequate translations of sentences should preserve their illocutionary force potential. Translations of performative verbs and illocutionary force markers into formulas of an ideal object-language, which is roughly that of λ-calculus with modalities and tense, are also intended to be useful for this purpose.[1]

I RELEVANT ENGLISH WORDS AND SYNTACTIC FEATURES

As Montague pointed out,[2] an indirect semantic analysis of a fragment of English in a logical semantics is made in three steps. In the first step, the *grammar* of the fragment is constructed. The grammar must generate the set of all well-formed expressions of that fragment. It must also associate with these expressions descriptions of their syntactic structure. The *lexicon* of the fragment of English which is under consideration in this chapter contains only a series of speech act verbs and a few other words, such as tense and modal operators, which express important recurrent features of English illocutionary forces. I will enumerate these basic expressions and define their syntactic categories. The rules of formation are intended to be those of the ordinary grammar of English. In the second step of an indirect semantic analysis, *rules of translation* are specified by the application of which each well-formed expression of the fragment that is considered can be associated with one (or, if it is ambiguous, several) formulas of the ideal language of the logical semantics. For the purposes of the

---

[1] I will develop this implementation and a theory of dialogue generation based on general semantics in a future paper with Michel de Rougemont.
[2] See R. Montague, "Universal grammar", *Theoria*, 36 (1970).

formalization, these rules of translation are formulated in a recursive definition, which is made by induction on the length of the well-formed expressions of the fragment. *Basic* words or syntactic features of the vocabulary (which are expressions of length zero) are first translated into formulas of the ideal language of the appropriate type. Next, specifications are given for translating the *complex* expressions that are obtained by the application of the rules of formation given the translations of the simpler expressions out of which they are composed.

Finally, in the third and last step of the indirect semantic analysis, a systematic study is made of the semantic laws of analyticity, consistency, validity, and entailment that are valid for the sentences of that fragment of English, given their translations and the logical semantics for the ideal language. The material adequacy of the logical semantics can then be evaluated by checking that its application to English succeeds in making true predictions of actual entailments and relative inconsistencies.

I will not analyze indirectly here all the illocutionary verbs that have already been analyzed directly in chapter 6 of volume I. Since my rules of translation for illocutionary verbs are intended to be a simple, adequate, syntactic reformulation of these previous direct semantic analyses, it would be quite redundant to reintroduce all these verbs here by syntactic rules. For the sake of brevity, I will concentrate on the few English performative verbs that are listed below:

The English assertives

"assert", "negate", "inform", "notify", "report", "retrodict", "predict", "forecast", "prophesy", "remind", "suggest", "conjecture", "swear", "testify", "admit", and "confess".

The English commissives

"commit", "pledge", "promise", "threaten", "vow", "swear", "accept", and "consent".

The English directives

"direct", "suggest", "advise", "recommend", "request", "ask", "urge", "beg", "supplicate", "implore", "entreat", "beseech", "pray", "tell (to)", "demand", "require", "command", "order", and "forbid".

The English declaratives

"declare", "renounce", "disclaim", "resign", "abdicate", "appoint", "nominate", "approve", "confirm", "sanction", "ratify", "bless", "curse", "abbreviate", "name", and "call".

The English expressives

"apologize", "thank", "condole", "congratulate", "complain", "lament", "boast", "deplore", "", "compliment", "disapprove", and "protest".

Any translation of English words in the ideal object-language of general semantics implies of course a certain *conceptual analysis* of their meaning within the logico-philosophical framework of that semantics. As we have seen, the apparent grammatical structure of English expressions can be misleading. Thus, important logical features of the illocutionary forces or senses expressed by English expressions are in many cases not directly apparent on the surface. On the one hand, logically complex illocutionary forces and senses are often named or expressed by syntactically simple words or features of the English vocabulary. On the other hand, logically simple illocutionary forces or senses can be deprived of names or only realized indirectly in syntactically complex English expressions.

The first task of translation is then to *decompose* the illocutionary forces or senses expressed or named by English expressions into their basic ultimate (non-logical) constituent features. Thus, in order to translate English performative verbs, one must first identify the *actual basic components* of English illocutionary forces. From a logical point of view, these components are like *coordinates* which determine the exact *place* that each English illocutionary force occupies in the *logical space* of all possible forces of English utterances. So the rule of translation for a performative verb must associate with that verb one (or, if it is ambiguous, several) ifids (preferably in normal form) whose constituent terms describe the logical forms of the components of the illocutionary force(s) named by that verb. Moreover, the logical relations of comparative strength between illocutionary forces with the same point must be diagrammatically reflected in the surface structure of the translations of performatives.

As I said earlier, the actual basic features of illocutionary forces of utterances can vary from one natural language to another. Indeed, what is linguistically significant for a linguistic population depends largely on its social, historical, and natural environment. However, for each actual natural language, *there are only finitely many basic components of actual illocutionary forces* in the contexts of use of that language. Otherwise, it would not be a human language that can be learned and understood by human beings with finitary cognitive capacities. In my translations of English performative verbs, I will first identify these ultimate basic constituent features of English illocutionary forces. Many other more complex components of English forces can be obtained from these basic features by the application of the universal Boolean and Abelian operations on components described in the logical theory.

Many basic components of English illocutionary forces are *recurrent* in the analysis of performative verbs. For example, the conditions that the propositional content is good or bad or is past, present, or future with respect to the moment of the utterance are *components* of a great number of English forces. This occurs especially when these components are transcendent or determined by illocutionary point. Other basic features of illocutionary forces are peculiar to English. When a recurrent basic feature of English illocutionary forces is immanent, I will leave it unanalyzed in the rules of translation. Following common practice, I will only translate the English words which are used to express or name that feature into *non-logical constants* of the ideal language L_ω of the appropriate type. However, if a recurrent basic feature of English illocutionary forces is also transcendent, I will in some cases try to analyze it further, when this does not complicate the formal model-theoretic apparatus too much. Thus, I will incorporate the principles of a logic of tense and of modalities in general semantics in order to analyze further the propositional content and preparatory conditions relative to time and action of English illocutionary forces.

Here are a few words or syntactic features that are especially important for the purpose of an applied semantics of English illocutionary forces. They can be translated as follows in the ideal object-language of general semantics.

(1) *The first and second singular pronouns: " I " and " you "*

In their central paradigmatic indexical meaning, " I " and " you " in English denote at each context of utterance, the *speaker and hearer(s)* of that context. Contrary to what is the case in Kaplan's logic of demonstratives, which admits direct reference, the indexical expressions " I " and " you " have senses in general semantics. Thus, their translations are formulas of type #*e*. The senses of the pronouns " I " and " you " in a context of utterance are context dependent. Their full apprehension implies a certain vivid acquaintance with the speaker and hearer of that context.[3]

(2) *The present, past and future tense operators*

" It is now the case ", " It will be the case (at least once after now) " and " It has been the case (at least once before now)." These three connectives (which I will abbreviate hereafter as " now ", " after " and " before ", respectively) are *indexical expressions*. They express unary temporal operations on propositions which compose complex propositions whose truth conditions are dependent on the moment of time of the context of the utterance. These truth conditions can be analyzed simply as follows:

A sentence of the form " It will be the case (at least once after now) that so and so " expresses a true proposition in a context of utterance *i* if and only if its clause ("that so and so") expresses in the same context a proposition which is true in at least one other context which is posterior to the context *i* but takes place in the same world as *i*. And similarly for the present and past operators.[4]

These tense operators are needed to express the propositional content conditions having to do with *time* which are determined by the world-to-words direction of fit. As we will see, they can be derived

---

[3] Thus, these pronouns have necessarily different senses in different contexts.

[4] This present tense operator (conceived as indexical) is studied by D. Kaplan in his logic of demonstratives. I have developed the logic of temporal indexicals in an unpublished paper with D. K. Johnston, "The logic of temporal indexicals".

syntactically from the corresponding standard indexical temporal connectives of type #*t*#*t* of the logic of demonstratives which express the corresponding operations on truth conditions.

(3) *The modal operator of physical or causal possibility*

"It is actually possible" (for short hereafter "possible"). This modal operator expresses a unary operation on propositions. It serves to compose complex propositions whose truth conditions are dependent on the causal order of events which prevail in the world of an utterance. Using the accessibility relation between possible worlds of modal logic, one can analyze these truth conditions simply, as follows: A sentence of the form "It is actually possible that so and so" expresses a true proposition in a context of utterance *i* if and only if its clause expresses in the same context a proposition which is true in at least one context *j* which is simultaneous with the context *i* and takes place in a world accessible from the world of *i*.

This modal operator is needed to express the preparatory conditions having to do with the *abilities* of the speaker or hearer. As we will see, it can be derived syntactically from the corresponding modal connective of type #*t*#*t* of the modal logic of Feys and von Wright.[5]

(4) *The action operator*

"Does something which makes it the case" (or for short hereafter "does"). This operator combines with names of individuals and "that" clauses, and expresses a binary function from senses of individuals and propositions into propositions which represent courses of action. Thus, for example, a sentence of the form "John does something which makes it the case that so and so" expresses a true proposition in a context of utterance if and only if the individual named by "John" in that context intentionally brings about at the moment of time of that utterance the state of affairs represented by the proposition expressed by the clause.

This action operator is needed to analyze further the propositional

---

[5] This modal connective was first studied by R. Feys and G. von Wright. See R. Feys, *Modal Logics*, Louvain: Nauwelaerts, 1965, and G. von Wright, *An Essay in Modal Logics*, Amsterdam: North-Holland, 1951. As Kripke pointed out, this modal connective is weaker than the S5 modal connective of universal possibility since the relation of accessibility used to analyze it semantically is not transitive or symmetric.

content conditions of illocutionary forces with the double and the world-to-words directions of fit.

(5) *Names of psychological modes*

"Belief", "desire", "wish", "will", "want", "intention", "knowledge", "regret", "pride", "content", "pleasure", "happiness", "discontent", "unhappiness", "sorrow", "sadness", "intention", "approval", and "gratitude". These nouns, which name modes of mental states, are needed to name sincerity conditions. They will be translated into formulas of type τ.

(6) *The corresponding propositional attitude verbs in the third person singular of the present tense*

"Believes", "desires", and so on. These verbs express functions from senses of individuals and propositions into propositions which are true if and only if individuals have certain mental states at certain moments. They will be translated into formulas of type $\#e(pp)$.

(7) *The propositional operators*

"Has reasons for", "is good", "is good for", "is bad", "is bad for", "is responsible for", "is obliged (to)", and "has evidence for". These operators are needed to name other recurrent preparatory conditions of English illocutionary forces.

(8) *The performative verb phrases that consist of a performative verb in the third person singular of the present tense*

"Asserts", "denies", "informs", etc. These verb phrases combine with names of individuals and clauses to compose declarative sentences which report the performances of illocutionary acts. Thus, for example, a sentence of the form "John promises so and so" expresses a true report in the context of an utterance if and only if the individual called "John" makes at the moment of that utterance in the world of that context the promise expressed by the clause of that sentence in the same context. Such performative verb phrases are needed to express the preparatory conditions of illocutionary forces about the surrounding discourse. They will be translated into formulas of type $\#e(pp)$.

Illocutionary acts seldom occur alone in the use of natural languages. They are performed in the course of conversations such as arguments, jokes, deliberations or exhortations. A conversation is more than just a succession of isolated illocutionary acts, as is shown by the fact that at each stage of a conversation only some possible illocutionary acts are admissible or suitable replies in that conversation, given the previous speech acts and conversational purposes. Now, some pairs of illocutionary acts, such as offers and counter-offers, or requests and acceptances, are logically related by the fact that the performance of the second illocutionary act of the pair always presupposes the performance of the first in a conversation. For example, an acceptance (or a refusal) to perform an action presupposes a past request to perform that action. Such logical relations are part of the preparatory conditions of these illocutionary acts.

II TIME, MODALITIES, AND ACTION

In this section, I will proceed to the indirect semantic analysis of the indexical expressions, tense and modal operators, names of modes of mental states, and other propositional operators listed above. I will first state rules of translation which specify how to translate them into formulas of the ideal language of general semantics. In some cases, the word or syntactic feature is simply translated into an arbitrary non-logical constant of the ideal language, and the basic feature that it expresses is left unanalyzed in the rule of translation. In other cases (e.g. words for mental states), the rules of translation incorporate a preliminary conceptual analysis from which one can derive laws of entailment and of relative inconsistency. I will also enrich the structure of a model of general semantics by incorporating an elementary logic of time, modalities, and action which is useful for stating meaning postulates for the translations of tense, modal, and other propositional operators. This will enable general semantics to analyze further the nature of actual illocutionary forces, and to derive new universal laws for speech acts having to do with time, modalities, and action.

Rules of translation

In the following rules of translation, "$\mathrm{tr}(A) = B$" means that B is the translation of A.

Rule of translation for the personal pronouns

$\text{tr}(I) = c^1_{\#e}$ and $\text{tr}(\text{you}) = c^2_{\#e}$

Rule of translation for the standard temporal indexicals

$\text{tr}(\text{now}) = c^1_{\#t\#t}$, $\text{tr}(\text{before}) = c^2_{\#t\#t}$ and $\text{tr}(\text{after}) = c^3_{\#t\#t}$

Rule of abbreviation for the propositional temporal connectives

now $A_p =_{\text{def}} \lambda x_\gamma \lambda x_{\gamma t} \exists x_{\#t} (x_{\#t} = \text{tr}(\text{now})[A_p] \wedge \forall x_a (x_\gamma x_a \leftrightarrow (\langle A_p \rangle x_a \vee {}^\vee x_{\#t} \dashv {}^\vee [x_a])) \wedge \forall y_\gamma (x_{\gamma t} y_\gamma \leftrightarrow (\forall x_a ({}^\vee x_{\#t} \dashv {}^\vee [x_a] \rightarrow (y_\gamma x_a = 1_t))))$. And similarly for after A_p and before A_p

Rule of translation for the standard modal connective of causal possibility

$tr(\text{possible}) = c^4_{\#t\#t}$

Rule of abbreviation for the propositional connective of causal possibility

possible $A_p =_{\text{def}} \lambda x_\gamma \lambda x_{\gamma t} \exists x_{\#t} (x_{\#t} = \text{tr}(\text{possible})[A_p] \wedge \forall x_a (x_\gamma x_a \leftrightarrow (\langle A_p \rangle x_a \vee {}^\vee x_{\#t} \dashv {}^\vee [x_a])) \wedge \forall y_\gamma (x_{\gamma t} y_\gamma \leftrightarrow \forall x_a ({}^\vee x_{\#t} \dashv {}^\vee [x_a] \rightarrow (y_\gamma x_a = 1_t))))$

Rules of translation for propositional attitude verbs

$\text{tr}(\text{believes}) = c^1_{\#e(pp)}$

$\text{tr}(\text{knows}) = \lambda x_{\#e} \lambda x_p ((\text{tr}(\text{believes}) x_{\#e} x_p) \wedge x_p \wedge (\text{tr}(\text{has reasons for}) x_{\#e} x_p) \wedge (c^2_{\#e(pp)} x_{\#e} x_p))$

$\text{tr}(\text{desires}) = c^3_{\#e(pp)}$

$\text{tr}(\text{wishes}) = \lambda x_{\#e} \lambda x_p ((\text{tr}(\text{desires}) x_{\#e} x_p) \wedge (c^4_{\#e(pp)} x_{\#e} x_p))$ where $c^4_{\#e(pp)} x_{\#e} x_p$ is to be interpreted naively as naming the proposition that the truth of x_p is independent of $x_{\#e}$

$\text{tr}(\text{wants}) = \lambda x_{\#e} \lambda x_p ((\text{tr}(\text{desires}) x_{\#e} x_p) \wedge \text{tr}(\text{believes}) x_{\#e} \text{ possible } x_p)$

$\text{tr}(\text{intends}) = \lambda x_{\#e} \lambda x_p ((\text{tr}(\text{desires}) x_{\#e} x_p) \wedge c^5_{\#e(pp)} x_{\#e} x_p \wedge \text{tr}(\text{believes}) x_{\#e} \text{ possible } x_p \wedge \exists y_p ((x_p = \text{now } y_p) \vee x_p = \text{after } y_p))$

$\text{tr}(\text{is content with}) = \lambda x_{\#e} \lambda x_p ((\text{tr}(\text{believes}) x_{\#e} x_p) \wedge (\text{tr}(\text{desires}) x_{\#e} x_p))$

$\text{tr}(\text{is happy with}) = \lambda x_{\#e} \lambda x_p (\text{tr}(\text{is content with}) x_{\#e} x_p \wedge c^6_{\#e(pp)} x_{\#e} x_p)$

$\text{tr}(\text{is discontent with}) = \lambda x_{\#e} \lambda x_p (\sim \text{tr}(\text{is content with}) x_{\#e} x_p \wedge \text{tr}(\text{desires}) x_{\#e} \sim x_p)$

And similarly for the other propositional attitude verbs.

Rules of translation for psychological modes

If A_τ and $A_{\#e(pp)}$ are respectively the k-th name of psychological mode and the k-th propositional attitude verb, $\text{tr}(A_\tau) = \lambda x_p \lambda y_p \lambda x_{\#t} (y_p = x_p \wedge x_{\#t} = [\text{tr}(A_{\#epp})\text{tr}(I)x_p])$. Moreover, $\text{tr}(\text{will}) = \text{tr}(\text{want})$.

As I said earlier, some rules of translation incorporate an analysis of the logical form of mental states. Thus, for example, it follows from the rule of translation for knowledge that one cannot know a proposition unless that proposition is true and one believes it. And similarly, it follows from the rule of translation for intention that one cannot intend to do something unless one believes that one has the capacity of doing it.

Rule of translation for the action operator

In order to translate the action operator one must first introduce the intensional connective "because".

$$(A_p \text{ because of } B_p) =_{\text{def}} \sim\text{possible } (A_p \wedge \sim B_p)$$

$$\text{tr}(\text{does}) = \lambda x_{\#e} \lambda x_p (\text{tr}(\text{intends})x_{\#e} x_p \wedge (x_p \text{ because of } (\text{tr}(\text{intends})x_{\#e} x_p) \wedge \sim \Box x_p)$$

On this account, one cannot perform an action without intending to perform that action and the intention in question must be the cause of the performance of the action.

Rules of translation for performative verb phrases in the third person singular of the present tense

If Xs is the performative verb X in the third person singular of the present tense and X occurs in the k-th place in the alphabetic enumeration of the performative verbs of this chapter, then $\text{tr}(Xs) = c_{\#e(pp)}^{k000}$ when X is not ambiguous. Otherwise, Xs is translated into n different constants $c_{\#e(pp)}^{k100} \ldots, c_{\#e(pp)}^{kn00}$ where n is the number of different translations of X.

Rules of translation for other expressions

$$\text{tr(has reasons for)} = c^{100}_{\#e(pp)}$$

$$\text{tr(has evidence for)} = \lambda x_e \lambda x_p (c^{100}_{\#e(pp)} x_{\#e} x_p \wedge c^{101}_{\#e(pp)} x_{\#e} x_p)$$

$$\text{tr(is good)} = c^5_{pp}$$

$$\text{tr(is bad)} = \lambda x_p (\sim c^5_{pp} x_p \wedge c^6_{pp} x_p)$$

$$\text{tr(is good for)} = c^1_{p(\#ep)}$$

$$\text{tr(is bad for)} = \lambda x_p \lambda x_e (\sim c^1_{p(\#ep)} x_{\#e} x_p \wedge c^2_{p(\#ep)} x_{\#e} x_p)$$

In order to analyze adequately the meaning of tense and modal operators and of the verb of action, I will now incorporate an elementary logic of time, modalities, and action in the formal apparatus of general semantics. For this purpose, I will further develop the model-theoretical semantics for the ideal object-language L_ω. I will first enrich the definition of the structure of a model for that language so as to account for the fact that each context of use of a semantic interpretation has a speaker and a hearer, and that the utterances which are made in that context are made at a certain moment (or interval) of time and in a certain world. Next, I will specify meaning postulates for the standard modal and temporal operators and for the verb of action and the basic propositional attitude verbs.

All this leads to the following definition of a model:

An *improved standard model* for the language L_ω is any sequence $\mathfrak{M}' = \langle I, D, U, W, H, \| \, \| \rangle$ which is obtained from a standard model $\mathfrak{M} = \langle I, D, U, \| \, \| \rangle$ by adding to that model a non-empty set W and a function H from I into $U_e \times U_e \times U_\iota \times W$.

These new elements satisfy the following clauses:

(1) The set W is a non-empty set which represents the *set of possible worlds* which are considered in the model $\mathfrak{M}'$. It is provided with a binary reflexive relation R which represents the relation of *accessibility* in the model $\mathfrak{M}'$.

Thus, if w and w' are in W, wRw' means that the world w' is accessible from the world w according to the model $\mathfrak{M}'$. (In that case, all the laws of nature which hold in w also hold in w' according to that model.)

(2) For each context i, let $\langle a_i, b_i, t_i, w_i \rangle$ be the sequence of elements that is the value of the function H for that context. The elements a_i, b_i,

t_i, and w_i represent respectively the *speaker*, the *hearer*, the *moment* of utterance and the *world* of the context i in the model $\mathfrak{M}'$.

As in temporal logic, *anteriority* is represented by the relation of being a smaller integer.[6] Thus, if i and j are in I, $t_i > t_j$ means that the context j is anterior to the context i in the model $\mathfrak{M}'$. Similarly, $t_i = t_j$ means that the contexts i and j are simultaneous in the model $\mathfrak{M}'$.

(3) If $P \in U_p$, $w_i = w_j$ and $t_i = t_j$, then P is true in i under $\mathfrak{M}$ if and only if P is true in j under $\mathfrak{M}$. On this account, the world and the time of utterance of a context are the only two determinants of the truth values of propositions in that context.

(4) $\|^{\vee}\mathrm{tr}(I)\|_i^\sigma = a_i$ and $\|^{\vee}\mathrm{tr}(you)\|_i^\sigma = b_i$. The pronouns " I " and "you " name at each context senses of the speaker and the hearer of that context in an improved standard model.

(5) $\|\mathrm{tr}(\text{before})\|_i^\sigma(u_{\#t}^1)$ is the function $u_{\#t}^2 \in (U_t)^I$ such that $u_{\#t}^2(j) = \mathrm{T}$ if and only if there exists a context j' such that $t_{j'} < t_i, w_{j'} = w_j$, and $u_{\#t}^1(j')$ $= \mathrm{T}$ in $\mathfrak{M}'$.

(6) Similarly for tr(after) except that $t_i < t_{j'}$.

(7) Similarly for tr(now) except that $t_i = t_{j'}$.

(8) $\|\mathrm{tr}(\text{possible})\|_i^\sigma(u_{\#t}^1)$ is the function $u_{\#t}^2$ such that $u_{\#t}^2(j) = T$ if and only if there exists at least one context j' such that $w_j R w_{j'}$, $t_j = t_{j'}$ and $u_{\#t}^1(j') = T$ in $\mathfrak{M}$.

(9) $\{P/\mathrm{tr}(\text{believes})u_{\#e}P$ is true in a context i under $\mathfrak{M}\}$ is minimally consistent and closed under strong implication. $\{P/\mathrm{tr}(\text{desires})u_{\#e}P$ is true in a context under $\mathfrak{M}\}$ is closed under strong implication in the restricted sense that if it contains two propositions, then it also contains all non-tautological propositions that are strongly implied by them. Finally, $\{P/\mathrm{tr}(\text{intends})u_{\#e}P$ is true in a context under $\mathfrak{M}\}$ is both minimally consistent and closed under strong implication in the restricted sense defined above.[7]

(10) If A_ϕ is the n-th translation of a performative verb X analyzed in this chapter and $A_{\#e(pp)}$ is the n-th translation of the corresponding performative verb phrase in the third person singular of the present tense, then $\|A_{\#e(pp)}\|_i^\sigma(u_{\#e}, P)$ is the proposition Q that satisfies the following conditions. First, $id_1(Q) = \{u_a/id_2(u_a)(j) = \mathrm{T}$ if and only if $id_2(\|A_\phi\|_i^\sigma(P))(j) = \mathrm{S}\}$. Second, $id_2(Q) = \{f/f(u_a) = T$ if $u_a \in id_1(Q)\}$.

---

[6] For further reference on temporal logic, see A. N. Prior, *Past, Present and Future*, Oxford: Clarendon Press, 1967, and Kaplan, "On the logic of demonstratives".

[7] I am aware that the rules of translation and meaning postulates for the verb of action and the propositional attitude verbs only provide a partial semantic analysis of these notions. General semantics needs further developments in the logic of action and of mental states. I intend to develop further the logic of propositional attitudes in my next book, *Propositions and Conceptual Thoughts*.

(11) $\|\Sigma(\vdash)\|_i^\sigma = \|^\wedge\lambda x_p \lambda y_p y_p = (\text{tr(has reasons for)tr}(I)x_p)\|_i^\sigma$

(12) $\|\Psi(\vdash)\|_i^\sigma = \|\lambda x_\tau (\text{tr(belief)}) = x_\tau\|_i^\sigma$

(13) $\|\theta(\bot)\|_i^\sigma = \|^\wedge\lambda x_p \exists y_p x_p = \text{after tr(does)tr}(I)y_p\|_i^\sigma$

(14) $\|\Sigma(\bot)\|_i^\sigma = \|^\wedge\lambda x_p \lambda y_p y_p = \text{possible } x_p\|_i^\sigma$

(15) $\|\Psi(\bot)\|_i^\sigma = \|\lambda x_\tau \text{tr(intention)} = x_\tau\|_i^\sigma$

(16) $\|\theta(!)\|_i^\sigma = \|^\wedge\lambda x_p \exists y_p x_p = \text{after tr(does)tr(you)}y_p\|_i^\sigma$

(17) $\|\Sigma(!)\|_i^\sigma = \|\Sigma(\bot)\|_i^\sigma$

(18) $\|\Psi(!)\|_i^\sigma = \|\lambda x_\tau \text{tr(desires)} = x_\tau\|_i^\sigma$

(19) $\|\theta(\top)\|_i^\sigma = \|^\wedge\lambda x_p \exists y_p x_p = \text{now tr(does)tr}(I)y_p\|_i^\sigma$

(20) $\|\Sigma(\top)\|_i^\sigma = \|\Sigma(\bot) \ast \Sigma(\vdash)\|_i^\sigma$

(21) $\|\Psi(\top)\|_i^\sigma = \|\Psi(\vdash) \ast \Psi(\bot) \ast \Psi(!)\|_i^\sigma$

Clauses 4–10 express natural meaning postulates for the translations of the indexical expressions, standard tense and modal operators, the verb of action and the names for psychological modes of the vocabulary of English considered in this chapter. Thus, for example, according to clause 6, the truth condition expressed at a context of utterance i by a formula of the form tr(after)$[A_p]$ is true in a context j if and only if the proposition expressed by A_p in the context i is true in a context j' anterior to the context i and taking place in the same world as j. According to clause 9, the propositional content of a declaration must represent a present course of action of the speaker. Finally, clauses 11–20 specify the components which are determined by each illocutionary point.

As I said earlier, the preceding rules and meaning postulates incorporate an elementary logic of propositional attitudes in general semantics. Here are the main axioms that are valid for the psychological modes of belief, desire, and intention in that logic of propositional attitudes. For the sake of brevity, Bel, Des, and Int are used hereafter as abbreviations respectively for tr(believes), tr(desires) and tr(intends).

Axioms for belief

Axiom schema 1 $^\vee(\text{Bel } A_{\#e} A_p \to \sim \text{Bel } A_{\#e} \sim A_p)$

Axiom schema 2 $^\vee(\text{Bel } A_{\#e} A_p \wedge \text{Bel } A_{\#e} B_p) \to (((A_p \wedge B_p) \vdash C_p) \to$
$^\vee\text{Bel } A_{\#e} C_p)$

Axioms for desire

Axiom schema 1 $^\vee\mathrm{Des}\,A_{\#e}A_p \to \,\sim\mathrm{T}(A_p)$

Axiom schema 2 $^\vee(\mathrm{Des}\,A_{\#e}A_p \,\wedge\, \mathrm{Des}\,A_{\#e}B_p) \to ((((A_p \,\wedge\, B_p) \vdash C_p) \,\wedge\, \sim\mathrm{T}C_p) \to \,^\vee\mathrm{Des}\,A_{\#e}C_p)$

Axioms for intention

Axiom schema 1 The axiom schema 1 for belief and the two axiom schemas for desire are also axiom schemas for intention.

Axiom schema 2 $^\vee(\mathrm{Int}\,A_{\#e}A_p \to \mathrm{Bel}\,A_{\#e}\ \mathrm{possible}\ A_p)$

Axiom schema 3 $^\vee\mathrm{Int}\,A_{\#e}A_p \to \exists y_p(A_p = \mathrm{now}\ y_p \,\vee\, A_p = \mathrm{after}\ y_p)$

Incidentally, one can derive from these axioms the laws that Searle and I stated for these basic psychological modes in *Foundations*.[8]

III ENGLISH ASSERTIVES

I will now proceed to the indirect semantic analysis of the following assertive performative verbs: "assert", "negate", "inform", "notify", "report", "retrodict", "predict", "forecast", "prophesy", "remind", "suggest", "guess", "conjecture", "swear", "testify", "admit", and "confess". Similar rules of translation can be stated without difficulty for the other assertive verbs analyzed in the first volume.

(1) *assert*

The primitive assertive is "assert" which names the illocutionary force of assertion.

$\mathrm{tr}(\mathrm{assert}) = \vdash$

(2) *negate*

To negate a proposition is just to assert its negation.

$\mathrm{tr}(\mathrm{negate}) = \lambda x_p \vdash \sim_{pp} x_p$

---

[8] As Searle and I pointed out in *Foundations*, there is a strong parallelism between the logic of illocutionary points and the logic of the mental states that enter into the sincerity conditions determined by these points.

(3) *inform*

To inform is to assert to a hearer a proposition P while presupposing (the preparatory condition) that he does not already know P.

Thus, tr(inform) = $[^\wedge\lambda x_p \lambda y_p\, y_p = \sim_{pp}$ before (tr(knows) tr(you) $x_p)]\vdash$.

(4) *notify*

To notify is to assert to a hearer a proposition P with the additional mode of achievement that he be put on notice that P.

Thus, tr(notice) = $[^\wedge\lambda x_p \{^\vee(c^{20}_{\#e(pp)}\mathrm{tr(you)}x_p)\}]\vdash$, where $c^{20}_{\#e(pp)}\, A_{\#e}\, A_p$ is to be interpreted naively as naming the proposition that the individual $^\vee A_{\#e}$ is put on notice of A_p.

(5) *report*

To make a report is to assert a proposition which is about the past or the present.

Thus, tr(report) = $[^\wedge\lambda x_p \exists y_p ((x_p = \mathrm{now}\, y_p) \vee x_p = \mathrm{before}\, y_p)]\vdash$.

(6) *retrodict*

To make a retrodiction is to assert a proposition about the past, while presupposing (the preparatory condition) that one has evidence for its truth.

Thus, tr(retrodict) = $[^\wedge\lambda x_p \exists y_p\, x_p = \mathrm{before}\, y_p][^\wedge\lambda x_p \lambda y_p\, y_p = $ tr(has evidence for)tr(I)$x_p]\vdash$.

(7) *predict*

To predict is to assert a proposition about the future while presupposing (the special preparatory condition) that one has evidence for its truth.

Thus, tr(predict) = $[^\wedge\lambda x_p \exists y_p\, y_p = \mathrm{after}\, y_p]$
$[^\wedge\lambda x_p \lambda y_p\, y_p = $ (tr(has evidence for)tr(I)$x_p)]\vdash$.

(8) *forecast*

A forecast is a prediction which is generally about the weather or business (propositional content condition).

Thus, tr(forecast) = $[c^2_\theta]$ tr(predict).

(9) *prophesy*

Prophesying is to make a strong prediction as a prophet or by divine inspiration (mode of achievement).

$\quad$ tr(prophesy) $= [c_\mu^3] [+1_\downarrow]$tr(predict)

(10) *remind*

To remind is to assert to a hearer while presupposing (the preparatory condition) that he once knew and might have forgotten the truth of the propositional content.

$\quad$ Thus, tr(remind) $= [^\wedge \lambda x_p \lambda y_p\, y_p =$ (before tr(knows) tr(you)x_p) $\wedge$ (possible (tr(forgets) tr(you)x_p))]$\vdash$.

(11) *suggest*

Suggest has both an assertive and a directive use. In its assertive use, to suggest is to make a weak assertion. In its directive use, it is to make a weak attempt to get the hearer to do something.

$\quad$ Thus, tr(suggest) is the pair which contains the formulas $[-1_\downarrow]\vdash$ and $[-1_\downarrow]!$.

(12) *guess*

To make a guess is to assert a proposition weakly with the preparatory condition that it is probable.

$\quad$ Thus, tr(guess) $= [^\wedge \lambda x_p \lambda y_p\, y_p = (c_{pp}^7 x_p)] [-1_\downarrow]\vdash$ where c_{pp}^7 is intended to be the translation of the probability operator.

(13) *conjecture*

To conjecture is to assert a proposition weakly while presupposing (the preparatory condition) that one has evidence for its truth.

$\quad$ Thus, tr(conjecture) $= [^\wedge \lambda x_p \lambda y_p\, y_p =$ tr(has evidence for) tr(I)x_p] $[-1_\downarrow]\vdash$.

(14) *swear*

Swear has both an assertive and a commissive use. In each case, the speaker commits himself under an oath to the truth of the propositional content and the degree of strength is increased by this solemn mode of achievement.

Thus, tr(swear) is a pair which contains the formula $[^{\wedge}\lambda x_p \{^{\vee}(c^{21}_{\#e(pp)} \, \text{tr(I)}x_p)\}] [+1_\downarrow] \vdash$.

(15) *testify*

To testify is to swear (assertively) in one's capacity as a witness.

Thus, $\text{tr(testify)} = [^{\wedge}\lambda x_p \{^{\vee}((c^{21}_{\#e(pp)} \, \text{tr(I)}x_p) \wedge {}^{\vee}(c^{22}_{\#e(pp)} \, \text{tr(I)}x_p))\}] [+1_\downarrow] \vdash$.

(16) *admit*

To admit is to assert with the additional preparatory condition that the propositional content is bad.

Thus, $\text{tr(admit)} = [^{\wedge}\lambda x_p \lambda y_p \, y_p = \text{tr(is bad)}x_p] \vdash$.

(17) *confess*

To confess is to admit a proposition which predicates responsibility of the speaker for a certain state of affairs with the additional preparatory condition that that state of affairs is bad.

Thus, $\text{tr(confess)} = [^{\wedge}\lambda x_p \exists y_p \, (x_p = \text{tr(is responsible for)tr(I)}y_p] \text{tr}$ (admit).

(18) *and similarly for other assertive verbs.*

Given previous translations of assertives, one can easily verify that the following laws of comparative strength and of relative incompatibility are valid in all standard models.[9]

$\vDash \text{tr(assert)} \vartriangleright \text{tr(suggest}_1)$; $\vDash \text{tr(conjecture)} \vartriangleright \text{tr(suggest}_1)$; $\vDash \text{tr}$ (admit) $\vartriangleright \text{tr(assert)}$; $\vDash \text{tr(confess)} \vartriangleright \text{tr(admit)}$; $\vDash \text{tr(testify)} \vartriangleright \text{tr}$ (swear$_1$); $\vDash \text{tr(swear}_1) \vartriangleright \text{tr(assert)}$ and $\vDash \text{tr(predict)} \vartriangleright \text{tr(assert)}$; $\vDash \text{tr(forecast)} \vartriangleright \text{tr(predict)}$ and $\vDash \text{tr(prophesy)} \vartriangleright \text{tr(predict)}$.

[9] As in *Foundations*, "suggest$_k$" means the verb "suggest" taken in the sense where it has the k-th illocutionary point.

Moreover, in all improved standard models, $\models \text{tr(report)} \mathbin{\rangle\langle}$ tr(predict) and $\models \text{tr(assert)} \mathbin{\rangle\langle} \text{tr(negate)}$

IV ENGLISH COMMISSIVES

I will now analyze the following English performative verbs: "commit", "pledge", "promise", "threaten", "vow", "swear", "accept", and "consent".

(1) *commit*

The primitive commissive is "commit". Thus, $\text{tr(commit)} = \bot$.

(2) *pledge*

A pledge is a strong commitment to doing something. Thus, tr(pledge) $= [+1_\perp]\bot$.

(3) *promise*

A promise is a commitment that is made to a hearer to do something, with the special preparatory condition that it is for his benefit, and which is made in a way that creates an obligation for the speaker to do what he says. This special mode of achievement increases the degree of strength.

Thus, $\text{tr(promise)} = [^{\wedge}\lambda x_p \{^{\vee}\text{tr(is obliged to)} \text{ tr}(I)x_p\}]$

$[^{\wedge}\lambda x_p \lambda y_p\, y_p = (\text{tr(is good for)}x_p\, \text{tr(you)}))]\text{tr(pledge)}.$

(4) *threaten*

A threat is a commitment that is made to a hearer to do something with the special preparatory condition that it is bad for him.

Thus, $\text{tr(threat)} = [\lambda x_p \lambda y_p\, y_p = (\text{tr(is bad for)}x_p\, \text{tr(you)}))]\bot.$

(5) *vow*

A vow is an earnest pledge that is often made with solemnity.

Thus, $\text{tr(vow)} = [^{\wedge}\lambda x_p \{^{\vee}(c^{23}_{e(pp)}\, \text{tr}(I)x_p)\}][+1_\perp]\bot.$

(6) *swear*

The commissive use of "swear" is obtained from the primitive commissive in the same way the assertive use of "swear" is obtained from assertion.

Thus, tr(swear) is a pair whose second term is the ifid $[^\wedge\lambda x_p\{^\vee(c^{21}_{\#e(pp)}$ tr(I)$x_p)\}]\,[+1_s]\perp$.

(7) *accept*

To accept is in general to commit oneself to doing something with the special preparatory condition that one has been asked by the hearer to do it.

Thus, tr(accept) $= [^\wedge\lambda x_p\lambda y_p\,y_p =$ before (tr(requests) tr(you)$x_p)]\perp$.

(8) *consent*

To consent to do something is to agree to do it with the special preparatory condition that one has reasons not to do it.

Thus, tr(consent) $= [^\wedge\lambda x_p\lambda y_p(y_p =$ tr(has reasons for)tr(I) $\sim_{pp} x_p)]$ tr(accept).

(9) *and similarly for other commissives.*

Given these translations of commissives, one can derive the following valid laws of comparative strength and of relative incompatibility in general semantics:

$\models$ tr(swear$_2$) $\triangleright$ tr(vow); $\models$ tr(vow) $\triangleright$ tr(pledge); $\models$ tr(promise) $\triangleright$ tr(pledge); $\models$ tr(pledge) $\triangleright$ tr(commit); $\models$ tr(consent) $\triangleright$ tr(accept); $\models$ tr(accept) $\triangleright$ tr(commit) and $\models$ tr(promise) $\rangle\langle$ tr(threaten).

V ENGLISH DIRECTIVES

The directive performative verbs that I will analyze are: "direct", "suggest", "advise", "recommend", "request", "ask", "urge", "beg", "supplicate", "implore", "entreat", "beseech", "pray", "tell (to)", "demand", "require", "command", "order", and "forbid".

(1) *direct*

The imperative sentential type and the performative verb "direct" respectively express and name the primitive directive force.

tr(direct) = !

(2) *suggest*

As I said earlier, the directive use of "suggest" is obtained from the primitive directive in the same way as the assertive use of "suggest" is obtained from assertion.

(3) *advise*

To advise is to suggest that a hearer do something with the special preparatory condition that this is good for him or her.

Thus, $\text{tr(advise)} = [^{\wedge}\lambda x_p \lambda y_p \, (y_p = \text{tr(is good for)} x_p \, \text{tr(you)}))]\,[-1_!]\,!$

(4) *recommend*

To recommend is to advise with the additional preparatory condition that the propositional content is good in general (and not only for the hearer).

Thus, $\text{tr(recommend)} = [^{\wedge}\lambda x_p \lambda y_p \, y_p = \text{tr(is good)} x_p]\,\text{tr(advise)}$.

(5) *request*

To request is to make a linguistic attempt to get the hearer to do something in a way that gives him an option of refusal. By definition, a request can be granted or refused by the hearer. The special mode of achievement of request is named by the adverb "please" in English.

Thus, $\text{tr(request)} = [\text{tr(please)}]\,!$.

(6) *ask (a yes-no question)*

"Ask" has two distinct directive uses in English. In the first sense, to ask someone to do something is just to request that person to do it. In the second sense of asking a question, to ask is to request that the hearer give an answer to a question. An answer to a yes-no question whether P is in general an assertion or a denial of P.

Thus tr(ask) is the pair of the two ifids: tr(request) and $[\lambda x_p \exists y_p x_p$
$=$ after (tr(asserts)tr(you)y_p $\vee$ tr(denies) tr(you)y_p)]!, if we limit the
discussion to the simplest cases.

On this analysis, an interrogative sentence such as " Is it raining?"
and the corresponding positive declarative sentence " It is raining" do
not express illocutionary acts with the same propositional content. The
assertion expressed by the declarative sentence in a context is true in
that context if and only if it is raining at the time of the utterance in that
context while the question expressed by the interrogative sentence in
the same context is satisfied if and only if the hearer gives an answer to
that question.

Thus, if a declarative sentence like " It is raining" is translated into
$A_\phi A_p$, the corresponding yes-no interrogative sentence translates into
tr(request) after (tr(asserts)tr(you)A_p $\vee$ tr(denies)tr(you)A_p).

(7) *urge*

To urge a hearer to do something is to request strongly a future course
of action with the special preparatory condition that one has reasons for
that course of action.

Thus, tr(urge) $= [{}^\wedge\lambda x_p \lambda y_p\, y_p = $ tr(has reasons for)tr(I)$x_p]\,[+1_,]$tr
(request).

(8) *beg*

To beg as a directive has two distinct uses in English. In one sense, to
beg is to request humbly while expressing a strong desire. In the other
sense, it is to request politely while expressing a strong desire.

Thus, tr(beg) is the pair of the two ifids: $[{}^\wedge\lambda x_p\{{}^\vee(c^{25}_{e(pp)}\, \mathrm{tr}(I)x_p)\}]\,[+1_,]$
tr(request) and $[{}^\wedge\lambda x_p\{{}^\vee(c^{26}_{e(pp)}\, \mathrm{tr}(I)x_p)\}]\,[+1_,]$tr(request).

(9) *supplicate*

To supplicate is to beg very humbly.

Thus, tr(supplicate) $= [c^2_\mu]$ tr(beg$_2$).

(10) *implore*, (11) *entreat*, (12) *beseech*

To implore or to entreat or to beseech is to beg humbly and earnestly.

Thus, tr(implore) $=$ tr(entreat) $=$ tr(beseech) $= [\lambda x_p\{{}^\vee(c^{23}_{\#e(pp)}\, \mathrm{tr}(I)$
$x_p)\}]\,[\lambda x_p\{{}^\vee(c^{25}_{\#e(pp)}\, \mathrm{tr}(I)x_p)\}]\,[+1_,]$ tr(request).

(13) *pray*

To pray is to entreat God (or another supernatural entity).

Thus, $\quad$ tr(pray) = $[^{\wedge}\lambda x_p \exists y_p (x_p = (\text{after tr(does) tr(God)} y_p))]$tr (entreat).

(14) *tell (to)*

To tell a hearer to do something is to direct him in a mode which precludes option of refusal.

$\quad$ tr(tell(to)) = $[^{\wedge}\lambda x_p \{\sim [^{\vee}\text{tr(please)} x_p] \wedge {}^{\vee}c_p^1\}]!$

(15) *demand*

To demand is to tell a hearer to do something while expressing a strong wish.

$\quad$ Thus, tr(demand) = $[+1_{\text{J}}]$ tr(tell(to)).

(16) *require*

To require is to demand of the hearer that he do something with the preparatory condition that it needs to be done.

Thus, $\quad$ tr(require) = $[^{\wedge}\lambda x_p \lambda y_p y_p = \text{tr(has reasons for)tr(I)} x_p]$tr (demand).

(17) *command*

To issue a command is to demand of the hearer that he do something while invoking a position of authority over him.

Thus, $\quad$ tr(command) = $[^{\wedge}\lambda x_p \lambda y_p \, y_p = (c^1_{\#e(\#epp)}\text{tr(I)tr(you)} x_p)]$tr (demand).

(18) *order*

To give an order is to demand of the hearer that he do something while invoking a position of authority or of power. Unlike commands, the position of power invoked by the speaker of an order need not be institutionally established. It can for example be based on brute physical power.

Thus, tr(order) = $[^\wedge\lambda x_p \lambda y_p y_p = (c^1_{\#e(\#epp)}$ tr(I)tr(you)x_p) $\vee$ ($c^2_{\#e((\#ep)p)}$ tr(I)tr(you)x_p)]tr(demand).

(19) *forbid*

To forbid a hearer to do something is to order him not to do it.
Thus, tr(forbid) = $^\wedge\lambda x_p$(tr(order) $\sim x_p$).

Given these translations of directives, the following laws of entailment and of incompatibility are valid in all standard models:

$\vDash$ tr(pray) $\triangleright$ tr(entreat); $\vDash$ tr(supplicate) $\triangleright$ tr(beg); $\vDash$ tr(beg) $\triangleright$ tr(request); $\vDash$ tr(ask) $\triangleright$ tr(request); $\vDash$ tr(urge) $\triangleright$ tr(request); $\vDash$ tr(request) $\triangleright$ tr(direct); $\vDash$ tr(command) $\triangleright$ tr(order); $\vDash$ tr(order) $\triangleright$ tr(demand); $\vDash$ tr(require) $\triangleright$ tr(demand); $\vDash$ tr(demand) $\triangleright$ tr(tell to); $\vDash$ tr(tell to) $\triangleright$ tr(direct); $\vDash$ tr(direct) $\triangleright$ tr(suggest$_3$); $\vDash$ tr (recommend) $\triangleright$ tr(advise); $\vDash$ tr(advise) $\triangleright$ tr(suggest$_3$); $\vDash$ tr(forbid) $\rangle\langle$ tr(order) and $\vDash$ tr(request) $\rangle\langle$ tr(tell to).
If $\vDash$ tr(X) $\triangleright$ tr(request) and $\vDash$ tr(Y) $\triangleright$ tr(tell to) then $\vDash$ tr(X) $\rangle\langle$ tr(Y).

Thus, for example, $\vDash$ tr(supplicate) $\rangle\langle$ tr(demand).

VI ENGLISH DECLARATIVES

I will now analyze the following declaratives: "declare", "renounce", "disclaim", "resign", "abdicate", "appoint", "nominate", "approve", "confirm", "sanction", "ratify", "bless", "curse", "abbreviate", "name", and "call".

(1) *declare*

The primitive declarative is "declare", which names the illocutionary force of declaration.
tr(declare) = $\top$.

(2) *renounce*

To renounce is to declare that one gives up or abandons something (special propositional content conditions).
Thus, tr(renounce) = $[c^{10}_\theta]\top$.

(3) *disclaim*

When one disclaims something, one renounces any previous claim on it, thus making it the case by declaration that one no longer has rights to it.

Thus, tr(disclaim) = $[c_\theta^{20}]$tr(renounce).

(4) *resign*

To resign is to renounce one's tenure of a position thus making it the case that it is terminated. This special propositional content condition determines of course the preparatory condition that one occupies that position and that one has the power to relinquish it.

Thus, tr(resign) = $[c_\theta^{30}]$tr(renounce).

(5) *abdicate*

To abdicate is to renounce a throne or another supreme power or position.

Thus, tr(abdicate) = $[c_\theta^{40}]$tr(resign).

(6) *appoint*

To appoint is to declare that someone occupies a certain position (or office).

Thus, tr(appoint) = $[c_\theta^{50}]\top$.

(7) *nominate*

To nominate is to declare that someone is a candidate for a position or office.

Thus, tr(nominate) = $[c_\theta^{70}]\top$.

(8) *approve*

Approve in English has both a declarative and an expressive use. To approve something in the declarative use is to declare that it is good (or valid). To approve something in the expressive use is to express approbation.

Thus, tr(approve) is the set of the two ifids: $[^\wedge\lambda x_p \exists y_p x_p = $ tr(is good) $y_p]\top$ and $[^\wedge\lambda x_\tau($tr(approbation) $= x_\tau)]\dashv$.

(9) *confirm*

To confirm is to approve with the special preparatory condition that a declaration with the same propositional content has been performed by a speaker in a lesser position of authority than the present speaker in a certain institution.

$$\mathrm{tr(confirm)} = [c_{\Sigma}^{1}]\mathrm{tr(approve)}$$

(10) *sanction*

In one of its senses, to sanction is to confirm legally or officially making it the case by declaration that someone or something is to comply with legal obligations.

Thus, $\mathrm{tr(sanction)} = [c_{\mu}^{30}]\mathrm{tr(confirm)}$.

(11) *ratify*

To ratify is to confirm legally or officially in the required forms, most of the time a treaty, an amendment or another important document, making it the case by declaration that one is to comply with the obligations contained in that document.

Thus, $\mathrm{tr(ratify)} = [c_{\theta}^{80}]\mathrm{tr(sanction)}$.

(12) *bless*

To bless someone is to declare that he is placed in a state of God's grace.

$$\mathrm{tr(bless)} = [c_{\theta}^{4}]\top$$

(13) *curse*

To curse someone is to declare that he is placed in a state of God's malediction.

Thus, $\mathrm{tr(curse)} = [^{\wedge}\lambda x_{p}(\sim {^{\vee}}c_{\theta}^{4}x_{p} \wedge c_{\theta}^{5}x_{p})]\top$.

(14) *abbreviate*

To abbreviate is to declare that some linguistic expression shorter than another expression will be used instead of it.

Thus, $\mathrm{tr(abbreviate)} = [c_{\theta}^{6}]\top$.

(15) *name*, (16) *call*

To name is to declare that something has a certain linguistic expression as a name.

Thus, tr(name) = tr(call) = $[c_0^7]\top$.

VII ENGLISH EXPRESSIVES

I will analyze the following expressives: "apologize", "thank", "condole", "congratulate", "complain", "lament", "boast", "deplore", "compliment", "disapprove", and "protest".

(1) *apologize*

To apologize is to express sorrow or regret for something with the preparatory conditions that one is responsible for it and that it is bad for the hearer.

Thus, tr(apologize) = $[^\wedge \lambda x_p \lambda y_p (y_p = ((\text{tr(is responsible for) tr}(I)x_p)$
$\wedge (\text{tr(is bad for)} x_p \text{tr(you)})))] [\lambda x_\tau (\text{tr(sorrow)} = x_\tau \vee \text{tr(regret)} = x_\tau)]\dashv$.

(2) *thank*

To thank is to express gratitude for something with the preparatory condition that the hearer is responsible for it.

Thus, tr(thank) = $[^\wedge \lambda x_p \lambda y_p (y_p = \text{tr(is responsible for) tr(you)} x_p)]$
$[\lambda x_\tau \text{tr(gratitude)} = x_\tau)]\dashv$.

(3) *condole*

To send one's condolences is to express sympathy for something that concerns the hearer with the preparatory condition that it is bad (usually very bad) for him.

Thus, tr(condole) = $[^\wedge \lambda x_p \lambda y_p (y_p = \text{tr(is bad)} x_p \text{ tr(you)})] [\lambda x_\tau (\text{tr(sympathy)} = x_\tau)]\dashv$.

(4) *congratulate*

To congratulate is to express pleasure for something that concerns the hearer with the special preparatory condition that it is good for him.

Thus, tr(congratulate) = $[^\wedge\lambda x_p \lambda y_p \ (y_p = \text{tr(is good)} x_p \ \text{tr(you))}] [\lambda x_\tau$ tr(pleasure) = $x_\tau] \dashv$.

(5) *complain*

"Complain" in English has both an expressive and an assertive use. In the expressive sense, to complain is just to express discontent. In the assertive sense, to complain about a state of affairs is to assert that it is the case while expressing discontent. In both cases there is the special preparatory condition that what one complains about is bad.

Thus, tr(complain) is the set of the two ifids $[^\wedge\lambda x_p \lambda y_p \ (y_p = \text{tr(is}$ bad) $x_p)] [\lambda x_\tau \text{tr(discontent)} = x_\tau] \dashv$ and $[^\wedge\lambda x_p \lambda y_p \ (y_p = \text{tr(is bad)} x_p)]$ $[\lambda x_\tau \text{tr(discontent)} = x_\tau] \vdash$.

(6) *lament*, (7) *boast*

"Boast" and "lament", like "complain", have both an expressive and an assertive use. In the expressive sense, to boast is just to express pride for something while to lament is to express discontent and sadness. In the first case there is the special preparatory condition that the propositional content is good for the hearer, and in the second case that it is bad. In the assertive sense, to boast is to assert a proposition while expressing pride and to lament is to assert while expressing discontent and sadness.

Thus, tr(boast) is the set which contains the ifid $A_\phi = [^\wedge\lambda x_p \lambda y_p \ y_p = (\text{tr(is good for)} x_p \text{tr(I))}] [\lambda x_\tau \ (\text{tr(pride)} = x_\tau))] \dashv$ and the ifid B_ϕ which differs only from A_ϕ by the fact that it contains $\vdash$ instead of $\dashv$.

Similarly, tr(lament) is the set which contains the ifid $A_\phi = [^\wedge\lambda x_p \lambda y_p$ $y_p = \text{tr(is bad)} x_p] [\lambda x_\tau (x_\tau = \text{tr(sadness)} \lor x_\tau = \text{tr(discontent))}] \dashv$ and the ifid B_ϕ which differs only from A_ϕ by the fact that it contains $\vdash$ instead of $\dashv$.

(8) *deplore*

To deplore something is to express strong discontent or sorrow for something with the special preparatory condition that someone (not necessarily the hearer) is responsible for it and that it is bad.

Thus, tr(deplore) = $[^\wedge\lambda x_p \lambda y_p \ (y_p = \text{tr(is bad)} x_p \land \exists x_{\#e} \ (y_p = \text{tr}$ (is responsible for) $x_{\#e} x_p))] [\lambda x_\tau (x_\tau = \text{tr(sorrow)} \lor x_\tau = \text{tr(discontent))}]$ $[+1] \dashv$.

(9) *compliment*

To compliment is to express approval of the hearer for something with the preparatory condition that it is good.

Thus, tr(compliment) $= [^\wedge \lambda x_p \lambda y_p \, y_p = \text{tr(is good)} x_p] [\lambda x_\tau \, x_\tau = \text{tr(approbation)}] \dashv$.

(10) *disapprove*

To disapprove (in the expressive sense) is to express disapproval for something with the preparatory condition that it is bad.

Thus, tr(disapprove$_5$) $= [^\wedge \lambda x_p \lambda y_p \, y_p = \text{tr(is bad)} x_p] [\lambda x_\tau \, x_\tau = \text{tr(disapproval)}]$ tr(complain).

(11) *protest*

Protesting is a formal expression of disapproval. It has the preparatory condition that the speaker is responsible for the propositional content or at least could do something about it, and has not done so.

Thus, tr(protest) $= [c_\mu^{100}] [c_\Sigma^{90}]$ tr(disapprove).

Given these translations of expressives, the following laws of entailment are valid:

tr(compliment) $\triangleright$ tr(approve$_5$);   tr(protest) $\triangleright$ tr(disapprove);   tr(lament) $\triangleright$ tr(complain); and tr(deplore) $\triangleright$ tr(complain).

APPENDIX 1

A COMPLETENESS THEOREM FOR
ILLOCUTIONARY LOGIC

(with the collaboration of David K. Johnston)

The aim of this appendix is to prove that the axiomatic system V of illocutionary logic IL is complete in the sense that every logically true sentence of IL is a theorem of V.

Following Henkin's method, we will prove the completeness of V by showing how to construct, for any consistent set Γ of sentences of L, a model which satisfies that set. To this end, let us construct a sequence $(\Gamma_i)_{i \in \omega}$ of sets of sentences such that

(1) ω is the set of natural numbers;

(2) $\Gamma \subseteq \Gamma_0$;

(3) for each $i \in \omega$, Γ_i is a maximal consistent set of sentences of IL;

(4) for each $i \in \omega$ and each sentence $B(x_\alpha)$ (where x_α occurs), $\exists x_\alpha B(x_\alpha)$ $\in \Gamma_i$ if and only if $B(y_\alpha) \in \Gamma_i$ for some variable y_α which is free for x_α in $B(x_\alpha)$; and

(5) for each $i \in \omega$ and each sentence B, $\Diamond B \in \Gamma_i$ if and only if, for some $k \in \omega$, $B \in \Gamma_k$.

Such a sequence is easily constructed by adapting Gallin's construction for intensional logic.

Given such a sequence $(\Gamma_i)_{i \in \omega}$, a *canonical model* $\mathfrak{M}^{\ast}$ for Γ is defined as follows:

(1) Let the set I of $\mathfrak{M}^{\ast}$ be the index set of the sequence $(\Gamma_i)_{i \in \omega}$.

(2) Define, for each P-term A_p of L and each $i \in \omega$, the equivalence class $[A_p] = \{B_p | ((A_p \succ B_p) \wedge (B_p \succ A_p)) \in \Gamma_i\}$. Since it is easily shown that $[A_p]_i = [A_p]_j$; for all $i, j \in I$ (by axiom schema 17), we can write simply $[A_p]$. Let D be the set of these equivalence classes.

A completeness theorem for illocutionary logic

Now define the ordering $[A_p] \leqslant [B_p]$ if and only if $B_p \geqslant A_p \in \Gamma_i$ for all i. It is clear that axioms 11–15 ensure that $\leqslant$ is a partial ordering. It is also clear that a supremum $[A_p] \cup [B_p]$ exists for each pair of elements of D: this is simply $[A_p \vee B_p]$.

(3) Define, for each term A_τ of type τ and each $i \in \omega$, the equivalence class $[A_\tau]_i = (B_\tau / \square(A_\tau = B_\tau) \in \Gamma_i\}$. Let the set M of the canonical model $\mathfrak{M}^i$ be the set of these equivalence classes. (By definition of $(\Gamma_i)_{i \in \omega}$, $[A_\tau]_i = [A_\tau]_j$ for any $i, j \in \omega$.)

(4) For each type symbol α, the set U_α of entities of type α of the domain of the canonical model $\mathfrak{M}$ is defined as follows:

First, let $U_\tau = M$.

As for U_p, note that there is a one-to-one correspondence between P-terms and the sentences of the propositional calculus PC. Define PCmax as the set of maximal consistent sets of the propositional calculus of V generated by the set of P-terms: where $f \in PC$max, we define $f(A_p) = 1$ if and only if $A_p \in f$. We then define for each P-term A_p the triple $\langle [A_p], \{i \in I / t(A_p) \in \Gamma_i\}, \{f \in PC\text{max}/A_p \in f\}\rangle$ which we symbolize as $\langle A_p \rangle$. U_p is the set of triples thus defined.

$U_\mu = \mathscr{P}(I \times U_p)$
$U_\theta = (\mathscr{P}(U_p))^I$
$U_\Sigma = (\mathscr{P}(U_p))^{I \times U_p}$
$U_\psi = (\mathscr{P}(M))$
$U_\phi = (U_p \times \mathscr{P}(I))^{U_p}$
$U_\Omega = U_p \times \mathscr{P}(I)$
U_ι is the set of all equivalence classes $[A_\iota] = \{B_\iota / \vdash_V A_\iota = B_\iota\}$ for each IFC-term of type ι

(5) $\rangle\rangle = \{\langle i, \langle A_p \rangle\rangle / \geqslant A_p \in \Gamma_i\}$

(6) $\mathbb{E} = \{\langle i, [A_\tau], \langle A_p \rangle, [A_\iota]\rangle / E((A_\tau A_p)A_\iota) \in \Gamma_i\}$

(7) $\Pi_k = \{\langle i, \langle A_p \rangle\rangle / \pi^k A_p \in \Gamma_i\}$

(8) Define as follows the assignments σ for each variable of the type τ, ι, p:

$\sigma(x_\tau) = [x_\tau]$
$\sigma(x_\iota) = [x_\iota]$
$\sigma(x_p) = \langle x_p \rangle$ (Clearly $f \in id_3(\sigma(x_p))$ if and only if $f(x_p) = 1$.)

$\|A_\alpha\|^\sigma$ is then defined for each type α as follows:

$$\|A_p\|^\sigma = \langle A_p \rangle$$
$$\|A_\mu\|^\sigma = \{\langle i, \langle A_p \rangle\rangle / A_\mu A_p \in \Gamma_i\}$$
$$\|A_\theta\|^\sigma(i) = \{\langle A_p \rangle / A_\theta A_p \in \Gamma_i\}$$
$$\|A_\Sigma\|^\sigma(i)(\langle A_p \rangle) = \{\langle B_p \rangle / A_\Sigma A_p B_p \in \Gamma_i\}$$
$$\|A_\psi\|^\sigma = \{[A_\tau] / A_\psi A_\tau \in \Gamma_i \text{ for all } i\}$$
$$\|A_\iota\|^\sigma = [A_\iota]$$
$$\|A_\tau\|^\sigma = [A_\tau]$$
$$\|[(A_\mu, A_\theta, A_\Sigma, A_\psi), A_\iota, \ \pi^k]\|^\sigma(\langle A_p \rangle) = \langle\langle A_p\rangle, \{i/s(A_\phi A_p) \in \Gamma_i\}\rangle \text{ where}$$
$$A_\phi = [(A_\mu, A_\theta, A_\Sigma, A_\psi), A_\iota, \pi^k].$$
$$\|A_\Omega\|^\sigma = \|A_\phi\|^\sigma(\|A_p\|^\sigma) \text{ where } A_\Omega = A_\phi A_p$$

It can now be shown that given a consistent set Γ, a canonical model $\mathfrak{M}^x$ defined as above will satisfy that set:

Theorem: A sentence A is true in i under σ in the canonical model $\mathfrak{M}^x$ if and only if $A \in \Gamma_i$

The proof is by induction on the length of A and is straightforward in all cases. Let us consider a few examples.

Example 1 A is of the form $E(A_\tau A_p)A_\iota$

$E(A_\tau A_p)A_\iota$ is true in i on σ
  if and only if $\langle i, \|A_\tau\|^\sigma, \|A_p\|^\sigma \|A_\iota\|^\sigma\rangle \in \mathbb{E}$ (truth definition)
  if and only if $\langle i, [A_\tau], \langle A_p \rangle, [A_\iota]\rangle \in \mathbb{E}$ (by the definition of canonical $\| \ \|$)
  if and only if $E((A_\tau A_p)A_\iota) \in \Gamma_i$ (by the definition of canonical $\mathbb{E}$).

Example 2 A is of the form $A_p \rangle B_p$

  ($\Rightarrow$) Assume $A_p \rangle B_p$ is true in i on σ.
  $\therefore id_1(\|B_p\|^\sigma) \subseteq id_1(\|A_p\|^\sigma)$ by the truth definition.
  $\therefore [B_p] \leqslant [A_p]$ by definition of $\leqslant$.
  $\therefore A_p \rangle B_p \in \Gamma_i$.
  ($\Leftarrow$) Assume $A_p \rangle B_p \in \Gamma_i$.
  But $\vdash (A_p \rangle B_p) \to \Box(A_p \rangle B_p)$ by axiom schema 17.

$\therefore \Box(A_p \succ B_p) \in \Gamma_i \therefore A_p \succ B_p \in \Gamma_j$ for all j by construction of $(\Gamma_i)_{i \in \omega}$.

$\therefore [B_p] \leqslant [A_p]$ by definition of $\leqslant$.

$\therefore id_1(\|B_p\|^\sigma) \subseteq id_1(\|A_p\|^\sigma)$ for any σ, by definition of $\|A_p\|^\sigma$, $\|B_p\|^\sigma$.

$\therefore A_p \succ B_p$ is true in i on σ by the truth definition.

Example 3 A is of the form $(A_\alpha = B_\alpha)$

Example 3.1 $\alpha = \mu$

$\|A_\mu\|^\sigma = \|B_\mu\|^\sigma$

if and only if $A_\mu A_p \leftrightarrow B_\mu A_p \in \Gamma_i$ for all $i \in I$ and A_p (def. of $\|\ \|$)

if and only if $(\forall x_p)(A_\mu x_p \leftrightarrow B_\mu x_p) \in \Gamma_i$ for all i

if and only if $\Box(\forall x_p)(A_\mu x_p \leftrightarrow B_\mu x_p) \in \Gamma_i$ for all i

if and only if $A_\mu = B_\mu \in \Gamma_i$ by axiom 32 and the axioms for the quantifier $\forall$ and the modal connective $\Box$.

Example 3.2 $\alpha = \Sigma$

($\Rightarrow$) Suppose $A_\Sigma = B_\Sigma$ is true in i on σ.

$\therefore \|A_\Sigma\|^\sigma = \|B_\Sigma\|^\sigma$ by the truth definition.

$\therefore$ for all P, $\|A_\Sigma\|^\sigma(i, P) = \|B_\Sigma\|^\sigma(i, P)$ for all i.

$\therefore$ for all $A_p, B_p, A_\Sigma A_p B_p \in \Gamma_i$ if and only if $B_\Sigma A_p B_p \in \Gamma_i$ for all i by definition of $\|A_\Sigma\|^\sigma$.

$\therefore (\forall x_p)(\forall y_p)(A_\Sigma x_p y_p \leftrightarrow B_\Sigma x_p y_p) \in \Gamma_i$ for all i.

$\therefore \Box(\forall x_p)(\forall y_p)(A_\Sigma x_p y_p \leftrightarrow B_\Sigma x_p y_p) \in \Gamma_i$ for all i by Gallin's lemma 3.2.

$\therefore (A_\Sigma - B_\Sigma) \in \Gamma_i$ by axiom schema 33 and the axioms for the quantifier $\forall$ and the modal connective $\Box$.

($\Leftarrow$) Suppose $(A_\Sigma = B_\Sigma) \in \Gamma_i$.

$\therefore \Box(\forall x_p)(\forall y_p)(A_\Sigma x_p y_p \leftrightarrow B_\Sigma x_p y_p) \in \Gamma_i$ by axiom schema 33 and the axioms for $\forall$ and $\Box$.

$\therefore$ for all $A_p, B_p, A_\Sigma A_p B_p \in \Gamma_i$ if and only if $B_\Sigma A_p B_p \in \Gamma_i$ for all i.

$\therefore$ for any $i, P, \|A_\Sigma\|^\sigma(i, P) = \|B_\Sigma\|^\sigma(i, P)$ by definition of $\|A_\Sigma\|^\sigma$.

$\therefore \|A_\Sigma\|^\sigma = \|B_\Sigma\|^\sigma$.

Example 3.3 $\alpha = p$

$\|A_p\|^\sigma = \|B_p\|^\sigma$ if and only if $\langle A_p \rangle = \langle B_p \rangle$

if and only if $[A_p] = [B_p]$ and $(t(A_p) \leftrightarrow t(B_p)) \in \Gamma_i$ for all i and $A_p \leftrightarrow B_p$ is a theorem of *PC*

if and only if $(A_p \langle \rangle B_p) \wedge (t(A_p) \leftrightarrow t(B_p)) \wedge \mathbf{T}(A_p \leftrightarrow B_p) \in \Gamma_i$ for all i by definition of $\langle A_p \rangle$ and $\langle B_p \rangle$

if and only if $(A_p = B_p) \in \Gamma_i$ for all i by axiom 20.

Example 3.4 $\alpha = \Omega$

Where $A = (A_\Omega = B_\Omega)$, $A_\Omega = A_\phi A_p$ and $B_\Omega = B_\phi B_p$, $\|A_\phi A_p\|^\sigma = \|B_\phi B_p\|^\sigma$

if and only if $\|A_\phi\|^\sigma (\langle A_p \rangle) = \|B_\phi\|^\sigma (\langle B_p \rangle)$

if and only if $\langle A_p \rangle = \langle B_p \rangle$ and $(s(A_\phi A_p) \leftrightarrow s(B_\phi B_p)) \in \Gamma_i$ for all i

if and only if $(A_p = B_p) \wedge \square(s(A_\phi A_p) \leftrightarrow s(B_\phi B_p)) \in \Gamma_i$ for all i

if and only if $(A_\Omega = B_\Omega) \in \Gamma_i$ for all i by axiom 58.

The induction steps of the proof for sentences of the form $\sim A, (A_1 \vee A_2), \square A, \forall x_\alpha A$ are omitted, since they also present no difficulties.

This proves the theorem.

Thus given a consistent set Γ the associated canonical model as defined above will satisfy that set. We now need to show that the various meaning postulates governing $\rangle\rangle$, $\mathbb{E}$, Π_k, etc. hold. Again, this is straightforward in each case. Each of the postulates is guaranteed by particular axioms, and it is clear which axioms govern which postulates. We give a few examples here:

Example 1 $\{P/\langle i, P \rangle \in \rangle\rangle\}$ is closed under strong implication.

Proof By axiom schema 53.

Example 2 $\langle i, P \rangle \in \Pi_4$ only if P is contingently true.

Proof

Assume $\langle i, \langle A_p \rangle \rangle \in \Pi_4$.

$\therefore \pi^4 A_p \in \Gamma_i$.

$\therefore \sim \square t(A_p) \in \Gamma_i$ by axiom schema 47 and $t(A_p) \in \Gamma_i$ by axiom 48.

$\therefore \langle A_p \rangle$ is true and contingent.

Example 3 $\{P/\langle i, P\rangle \in \Pi_1\}$ is minimally consistent.

Proof By axiom schema 44

Example 4

$\{P/\langle i, P\rangle \in \Pi_1\}$ is closed under strong implication, and contains a unique maximal element.

Proof By axiom schema 45

Example 5 $\langle i, P\rangle \in \|1_\mu\|^\sigma$

Proof $\langle i, P\rangle \in \|1_\mu\|^\sigma$ if and only if $1_\mu A_p \in \Gamma_i$ where $\langle A_p\rangle = P$.
But $1_\mu A_p \in \Gamma_i$ for all A_p, i, since $\vdash_V \square(1_\mu A_p)$ for all A_p by axiom schema 35.
$\therefore \langle i, P\rangle \in \|1_\mu\|^\sigma$ for all i, P.

Example 6 $\langle i, P\rangle \notin \|0_\mu\|^\sigma$ for all i, P.

Proof By axiom schema 36

Example 7

$\|A_\theta \ast B_\theta\|^\sigma(i) = \|A_\theta\|^\sigma(i) \cap \|B_\theta\|^\sigma(i)$.
Proof By axiom schema 37

We omit the rest of the proofs of the meaning postulates. The reader can easily verify that axiom schemas 32 to 58, together with the axioms of quantified modal logic with identity, guarantee that the various postulates for the valuation function $\|\ \|$ also hold on the canonical model.

Thus, every consistent set Γ of sentences of V has a standard model and consequently every valid sentence is a theorem of the axiomatic system V.

APPENDIX 2

THE GENERAL COMPLETENESS

OF THE

AXIOMATIC SYSTEM

(with the collaboration of David K. Johnston and François Lepage)

In this appendix, we will prove the *general completeness* of the axiomatic system GS of general semantics. we will also show that GS is a *conservative extension* of Gallin's intensional logic.

Following Henkin's method, we will prove the completeness of the axiomatic system GS by defining for each consistent set Γ a canonical model which satisfies that set. The construction is an extension of that of Gallin for intensional logic and familiarity with this work will be assumed here. It is necessary to augment Gallin's construction in a number of ways:

(A) For each type α, Gallin defines a set U_α and a mapping $f_\alpha : L_\alpha \times I \to U_\alpha$ (where L_α is the set of formulas of type α of L_ω and I is the index set of the canonical model) which has the following properties:

    (1) for each $i, j \in I$ and each variable x_α, $f_\alpha(x_\alpha)(i) = f_\alpha(x_\alpha)(j)$

    (2) for each $i \in I$ and $u_\alpha \in U_\alpha$, there is a variable x_α such that $f_\alpha(x_\alpha)(i) = u_\alpha$

    (3) for each $i \in I$ and all formulas A, B of type α, $f_\alpha(A)(i) = f_\alpha(B)(i)$ if and only if $(A = B) \in \Gamma_i$, where Γ_i is a maximal consistent set.

The definitions of U_α and f_α must be extended in order to accommodate the types s and a.

(B) It must be shown that the valuation $\| \ \|$ defined on the canonical model obeys the conditions set out for the logical constants. It must also be shown that the meaning postulates hold on the canonical model. I will now undertake each of these tasks in turn.

(A) The sets U_s and U_a and the mappings f_s and f_a must be defined. First, let $U_s = \{S, \mathcal{S}\,\}$, and let $f_s(A_s)(i) = S$ if $(A_s = 1_s) \in \Gamma_i$ and $\mathcal{S}$ otherwise. It must now be shown that properties 1 to 3 obtain.

(1) Suppose $f_s(x)(i) = S$ for an arbitrary i.

$\therefore (x = 1_s) \in \Gamma_i$.

$\therefore \Box(x = 1_s) \in \Gamma_i$ by theorem schema 19, since $(x = 1_s)$ is modally closed.

$\therefore (x = 1_s) \in \Gamma_j$ for any j by Gallin's property vi of the sequence of Γ_i's.

$\therefore f_s(x)(i) = f_s(x)(j)$ for all j.

Suppose $f_s(x)(i) = \mathcal{S}$ for an arbitrary i.

$\therefore (x = 1_s) \notin \Gamma_i$.

$\therefore \sim(x = 1_s) \in \Gamma_i$ since Γ_i is maximal.

$\therefore \Box \sim(x = 1_s) \in \Gamma_i$ by theorem schema 19 as above.

$\therefore (x = 1_s) \notin \Gamma_j$ for any j by property vi of the sequence of Γ_i's.

$\therefore f_s(x)(i) = f_s(x)(j)$ for all j.

(2) By theorem schema 12, $(\exists x_s(1_s = x_s)) \in \Gamma_i$ for each i.

$\therefore (y_s = 1_s) \in \Gamma_i$ for some variable y_s by Gallin's property iii of the sequence of Γ_i's.

$S = f_s(y_s)(i)$ for some variable y_s for each i.

Similarly, $(\exists x_s(0_s = x_s)) \in \Gamma_i$ for each i by theorem schema 12; thus we can also show that

$\mathcal{S} = f_s(y_s)(i)$ for some variable y_s for each i.

(3) ($\Rightarrow$) Assume $f_s(A_s)(i) = f_s(B_s)(i) = S$ for an arbitrary i.

$\therefore (A = 1_s) \in \Gamma_i$ and $(B = 1_s) \in \Gamma_i$ $\therefore (A = B) \in \Gamma_i$.

Assume $f_s(A)(i) = f_s(B_s)(j) = \mathcal{S}$.

$\therefore \sim(A = 1_s) \in \Gamma_i$ and $\sim(B = 1_s) \in \Gamma_i$.

$\therefore (A = 0_s) \in \Gamma_i$ and $(B = 0_s) \in \Gamma_i$ by axiom 8.

$\therefore (A = B) \in \Gamma_i$.

($\Rightarrow$) Assume $(A = B) \in \Gamma_i$ for an arbitrary i.

If $f_s(A)(i) = S$ then $(A = 1_s) \in \Gamma_i$. So $(B = 1_s) \in \Gamma_i$ and $f_s(B)(i) = S$.

If $f_s(A)(i) = \cancel{S}$ then $(A = 0_s) \in \Gamma_i$ as above.

So $(B = 0_s) \in \Gamma_i$ and thus $f_s(B)(i) = \cancel{S}$

As for U_a, define for every variable x_a the equivalence class $\langle x_a \rangle_i = \{y_a / x_a \simeq y_a \in \Gamma_i\}$.

Let $|x_a| = \{i/{}^{\vee}[x_a] \in \Gamma_i\}$.

Now define f_a as follows: $f_a(A_a)(i) = \langle\langle x_a \rangle_i, |x_a|\rangle$ where $(A_a = x_a) \in \Gamma_i$.

Properties 1 and 2 follow simply from the fact that $\vdash_{GS} x_a = x_a$ for any variable x_a.

Modal closure ensures that $\langle x_a \rangle_i = \langle x_a \rangle_j$ for all i and $j \in I$.

As for property 3, $f_a(A_a)(i) = f_a(B_a)(i)$

if $\langle x_a \rangle = \langle y_a \rangle$ and $|x_a| = |y_a|$ where $(A = x_a)$ and $(B = y_a) \in \Gamma_i$,

if and only if $(x_a \simeq y_a) \in \Gamma_j$ and ${}^{\vee}[x_a] = {}^{\vee}[y_a] \in \Gamma_j$ for all $j \in I$,

if and only if $(x_a \simeq y_a) \in \Gamma_i$ and $\Box({}^{\vee}[x_a] = {}^{\vee}[y_a]) \in \Gamma_i$,

if and only if $(x_a \simeq y_a) \wedge [x_a] = [y_a] \in \Gamma_i$, since $\vdash_{GS}(\Box({}^{\vee}A_{\#\gamma} = {}^{\vee}B_{\#\gamma})) \leftrightarrow A_{\#\gamma} = B_{\#\gamma})$ where $A_{\#\gamma}$ and $B_{\#\gamma}$ are modally closed,

if and only if $x_a = y_a \in \Gamma_i$ by the axiom schema 12 stating the law of identity for atomic propositions,

if and only if $A_a = B_a$ by the theorems for identity.

Finally, let D be the set of all equivalence classes $\langle x_a \rangle$ as defined above, and let U_a be the set of all pairs $\langle\langle x_a \rangle, |x_a|\rangle$ in a canonical model.

In order to show that the canonical valuation $\| \|$ fulfills the conditions for the logical constants 1_s, $\{\}_{ts}$, $\simeq_{a(at)}$ and $[]_{a\#t}$, it is enough to show that the associated f_γ has the required property. This is straightforward in each case.

Lemma 1 $\|1_s\|_i^\sigma = S$ (clause iii)

Proof Clearly $\|1_s\|_i^\sigma = f_s(1_s)(i)$.

But $f_s(1_s)(i) = S$ if $(1_s = 1_s) \in \Gamma_i$.

Lemma 2 $\|\{\}_{ts}\|_i^{\sigma}(u_t) = S$ if and only if $u_t = T$ (clause iii)

Proof $\|\{\}\|_i^{\sigma}(u_t) = S$ if and only if $f_{ts}(\{\})(i)(u_t) = S$

if and only if $f_s(\{x_t\})(i) = S$, where $f_t(x_t) = u_t$

if and only if $(\{x_t\} = 1_s) \in \Gamma_i$

if and only if $[\{x_t\}] \in \Gamma_i$

if and only if $x_t \in \Gamma_i$ since $\vdash_{GS}[\{A_t\}] = A_t$

if and only if $f_t(x_t)(i) = T$

if and only if $u_t = T$.

Lemma 3 $\|A_a \simeq B_a\|_i^{\sigma} = T$ if and only if $id_1(\|A_a\|_i^{\sigma}) = id_1(\|B_a\|_i^{\sigma})$.

By the previous definitions and the axioms of GS for $\simeq$.

Lemma 4 $\|[A_a]\|_i^{\sigma} = id_2(\|A_a\|_i^{\sigma})$.

Proof $f_{a\#t}([\,])(i)(u_a)(j) = T$

if and only if $f_{\#t}([x_a])(i)(j) = T$ where $u_a = f_a(x_a)(i)$,

if and only if $f_t(^{\vee}x_{\#t})(j) = T$ where $(x_{\#t} = [x_a]) \in \Gamma_i$,

if and only if $^{\vee}x_{\#t} \in \Gamma_j$,

if and only $^{\vee}[x_a] \in \Gamma_j$ since $\square(x_{\#t} = [x_a]) \in \Gamma_i$ by modal closure,

if and only if $j \in |x_a|$,

if and only if $j \in id_2(u_a)$.

The meaning axioms governing the logical constants π_{μ}^n, $\gg_{pt}$ and $E_{\xi_{\iota}s}$ are also each guaranteed by particular axioms. Again, the proofs are straightforward in each case.

For example, the set $\{P/\|\pi^1\|_i^{\sigma}(j, P) = S\}$ is closed under strong implication.

Proof Assume $f_{\mu}(\pi^1)(i)(j)(P) = S$ where $P \in U_p$.
$\therefore f_{ps}(^{\vee}x_{\mu})(j)(P) = S$ where $(\pi^1 = x_{\mu}) \in \Gamma_i$.

Assume $Q \in U_p$ and P strongly implies Q (or for short hereafter $P \vdash Q$) in the canonical model.

In that case $x_p \vdash y_p \in \Gamma_i$ where $P = f_p(x_p)(i)$ and $Q = f_p(y_p)(i)$.

$\therefore f_s(^{\vee}x_\mu x_p)(j) = S.$

$\therefore [^{\vee}x_\mu x_p] \in \Gamma_j.$

But $\square(x_p \vdash y_p) \in \Gamma_i$ and $\square(\pi^1 = x_\mu) \in \Gamma_i$ by modal closure.

$\therefore (x_p \vdash y_p) \in \Gamma_j$ and $\pi^1 = x_\mu \in \Gamma_j.$

But $\vdash_{GS} (x_p \vdash y_p) \to ([^{\vee}\pi^1 x_p] \to [^{\vee}\pi^1 y_p])$ by axiom schema 15.

$\therefore ([^{\vee}x_\mu x_p] \to [^{\vee}x_\mu y_p]) \in \Gamma_j$ and hence $[^{\vee}x_\mu y_p] \in \Gamma_j.$

$\therefore f_{ps}(^{\vee}x_\mu)(j)(Q) = S.$

$\therefore f_\mu(\pi^1)(i)(j)(Q) = S.$

The proofs for the other postulates are omitted. The reader will have no difficulty determining which axioms go with which postulates.

As I have announced above, we can infer from the general completeness of general semantics the following results:

Thesis General semantics (GS) is a conservative extension of intensional logic (GL).

Suppose A is not a theorem of Gallin's intensional logic GL. Then $\sim A$ is consistent in that intensional logic, and by Gallin's result has a model. But this model can be expanded into a model for GS simply by adding the required structures and extending the truth definition. Thus $\sim A$ is also consistent in GS. Hence A is not a theorem of GS because GS is consistent.

APPENDIX 3

LIST OF SYMBOLS

Numbers in brackets refer to pages in this book.

a is the logical type of atomic propositions (76)

a_i names the speaker of context of utterance i (148)

b_i names the hearer of context of utterance i (148)

c_α, c_α^1, c_α^2, ... are constants of type α of the ideal object-languages of illocutionary logic and of general semantics (23, 78)

e is the type of individuals (76–7)

f, f_1, f_2, ... are variables for illocutionary force markers

$f(p)$, $f_1(p_1)$, $f_2(p_2)$, ... range over elementary sentences

g, g_1, g_2 and h, h_1, h_2, ... are variables for functions

i, i_1, i_2, ... and j, j_1, j_2 are variables for contexts of utterance

$id_k(X)$ names the k-th term of the sequence named X (37, 96)

k is a variable for natural numbers or integers

m, m_1, m_2, ... are variables for psychological modes of mental states

$m(P)$ names the propositional attitude with psychological mode m and propositional content P

n is a variable for natural numbers or integers

p is the logical type of propositions (23, 77)

p, p_1, p_2, ... are variables for clauses expressing propositions

r is a variable for natural numbers or integers

s names the logical type of success values (76)

$s(A_\phi A_p)$ names the success value of the illocutionary act named by $A_\phi A_p$ (32, 89)

$t(A_\phi A_p)$ names the satisfaction value of the illocutionary act named by $A_\phi A_p$ (33, 90)

$t(A_p)$ names the truth value of the proposition named by A_p (26)

$u, u_1, u_2, \ldots$ are meta-variables for entities of the domain of a model (96)

u_α range over entities of type α of a model (96)

$v, v_1, v_2, \ldots$ range over variables of logical object-languages

$w, w_1, w_2, \ldots$ are variables for possible worlds (148)

$x_\alpha, x_\alpha^1, x_\alpha^2, \ldots y_\alpha, y_\alpha^1, y_\alpha^2, \ldots z_\alpha, z_\alpha^1, z_\alpha^2, \ldots$ are variables of the ideal object-languages for entities of type α (23, 78)

CAPITAL LETTERS

$A, A_1, A_2, \ldots B, B_1, B_2, \ldots C, C_1, C_2, \ldots$ are meta-variables for formulas of the ideal logical languages (79)

$[(A_\mu, A_\theta, A_\Sigma, A_\psi), A_\iota, \pi^k]$ names the weakest illocutionary force with the illocutionary point named by π^k, the degree of strength named by A_ι, the mode of achievement named by A_μ and the propositional content, preparatory and sincerity conditions respectively named by A_θ, A_Σ and A_ψ (25, 87)

$[A_\zeta]A_\phi$ names the illocutionary force obtained by adding the component named by A_ζ to the illocutionary force named by A_ϕ, when $\zeta = \mu, \theta, \Sigma$, or ψ (31, 88)

$[A_\iota]A_\phi$ names the illocutionary force obtained by adding the integer named by A_ι to the degree of strength of the illocutionary force named by A_ϕ (31, 88)

$[A_p]$ names the truth conditions of proposition A_p (83)

$A_\phi A_p$ names the illocutionary act with the force named by A_ϕ and the propositional content named by A_p (25, 87)

$\{A_\phi A_p\}$ names the conditions of success of the illocutionary act $A_\phi A_p$ (88)

$[A_\phi A_p]$ names the conditions of satisfaction of the illocutionary act $A_\phi A_p$ (90)

$\{A_\tau A_p\}$ names the conditions of possession of mental state $A_\tau A_p$ (91)

$\bar{A}_\zeta$ names the Boolean complement of the component named by A_ζ (56, 134)

D is the set that represents the set of all possible contents of a possible interpretation of illocutionary logic, or the function that gives as value, for each type symbol α, the set D_α of entities which are propositional constituents of type α in a possible interpretation of general semantics (36, 96)

E is the logical constant for expression of mental states (26, 78)

F, F_1, F_2, ... are variables for illocutionary forces

$F(P)$ names the elementary illocutionary act with the illocutionary force F and the propositional content P

GS is the axiomatic system of general semantics (128)

H is the function of an improved standard model that associates with each context i the sequence $\langle a_i, b_i, t_i, w_i \rangle$ (148)

I names the set of all possible contexts of utterance (36, 95)

IL is the first order illocutionary logic formulated in chapter 2 (22)

$\mathcal{J}$ is a variable for sets of contexts of utterance

$KA_\phi A_p$ names the proposition that the illocutionary act $A_\phi A_p$ is performed (91)

L names the ideal object-language of first order illocutionary logic

L_ω names the ideal object-language of general semantics (75)

M names the set of all psychological modes (37)

P, P_1, P_2, ... are variables for propositions

PC is the part of axiomatic system V that corresponds to the propositional calculus (42)

Q, Q_1, Q_2, ... are variables for propositions

R names the relation of accessibility between possible worlds (148)

S names success (96)

$\mathcal{S}$ names insuccess (96)

T names the true (96)

$\mathcal{T}$ names the false (96)

U is a function which associates with each type symbol α the set U_α of all entities which are possible denotations of terms of type α in a possible interpretation of illocutionary logic or of general semantics (37–8, 96)

V is the axiomatic system of first order illocutionary logic (42)

W is the set of all possible worlds (148)

Z is the set of integers

GREEK SYMBOLS

α, α_1, α_2 and β, β_1, β_2, ... are variables for logical types (23, 76)

#α names the logical type of intensions whose extensions are of type α (77)

($\alpha\beta$) names the logical type of functions from entities of type α into entities of type β (76)

γ is the type of sets of atomic propositions and of truth value assignments to atomic propositions (77)

$\eta(A_\phi)$ names the degree of strength of the sincerity conditions of the illocutionary force named by A_ϕ (59, 90)

ζ is a variable for types of components of illocutionary forces (23)

θ is the logical type of propositional content conditions (23, 77)

$\theta(A_\phi)$ names the set of propositional content conditions of the illocutionary force named by A_ϕ (89)

ι is the logical type of integers (23, 77)

λ is the operator of functional abstraction of intensional logic (79)

μ is the logical type of illocutionary points and modes of achievement (23, 77)

$\mu(A_\phi)$ names the set of modes of achievement of the illocutionary force named by A_ϕ (89)

ξ is the logical type of propositional attitude (23, 77)

π^1 is the logical constant which names the assertive illocutionary point (23, 78)

π^2 is the logical constant for the commissive point (23, 78)

π^3 is the logical constant for the directive point (23, 78)

π^4 is the logical constant for the declarative point (23, 78)

π^5 is the logical constant for the expressive point (23, 85)

$\sigma, \sigma', \sigma'', \ldots, \sigma_1, \sigma_2, \ldots$ are assignments of values to variables (39, 96)

τ is the logical type of psychological modes (23, 77)

ϕ is the logical type of illocutionary forces (25, 77)

ψ is the logical type of sincerity conditions (23, 77)

$\psi(\pi^k)$ names the sincerity condition determined by the illocutionary point named by π^k (86)

$\psi(A_\phi)$ names the set of sincerity conditions of the force named by A_ϕ (90)

ω names the set of natural numbers

Γ and Δ are meta-variables for sets of sentences, of propositions, of illocutionary acts etc.

Π_1 is the relation that determines the conditions of achievement of the assertive illocutionary point in a model (38)

Π_2 is the relation that determines the conditions of achievement of the commissive illocutionary point in a model (38)

Π_3 is the relation that determines the conditions of achievement of the directive illocutionary point in a model (38)

Π_4 is the relation that determines the conditions of achievement of the declarative illocutionary point in a model (38)

Π_5 is the relation that determines the conditions of achievement of the expressive illocutionary point in a model (38)

$\pi(A_\phi)$ names the illocutionary point(s) of the illocutionary force A_ϕ (89)

Σ is the logical type of preparatory conditions (23, 77)

$\Sigma(A_\phi)$ names the set of preparatory conditions of the force named by A_ϕ (90)

Ω is the logical type of illocutionary acts (25, 77)

MATHEMATICAL SYMBOLS

$=$ is the sign of equality (24, 79)

$\neq$ is the sign of inequality

$k \geqslant n$ means that k is equal to or greater than n

$k > n$ means that k is greater than n

$>$ also names the temporal relation of posteriority (149)

$k \leqslant n$ means that k is equal to or smaller than n

$\leqslant$ also names the temporal relation of being anterior to or simultaneous with (149)

$k < n$ means that k is smaller than n

$<$ also names the temporal relation of anteriority (149)

1 names the integer one

1_α names the neutral component of type α, whenever $\alpha = \mu, \theta, \Sigma, \psi$ or ι (23, 85–6)

0 names the integer zero

0_ϕ names the impossible illocutionary force (62)

0_α names the absorbent component of type α whenever $\alpha = \mu, \theta, \Sigma, \psi$ or ι (23, 85–6)

$\varnothing$ names the empty set

$\varnothing(A_\phi)$ means that the illocutionary force named by A_ϕ has the empty direction of fit (33, 89)

$\in$ is the sign of membership

$\subseteq$ is the sign of inclusion

$\subset$ is the sign of proper inclusion

$\{X, Y, \dots, Z\}$ names the set which contains $X, Y, \dots$ and Z

$\{X/A(X)\}$ names the set of entities X which have the property expressed by the predicate $A(X)$

$\langle X, Y, ..., Z \rangle$ names the sequence whose first, second, ..., and last terms are respectively X, Y, ..., and Z

$\cap$ is the sign of intersection

$\cup$ is the sign of union

$X \times Y$ names the Cartesian product of sets X and Y

$\mathscr{P}(X)$ names the power (i.e. the set of all subsets) of the set X

$(X)^Y$ and X^Y name the set of all functions from the set Y into the set X

$'$ names the function that associates with each integer its immediate predecessor whenever it precedes a numeral, and the function that associates with each integer its immediate successor whenever it follows a numeral (24)

$+$ names the operation of addition between integers (34)

$\therefore$ means therefore

LOGICAL SYMBOLS

$\sim$ is the sign of truth functional and of propositional negation (24, 27, 82–4)

$\wedge$ is the sign of truth functional and of propositional conjunction (28, 82–4)

$\vee$ is the sign of truth functional and of propositional disjunction (24, 27, 82–4)

$\rightarrow$ is the sign of truth functional and of propositional material implication (28, 82)

$\leftrightarrow$ is the sign of truth functional and of propositional material equivalence (28, 82)

$\square$ is the sign of universal necessity (27–8, 84)

$\diamondsuit$ is the sign of universal (or logical) possibility (28, 84)

$\dashv$ is the sign of strict implication (29, 84)

$\dashv$ also names the relation of determination between components of illocutionary force and the relation of being a component of an illocutionary force (32, 56–7)

⊣ also names the relations of inclusion of success conditions and of inclusion of satisfaction conditions (89, 91)

⊢⊣ is the sign of strict equivalence (29, 84)

⊢⊣ is the sign of strong implication (29, 85)

∀ is the universal quantifier (27, 82)

∃ is the existential quantifier (30, 82, 109)

∃! is the quantifier "there exists one and only one" (30, 83)

ᴉ is the operator of definite description (83)

⊃ is the sign of inclusion of content (27, 83)

$\simeq_{a(at)}$ names the relation of having the same propositional constituents (78)

T is the sign for tautologies (29, 84)

1_s is the logical constant for success (78)

1_t names the true (82)

0_s names insuccess (85)

0_t names the false (82)

$\{\}_{ts}$ is the logical constant naming the function that associates success with the true and insuccess with the false (78)

$[\,]_{a\#t}$ is the logical constant naming the function that associates with each atomic proposition its truth conditions (78)

$[A_s]$ names the true when A_s names success and the false when A_s names insuccess (85)

≫ is the logical symbol for presupposition (26, 78)

✻ names the Boolean operations of conjunction between modes of achievement, of intersection of propositional content conditions and of union of preparatory or sincerity conditions, and the operation of addition between integers (24–5, 86)

The parentheses ( ) name functional operation in formulas of the form $(A_{\alpha\beta} A_\alpha)$ (79)

∧ is the cap operator of intensional logic. It expresses functional abstraction over contexts (80)

∨ is the cup operator of intensional logic. It is the inverse of the preceding cap operator (80)

$^\vee A_p$ names the truth value of proposition A_p (83)

$|A_p|$ names the truth functional algorithm of the proposition A_p (83)

$\langle A_p \rangle$ names the content of the proposition A_p (83)

⊢ names the primitive illocutionary force of assertion (30, 87)

⊥ names the primitive commissive illocutionary force (30, 88)

! names the primitive directive illocutionary force (30, 88)

T names the primitive illocutionary force of declarations (30, 88)

⊣ names the primitive expressive illocutionary force (30, 88)

↓ is the symbol for the words-to-world direction of fit (32, 89)

↑ is the symbol for the world-to-words direction of fit (32, 89)

↕ is the symbol for the double direction of fit (32, 89)

▷ names the relation of strong commitment between speech acts, or between mental states, or the relation of illocutionary entailment between illocutionary forces (33, 90)

)(names the relation of incompatibility between illocutionary forces (34)

)($_t$ names the relation of having incompatible conditions of satisfaction (34)

)($_s$ names the relation of having incompatible conditions of success (34, 90)

META-LOGICAL SYMBOLS

$\mathfrak{M}$, $\mathfrak{M}_1$, $\mathfrak{M}_2$, ... are variables for possible interpretations or models (36, 95)

⟩⟩ is the relation determining which propositions are presupposed in each context of a model (39)

𝔼 is the relation determining which mental states are expressed in each context of a model (39)

‖ ‖ is the evaluation function which defines recursively the meanings of all formulas in a model (39, 98–9)

$\|A_\alpha\|_i^\sigma$ names the denotation of the formula A_α under the assignment σ at the context i in a model (98)

⊢$_V$ A_t means that the formula A_t is provable in the axiomatic system V (48)

⊢$_{GS}$ A_t means that A_t is provable in GS (131)

And similarly for other axiomatic systems

⊨ A_t means the formula A_t is logically valid (42, 100)

⊨ is also the symbol for truth conditional entailment between sentences (or formulas of type Ω) (102)

⊭ A means that A is not valid

⊨$_s$ is the symbol for strong truth conditional entailment (102)

⊩ is the symbol for illocutionary entailment between sentences (102)

⊩$_s$ is the symbol for strong illocutionary entailment (102)

List of symbols

⊫ is the symbol for illocutionary entailment of satisfaction (102)

⊫$_s$ is the symbol for strong illocutionary entailment of satisfaction (102)

⫤ is the symbol for truth conditional entailment of success (102)

⫤$_s$ is the symbol for strong truth conditional entailment of success (102)

BIBLIOGRAPHY

Austin, J. L., *How to do Things with Words*, Oxford: Clarendon Press, 1962

"Performatif-constatif", in *Cahiers de Royaumont*, Philosophie no. IV, *La Philosophie analytique*, Paris: Editions de Minuit, 1962

Bach, E. and R. Harnish, *Linguistic Communication and Speech Acts*, Cambridge, Mass.: M.I.T. Press, 1979

Bar-Hillel, Y., "Indexical expressions", *Mind*, 63 (1954)

Bealer, G., *Quality and Concept*, Oxford University Press, 1982

Belnap, N., "Declaratives are not enough", forthcoming in *Philosophical Studies*

Belnap, N. and T. Steel, *The Logic of Questions and Answers*, Yale University Press, 1976

Boole, G., *The Mathematical Analysis of Logic*, Oxford: Basil Blackwell, 1965 (original edition 1847)

Boolos, G. and R. Jeffrey, *Computibility and Logic*, Cambridge University Press, 1974

Carnap, R., *Meaning and Necessity*, University of Chicago Press, 1956

Church, A., "A formulation of the logic of sense and denotation", in P. Henle et al. (eds.), *Structure, Method and Meaning*, New York: Liberal Arts Press 1951

Introduction to Mathematical Logic, Princeton University Press, 1956

Cohen, P. R. and H. J. Levesque, "Rational interaction as the basis for communication", in P. R. Cohen, M. Pollack, and J. Morgan (eds.), *Intentions in Communication*, Cambridge, Mass.: Bradford Books, M.I.T., 1990

Davidson, D., *Enquiries into Truth and Interpretation*, Oxford: Clarendon Press, 1984

Descartes, R., *Discours de la méthode*, in R. Descartes, *Oeuvres et Lettres*, ed. A. Bridoux, Bibliothèque de la Pléiade, Paris: Editions Gallimard, 1953

Bibliography

Destutt de Tracy, *Eléments d'Idéologie*, Paris: Vrin, 1974

Dummett, M., *Truth and other Enigmas*, Cambridge, Mass.: Harvard University Press, 1978

Feys, R., *Modal Logics*, Louvain: Nauwelaerts, 1965

Frege, G., "Gedankengefüge", in *Beiträge zur Philosophie des Deutschen Idealismus*, 3 (1923–6)

Foundations of Arithmetic, Oxford: Basil Blackwell, 1958

The Basic Laws of Arithmetic, Los Angeles and Berkeley: University of California Press, 1967

Begriffschrift, in J. van Heijenoort (ed.), *From Frege to Gödel*, Cambridge, Mass.: Harvard University Press, 1967

"The thought. A logical inquiry" in P. F. Strawson (ed.), *Philosophical Logic*, Oxford University Press, 1967

"Negation" in P. Geach and M. Black (eds.), *Translations from the Philosophical Writings of Gottlob Frege*, Oxford: Basil Blackwell, 1970

Gallin, D., *Intensional and Higher-Order Modal Logic*, Amsterdam: North-Holland, 1975

Geach, P. and M. Black (eds.), *Translations from the Philosophical Writings of Gottlob Frege*, Oxford: Basil Blackwell, 1970

Gentzen, G., "Untersuchungen über das Logische Schliessen", *Mathematische Zeitschrift*, 39 (1934)

Gödel, K., "On formally undecidable propositions of *Principia Mathematica* and related systems I", in J. van Heijenoort, *From Frege to Gödel*, Cambridge, Mass., Harvard University Press, 1967

Groenendijk, J., and M. Stockhof, "On the semantics of questions and the pragmatics of answers", in F. Landman and F. Veldman (eds.), *Varieties of Formal Semantics*, Dordrecht, Netherlands: Foris, 1984

Hamblin, C. L., "Questions", *Australian Journal of Philosophy*, 36 (1958)

"Questions in Montague English", *Foundations of Language*, 10 (1973), 41–53

Harrah, D., "The logic of questions", in D. Gabbay and F. Guenthner (eds.), *Handbook of Philosophical Logic*, vol. II, Extensions of Classical Logic, Dordrecht, Netherlands: Reidel, 1984

Hausser, R., "Surface compositionality and the semantics of mood", in J. R. Searle, F. Kiefer, and M. Bierwisch (eds.), *Speech Act Theory and Pragmatics*, Dordrecht, Netherlands: Reidel, 1980

Henkin, L., "The completeness of the first-order functional calculus", *Journal of Symbolic Logic*, 14 (1949)

"Completeness in the theory of types", *Journal of Symbolic Logic*, 15 (1950)

Kaplan, D., "On the logic of demonstratives", *Journal of Philosophical Logic*, 8, 1 (1970), 81–98

Karttunen, L., "Syntax and the semantics of questions", *Linguistics and Philosophy* (1977)

Kripke, S., "Naming and necessity", in D. Davidson and G. Harman (eds.), *Semantics of Natural Language*, Dordrecht, Netherlands: Reidel, 1972

Lewis, C. I., *A Survey of Symbolic Logic*, Berkeley and Los Angeles: University of California Press, 1918

Lewis, D., "General semantics", in D. Davidson and G. Harman (eds.), *Semantics of Natural Language*, Dordrecht, Netherlands: Reidel, 1972
  Counterfactuals, Oxford: Basil Blackwell, 1973

Lewis, D. and S. Lewis, "Review of Olson and Paul, *Contemporary Philosophy in Scandinavia*", *Theoria*, 41 (1975)

Montague, R., "Universal grammar", *Theoria*, 36 (1978)
  "English as a formal language", in B. Visentini *et al.*, *Linguaggi nella Società e nella Tecnica*, Milan: Edizioni di Comunità, 1970
  Formal Philosophy, Yale University Press, 1974

Peirce, C. S., *Collected Papers*, Cambridge, Mass.: Harvard University Press, 1931–35

Plantinga, A., *The Nature of Necessity*, Oxford University Press, 1974

Prior, A. N., *Past, Present and Future*, Oxford: Clarendon Press, 1967
  Objects of Thought, Oxford: Clarendon Press, 1971

Prior, A. N. and Kit Fine, in *Worlds, Times and Selves*, Amherst, Mass.: University of Massachusetts Press, 1977

Quine, W. V., *Word and Object*, Cambridge, Mass.: M.I.T. Press, 1960
  Philosophy of Logic, Englewood Cliffs, N.J.: Prentice-Hall, 1970

Rescher, N., *The Logic of Commands*, London: Routledge & Kegan Paul, 1966

Ross, J. R., "On declarative sentences", in R. A. Jacobs and P. S. Rosenbaum (eds.), *Readings in English Transformational Grammar*, Waltham, Mass.: Ginn & Co., 1970

Searle, J. R., *Speech Acts*, Cambridge University Press, 1969
  "A taxonomy of illocutionary acts", in *Language, Mind, and Knowledge, Minnesota Studies in the Philosophy of Science*, vol. VII, Minneapolis: University of Minnesota Press, 1975
  Expression and Meaning, Cambridge University Press, 1979
  "How do performatives work", forthcoming in *Linguistics and Philosophy*

Searle, J. R., F. Kiefer and M. Bierwisch, *Speech Act Theory and Pragmatics*, Dordrecht, Netherlands: Reidel, 1980

Searle, J. R. and D. Vanderveken, *Foundations of Illocutionary Logic*, Cambridge University Press, 1985

Shoenfield, J. R., *Mathematical Logic*, Reading, Mass.: Addison-Wesley, 1967

Tarski, A., "The semantic conception of truth and the foundations of semantics", *Philosophy and Phenomenological Research*, 4 (1944), 341–76
  "Contributions to the theory of models. Part I", *Indagationes Mathematicae*, 16 (1955)
  Logic, Semantics and Meta-Mathematics, Oxford: Clarendon Press, 1956

Vanderveken, D., "Illocutionary logic and self-defeating speech acts", in *Speech Act Theory and Pragmatics*, Dordrecht, Netherlands: Reidel, 1980

"A model-theoretical semantics for illocutionary forces", *Logique et Analyse*, 103–4 (1983), 359–94

"What is an illocutionary force?", in M. Dascal (ed.), *Dialogue: an Interdisciplinary Study*, Amsterdam: Benjamins, 1985

Les Actes de Discours, Brussels: Editions Pierre Mardaga, 1988

"On the unification of speech act theory and formal semantics", in P. Cohen, M. Pollack, and J. Morgan (eds.), *Intentions in Communication*, Cambridge, Mass.: M.I.T. Press, 1990

"Non literal speech acts and conversational maxims", in E. LePore and R. Van Gulick (eds.), *John R. Searle and his Critics*, Oxford: Blackwell, 1990

"*Illokution. Illocutionary Force. Force illocutoire*", in M. Dascal *et al.* (eds.), *Sprachphilosophie. Philosophy of Language. Philosophie du Langage*, Berlin: W. De Gruyter, forthcoming

von Wright, G., *An Essay in Modal Logic*, Amsterdam: North-Holland, 1951

Whitehead, A. N. and B. Russell, *Principia Mathematica*, Cambridge University Press, 1910

Wittgenstein, L., *Tractatus logico-philosophicus*, London: Routledge & Kegan Paul, 1961

Philosophical Investigations, Oxford: Basil Blackwell, 1968

Zadeh, L. A., "Fuzzy logic", *Computer*, 21, 4 (1988), 83–92

Zaefferer, D., "On a formal treatment of illocutionary force indicators", in H. Parret, M. Sbisa, and J. Verschueren (eds.), *Possibilities and Limitations of Pragmatics*, Amsterdam: Benjamins, 1982

"The semantics of non-declaratives: investigating German exclamations", in R. Bäuerle, C. Schwarze, and A. von Stechow (eds.), *Meaning, Use and Interpretation of Language*, Berlin: W. de Gruyter, 1983

"The semantics of sentence mood in typologically differing languages", in Shiro Hattori and K. Inoue (eds.) *Proceedings of the XIIIth International Congress of Linguists*, Tokyo, August 29–September 4, 1982, published under the auspices of the Committee, Tokyo, 1984

Frageausdrücke und Fragen im Deutschen, Munich: Wilhelm Fink Verlage, 1984

INDEX

abbreviate, 162
abbreviation, *see* rules of
abdicate, 161
Abelian group, 44, 57, 141
absorbent components, 24, 40, 45, 56–7, 62, 85–6
accept, 156
accessibility, 143, 148
act: *see* illocutionary; speech act; utterance
action: logic of, 149; verb, 147, 149–50
actual, *see* language
admit, 154
advise, 157, 160
after, 142, 146, 149
ambiguity, 93
analyticity: illocutionary, 101; truth conditional, 101; *see also* laws for
answer, 8–12, 157, 158
anteriority, 149
a posteriori truth, 46, 108
apologize, 163
appoint, 161
approve, 161
a priori: knowledge, 55, 64, 69–70, 108; truth, 55, 71
arithmetic, 34, 39, 45, 53–4, 64, 71, 77, 87, 100, 125
artificial intelligence, 4, 137–8
ask, 11, 157, 158
assert, 151, 154
assertion, 1, 6, 9–10, 30, 87, 92–3
assertive: point, 24, 38, 46, 78, 80, 89, 92, 99–100; speech acts, 2, 151–5; verbs, 151–5

assignment: of truth values: to atomic propositions, 36, 77, 97, to propositional constants and variables, 36; of values to variables, 39, 95, 98
atomic proposition, 22, 76–7, 83, 96–7, 99, 129, 134
attribute, 77, 96
Austin, J. L., 74, 186
automatic translation, 138
axiomatic system: of general semantics, 128–31; of illocutionary logic, 42–8
axioms: for atomic propositions, 129; for components of force, 45–6; of extensionality, 129; for identity, 43, 129; for illocutionary acts, 47; for illocutionary forces, 47; for illocutionary points, 46, 130; for integers, 45; of intensional logic, 129; of modal logic, 43; of the first-order predicate calculus, 43; for presupposition, 47, 130; for propositional attitudes, 150–1; for propositions, 43–4; of protothetics, 129; for psychological expression, 47; of reducibility, 96; for sincerity conditions, 131; for success values, 129; of truth functional logic, 42; *see also* axiomatic system

Bach, E., 74
bad, 148
Barcan Marcus, R., x
Bayart, A., x
Bealer, G., 186

Index